O6

The Victorians

THE CONTEXT OF
ENGLISH LITERATURE

The Victorians

EDITED BY
LAURENCE LERNER

METHUEN & CO LTD
LONDON

First published in 1978
by Methuen & Co Ltd
11 New Fetter Lane London EC4P 4EE

©1978 Laurence Lerner, J. W. Burrow, Carol Dyhouse,
Geoffrey Hemstedt, Barry Supple

Photoset by Red Lion Setters, Holborn, London
Printed in Great Britain
at the University Press
Cambridge

ISBN 0 416 56210 8 (hardback)
ISBN 0 416 56220 5 (paperback)

Contents

Illustrations

The illustrations appear between pages 148 and 149

Preface

Although my name stands on the title-page as editor, this book is the cooperative product of its five authors. We planned it together, and we have read and criticized one another's contributions. It would not have been possible if we had not all been colleagues at the same university, able to draw on our experience in teaching together on some of the interdisciplinary courses that Sussex has developed over the years. It is a constant aim of our courses in literature and history to explore connections without being reductive: not to use literature as mere illustration for social and economic conditions, nor to assume that the insights of the novelist into the workings of his society are necessarily correct. The former would be to reduce literature to historical documents, the latter would give it a privileged (and unmerited) status in the study of society.

The plan of the book flows from these beliefs. The first section is intended as literary history, and its two chapters treat fiction and poetry with complete respect for their autonomy as art. The second section is concerned with the material reality, the institutions and the social and intellectual movements of Victorian Britain. The third section tries to show something of the complexity of relating a work of literature to its society.

But the sections, though their aims are distinct, do not ignore one another's existence. Though questions of literary form are paramount in Chapter 1, the social reality that the novelists

transformed into art cannot be ignored, and the difference
between, for example, Gissing's sober awareness of the nature of
poverty and his wild fantasy of the corruptibility of a man of the
people (between, say, *The Nether World* and *Demos*) is both a
literary matter and a question of social perception. Poetry may seem
less immediately connected to society than fiction, and Chapter 2
can therefore deal more with a self-contained world of verbal
conventions and personal emotion;but even here there is a basis in
social experience — in the last analysis in all forms of poetry, and
most obviously and immediately in the poems dealt with in the
fourth section, those arising from the nineteenth-century battle
between Christianity and scepticism, so that this section is best read
in conjunction with Chapter 8.

Section II is the longest: it is the 'context' which the title
announces. We have preferred to split it into a series of mono-
graphs, so that each chapter concentrates on one aspect of the
society and one set of problems, and is thus enabled to develop a
coherent argument. These chapters make frequent reference to
what the imaginative writers had to say: thus Chapter 3 can almost
be read as a historian's commentary on Carlyle, who more than
anyone else made the reading public aware of the 'Condition-of-
England question'. Literary references are rather more frequent in
Chapter 3 than in Chapter 4, simply because the literary imagination, under the first shock of industrialism, had more to say about
material conditions and the standard of living in the 1840s than in
the 1880s; but Chapter 4 none the less offers an invaluable
background to the reading of those authors (Shaw and Wells on the
one hand, James and Conrad on the other) whose work responds to
new political movements and the rise of socialism. Chapter 5 deals
with the institutions of Victorian England, those aspects of the
body politic (governing, electing, administering, educating, fighting, keeping the peace) that the novelists and their readers took for
granted, and that we now need to be told about. Chapter 6 is
essential to an understanding of the age, which had acquired a
sense of history as no previous generation had ever done: almost all
the great novelists tried their hand at historical novels, just as
almost all the leading architects used the gothic. Chapter 7 is
concerned not only with Victorian painting for its own sake but also
with its overlap with literature: painting invades fiction in the

illustrations to the novels, and is invaded by fiction and history in the narrative paintings that are so central to the period. Chapter 8 deals with what everyone knows to be the great controversy of the age, one which, as it happens, features more prominently in the poetry than in the fiction. It is present in Hardy and Butler but surprisingly absent from George Eliot: *Robert Elmsmere*, by Mrs Humphrey Ward, is the nearest thing to the great agnostic novel that one feels George Eliot should have written. Chapter 9 provides the background to almost any of the novels, since it deals with that most revered of all Victorian institutions, the family. All these chapters, then, offer to the literary student the social context that he needs for the full understanding of the Victorians; but we have to say emphatically that they have not been written merely as background to Victorian literature. Their concern is with the social reality itself, with what Victorian England was like before the novelists got hold of it.

Only the third section addresses itself directly to interdisciplinary questions. Two short essays, one on a novel, the other on a long poem, look both at the social issues dealt with by that work and at questions of form, style and emotional impact, and attempt to explore some of the relations between the two. We felt that this section should analyse particular works for two reasons. First, only in relation to an individual work can the parallels and tensions between form and content be adequately raised; and, second, by turning to each essay after a reading or a rereading of the book in question, the reader will find himself able to argue back on equal terms in a way that is never possible with a survey.

In a book of this length much has to be omitted. We would have liked, for instance, to have had a chapter on the White Man's Burden, discussing attitudes to foreigners and to colonized peoples, and treating of Conrad and Kipling; or one on Victorian science, which is considered in relation to problems of religious belief in Chapter 8, but is also worth discussing for its own sake, as well as for its effect on social institutions and poetic imagery. We have also had to abandon all attempt at factual coverage, so that the reader who wants to know when Gladstone was Prime Minister, or the names of the contributors to *Essays and Reviews*, will have to turn to the appropriate reference books. The short reading lists after each chapter are highly selective, and include only the most appropriate books. References to works by modern scholars are footnoted, but not those to Victorian works that our readers may already know or will probably want to read. These are identified by date when first mentioned in the text, the date being that of first publication.

Laurence Lerner
University of Sussex
May 1977

Part I

The literature

1 The novel

GEOFFREY HEMSTEDT

Novelists before the Victorian period had triumphantly demonstrated the suppleness of the genre, especially as it offered perspectives
of social experience. The novel's development in England had been
closely associated with varieties of realism: Defoe's documentary
concreteness, Richardson's immolating psychology, the dramatic
picaresque in Fielding and Smollett, Jane Austen's refining observation of the comedy of manners, and Scott's revelation of
historical causes and conditions. Although all these afforded
valuable models, the Victorians were to go further. For them the
novel became, in a sense, epic: not in the sense of making conscious
burlesqueing reference to epic conventions, as in Fielding, but
because it performed a function — the comprehensive unfolding of
interrelated destinies — analogous to the traditional functions of
epic. Two writers, pre-eminently, achieved comprehensiveness by
seeking to contain in single works total pictures of society. Dickens,
by the forced marriage of the old romance plots with a visionary
symbolism; and George Eliot, who created a new realism on
structures learned from positivism and scientific inquiry.

We should add to these 'great expectations' of the novelists the
immense popularity of the form. We can distinguish the rare from
the demotic in Victorian literature easily enough in particular cases,
but we do not look to such discriminations for evidences of cultural
polarity as we do, say, to Defoe and Fielding. We soon recognize
instead a Victorian currency of conventional rhetoric which passed

freely across categories and among genres, and was not shunned by serious artists and writers. Though we have made a canon of our own century's literature largely of works that found little popular favour in their time, we have necessarily taken from the Victorians what they themselves widely enjoyed. Tennyson had more readers in his lifetime than any other English poet has had. Paintings at the Royal Academy — new paintings — had to be roped off from eager crowds. If Art was popular, to discover that there was a further 'popular literature' down-market from *David Copperfield* and *The Mill on the Floss* is to recognize that all partly shared a rhetoric and an audience. The shorthand of sentimental tableau was long a vital element of serious literature, and it will be found, elegantly revamped, in Meredith, and vestigially even in James.

But an account of the Victorian novel must still be mainly of evolution and variety, of a form repeatedly stretched and reshaped to accommodate new aspects of experience. In a few cases — Dickens, George Eliot, James — we can follow a grand evolution in a single *oeuvre*. In others — Thackeray, Charlotte and Emily Brontë, Elizabeth Gaskell, Trollope, Gissing, Hardy — though some of them are decently prolific, we recognize unique and fulfilled expressions of their particular sensibility. In every case we can measure the individual contribution in terms of technical authority, the successful rendering of problematic subjects.

All this — abundance, variety, popularity, artistic growth — is found nowhere more sensationally than in Dickens. The processes of change in his work have been partly reflected in shifts of critical taste, and our own mythic sense of what Victorian England was like has been importantly shaped by his works, which themselves have been abstracted into myths. It is true that the Dickens celebrated by Chesterton, the creator of Pickwickian pastoral, of menus and Mrs Gamp, can be found abundantly in the early works, and that subsequent critical accounts of Dickens as symbolist, developing themes of the city, death, money, prisons, have properly emphasized the later novels. But such a distinction can mislead. The first novels, up to *Martin Chuzzlewit* (1843-4), display Dickens's affinities with earlier writers, for example Smollett. He deploys elements of romance and the picaresque with confidence, to construct linear plots ending in what Orwell called 'radiant idleness'. He addresses himself to the exposure of institutional abuses (debtors' prisons, the Poor Law, Yorkshire schools), but already, as in the later works, such themes were often more figurative than topical. His art thrives on popularity, from the moment of the famous and phenomenal success of Sam Weller. This is the period of Little Nell, with the great actor Macready flicking through the serial pages, glimpsing 'a picture of the dear, dead child', and dreading to read on. His choice of subjects shows an eye on the market, and the successes of writers like Ainsworth and Bulwer Lytton; *Oliver Twist* (1837-8) is a novel of criminal life, *Barnaby Rudge* (1841) a historical novel of the Gordon Riots. But in the midst of this turmoil of production, remorselessly paced by serial deadlines, Dickens was initiating the themes he was to pursue for the next thirty years.

When Oliver Twist goes with the undertaker Sowerberry to prepare for a pauper's funeral he passes

> houses which had become insecure from age and decay, [and] were prevented from falling onto the street by huge beams of wood reared against the walls.... The kennel was stagnant and filthy. The very rats, which lay here and there putrefying in its rottenness, were hideous with famine.   (chapter 5)

The pauper is buried in a grave 'so full, that the uppermost coffin was within a few feet of the surface'. Though this all takes place in the provincial town where Oliver was a foundling, its source is plainly in that same London where Ralph Nickleby, going to his suicide, passes a graveyard

> where the very grass and weeds seemed, in their frowzy growth, to tell that they had sprung from paupers' bodies, and had struck roots in the graves of men, sodden while alive in steaming courts and drunken, hungry dens.... Here they lay, cheek by jowl with life, no deeper down than the throng that passed there every day, and piled high as their throats.
> (chapter 62)

In these passages we can see Dickens taking hold of an idea (or perhaps it is truer to say that the idea takes hold of him) and moulding it to enforce a violent poetic conjunction of images and insights. He must wait until *Bleak House* (1852-3) before he commanded the structures which were to reveal the full symbolic truth of these interlocking themes. There he has Jo take Lady

Dedlock to the wretched graveyard in Tom-All-Alone's where her lover is buried, and show her the rat that goes into the ground to feed on corpses, and emerges to spread disease 'through every order of society, up to the proudest of the proud'. From this base he releases a language of revolutionary apocalypse ('Verily, what with tainting, plundering and spoiling, Tom has his revenge'), and weaves the theme of poverty avenged in pestilence tightly into the incidents of the plot. It should be noted that insanitary inner-city graveyards were a contemporary scandal. Dickens's power as a symbolist lay not only in his architectonic skill (the fog of *Bleak House*, the prisons of *Little Dorrit*) but in his discovery of the poetic charge of real social phenomena (the graveyard here, the dustheaps of *Our Mutual Friend*). We also see that this use of the graveyard provides a central insight into the modern mass urban experience. Dickens sees a civilization so unnatural that it cannot bury its dead except with obscene haste. He anticipates the sprouting corpse of *The Waste Land* and the choked incinerators of *La Peste*.

The growing intricacy of plotting from *Bleak House* on reflects his increasingly complex apprehension of social and political structures. His language was naturally rich, his didactic manner sonorous and facetious by changes, but because the early books are largely episodic they do not achieve an organic relation of language and plot. *Oliver Twist*, particularly the world of Fagin and Sykes, comes nearest to the terrifying and total animism that lies at the heart of this relation. It may be that serial writing frustrated holistic design, and he complained of its constraints when in 1841 he wound up the weekly serials in *Master Humphrey's Clock*. But the monthly number was increasingly a stimulus to technical success. In 1865 he spoke of himself as 'the story weaver at his loom', an image which suggests the holding in the mind of the full pattern as the first threads are woven, and the opening paragraphs of *Bleak House* or *Little Dorrit* or *Our Mutual Friend* declare the impending fiction and adumbrate the key language of the whole. These forms were developed not so much to give a resolved account of social connections, (and here we will see George Eliot as something of a contrast), but to imitate volatility and violent paradox. Fielding and Jane Austen had been able to choose comedy, because, for all that they were sharply aware of the manners and pretensions of social mobility, theirs was finally an aesthetic founded on stability, and thus properly expressed in the cyclical regenerations of comic plotting. Dickens saw a society which seemed to have lost its vital instincts of community, an ungovernable chaos where 'civilization and barbarism walked this beautiful island together'. His sensational plots, with their mysteries and Byzantine mazes of coincidence, were of course the stuff of popular art, but they also served to enforce connections and a sense of community in the teeth of selfish materialism.

The struggle to control such material produced many contradictions and conflicts. First, Dickens often seems to be aligned with the reformist spirit of the forties and fifties, in his novels as in his public speeches, when he treats such topics as education, the law, prostitution or industrialism. But the platform of reform cannot bear his weight when he assumes a prophetic diction, to conjure the miasmal putrefaction of the inner city. Yet even that landscape, 'a desert region blasted by volcanic fires', is made to seem less appalling when we are guided by Inspector Bucket in *Bleak House*, or in the report of a night 'On Duty with Inspector Field'. These men reflect something of Dickens's own pride of familiarity with the uncharted slums, and a reformist will to bring savage territory under control. There is also an apparent contradiction between castigating prophecy and the emollient language of pathos: the sentimental tableaux, the hosts of put-upon children and idiots. Like the conventions of romance, these effects survive to the very end of Dickens's career, combining with visionary symbolism to produce a kind of demagogic high style. Dickens gave equally serious attention to both elements, and was more than anybody responsible for the currency of such popular set pieces as the prostitute by the river or the enshrined hearth, and, notoriously, the deathbed seen through a blur of tears. We shall see other writers mistrustful of them, not as being insufficiently grave, but as incompatible with various critical conditions of realism. No such hesitations seem to have inhibited Dickens, however. Many commentators have remarked on the childlike qualities of his imagination, its animism, the vivid apprehension which could be expressed in the grotesque, or in the totality of recreated emotion, terror, loneliness, the sense of comfort. The essential simplicity of the child's dialectic psychology underlies the contrasts I have noted: the nightmare which terrifies or excites (a world of prisons, the mob grinding the guillotine), and the reassuring fantasy (Wemmick's castle, a goose for the Cratchits).

If the account of Dickens as social novelist seems to exclude the second main subject of fiction, the growth and consciousness of the individual, it may be answered that his own processes of mind are everywhere revealed, and that his account of social forces is inseparable from his sense of his private sufferings and deprivations. But famously too he explores the minds of children themselves, most remarkably in *David Copperfield* (Freud's favourite among his novels as well as his own) and *Great Expectations*. The idea of the shaping of personality in coherent development from childhood through youth to maturity, demonstrated by Rousseau, had been an important Romantic theme. For Victorian novelists it was intimately connected with a public measure of experience, just as themes like love and marriage, the relationship with parents, education and sexual status, were explored in a public, quasi-political and thus realist context. *David Copperfield* (1849-50) moves with the expansive scale of the monthly serial between personal exorcisms (the bottling warehouse, the child-wife killed off) and public issues, notably prostitution, and achieves a degree of thematic coherence in the public and private connections of sexuality and of the 'wayward heart'. The social determination of the inner life is clearer in the shorter *Great Expectations* (1860-1), the most disciplined and concentrated of the novels. Pip's emotional and psychological development is shown with penetrating dispassion. The early Satis House scenes are coloured with the psychic chiaroscuro of childhood, so different from Wordsworth's radiance. But the elements of myth and fantasy are made the grounds of a social fable, a fable for the age. Pip's agony is one of class shame mixed with adolescent yearning — it is the beautiful Estella who says 'He calls knaves jacks, this boy, and wears thick boots' — and it forces him to betray the most basic loyalties and affections until he might climb Miss Havisham's stairs 'in lighter boots than of yore'. Pip's is a snob's progress, but pretension is not, as traditionally for Ben Jonson or Fielding, the occasion for satiric comedy. Dickens wrote to his biographer John Forster of the 'grotesque tragi-comic conception' of the plot, and embarrassment claims something of the status of tragic emotion. The reader recognizes a new central myth in social mobility. Everything bears

on this theme — Wopsle's pathetically inadequate Hamlet, the
mockery of Trabb's boy, Orlick's advancement. Pip's friendship
with Herbert Pocket is moving precisely because of it. They must
develop rituals of studied kindness, of giving and accepting, the
gifts being initiations into the mysteries of etiquette. But the
contrast remains between such secondary characteristics of affection
and the primal love they have replaced, that between Jo and Pip.
Dickens conceived Pip's world as an alienating one, his earliest
nurture harsh and reluctant. When Peggotty strains the child David
to her breast the buttons pop off the back of her dress, suggesting a
willing and fruitful embrace. Pip's sister, with her 'trenchant way
of cutting bread', the loaf clasped to her apron, feeds him pins and
needles. As first written, the novel ended with Pip's inevitable
loneliness. Like Clennam in *Little Dorrit* he experiences the isolation
compulsively explored by the modernists, and if we begin by comparing Dickens with Smollett we end with a glimpse of Kafka.

Dickens offers revelation rather than analysis. His style is declara-
tive, his development one of depth and force, not of internal
critical qualification. Thackeray has traditionally been contrasted
with him, first by the Victorians themselves. In 1851 the critic
David Masson saw Dickens as practising the 'ideal' style, which
'strikes, not by recalling real scenes and occurences, but by taking
the mind out of itself into a region of higher possibilities.'
Thackeray, he said, was a realist, whose aim was 'to reproduce
pictures that shall impress by their close and truthful resemblance
to something or other in real nature or life.' The convincingness of
Thackeray has been challenged by post-Jamesian critics like
Lubbock and Forster, who complained that he subverted the
autonomy of his fictions by persistent commentary and interpola-
tion. His style, as Trollope said, 'smells of the lamp'. His manipu-
lation of character often recalls earlier, satiric modes, where the
character is allowed only a functional or typological being. When
we are conscious of this, and of wit, and of Thackeray's apprenticeship in journalism and burlesque, we may find it hard to see how
central he was to the development of European realism. We may
regret the shift of balance from satire to sentiment in his work, but
there was not always enough sentiment to content his first readers.
G.H. Lewes complained of his 'terrible impartiality' and 'perpetual
laughter', and he spoke for a public who wanted reassurance that a

writer was being serious about serious matters, and who distrusted satire for that reason. The *Westminster Review* of 1837 attacked caricature and satire as 'depreciation viewed as art', and throughout the period we should be aware of a demand for what Luke Fildes was to call in the sixties 'a graver style of art'. In Thackeray the conditions of satire and realism were intimately connected, but his was not the satire of *saeva indignatio* or the nightmare figures of a world turned upside down. He sought an emotionally disciplined rhetoric, claiming that the novel, generically, had its own decorum of language, which is essentially prosaic. He is for ever, in E.M. Forster's phrase, 'cooling things down'. He delights in private jokes and schoolboy absurdities. He decorates the letterpress of *Vanity Fair* (1847-8) with fantastical vignettes, comparing the characters to clowns and dolls and puppets. He delays the rendering of the expected scene, as for example when Rawdon is to discover his wife alone with Lord Steyne, until the reader knows it has occurred, and the tension is dissipated. He omits death scenes (Sedley, old Osborne, Sir Pitt Crawley), and subsumes them somehow into the flow of narrative or commentary. Notoriously he kills George Osborne off at Waterloo in a subordinate clause. The reader has little occasion to indulge the tearful thrills he might find in Dickens. Thackeray offers him instead a regretful cynicism, and urbane intimacies spoken as to a clubfellow. *Vanity Fair*'s subtitle, 'Pen and Pencil Sketches of English Society', suggests an intermittent and shifting focus, and a sinewy patter pulls the whole together.

How does this square with the conditions of realism? It is a realism of critical attitude, censoring severely the excitements of dramatic illusion, and demanding analysis from sentence to sentence, if only in the recognitions of wit. It is antiheroic, most successfully in the choice of the Waterloo years for the setting of *Vanity Fair*, where he sought to expose not only Napoleon, as the great historic type of vanity, but the gross complacency of the British as they looked back to a famous victory with their 'braggart heathen allegories, commemorating the fallen in St Paul's'. Lukács has identified 'the exposure of false heroism, in particular the reputed heroism fostered by historical legend',[1] as the basis of his style.

1 *The Historical Novel* (London, 1962), p.202.

Thackeray suggests that historical painters should concentrate on genre scenes from the British expedition to Belgium, not on scenes of martial glory. In the novel the great battle is heard only at a distance, and the measure of the heroic is in Mrs Major O'Dowd packing her husband's kit ('Venus preparing the armour of Mars'). He shares with traditional mock-heroic modes a concern with proportion, and the use of deliberate disproportion to expose falsity. His realism of selection, the historical event viewed through details taken from its periphery, recalls Stendhal's account of Waterloo in *La Chartreuse de Parme*, and becomes an essential condition of epic celebration in *War and Peace*.

Beyond this, Thackeray's chief theme is the corruption of values, the mean admiration of mean things. Though their styles are so contrary, Carlyle's influence is felt here too. He takes the flunkeys of Brussels and the Regency, the complacency of city men, the *opera buffo* world of Pumpernickel, and fills every crevice with a binding mortar of snobbism. He gives a cumulative sense of haggard emptiness, of real spiritual exhaustion underlying the uproarious glittering surface, chiefly dramatized by Becky Sharp, that very Victorian type of talent nurtured by environment. She has 'the dismal precocity of poverty'. What gave his argument uncomfortable edge to his first readers is that he does not confine his attack to the undemocratic viciousness of privilege, entrusting social virtue to the endeavour and morality of the burgess, but sees the middle class as corrupted by political advance and wallowing in stupid materialism. He has a fine sense of the tribal accoutrements of class, and can measure the gross weight of mahogany and brass. Better than any Victorian novelist he conveys the intimacy of domestic geography, and the life-sentence of family life where bonds of duty are stronger than love.

These skills serve him well in *The Newcomes* (1853-5), where he displays a developed understanding of the collective dynastic ascendancies and jealousies of the middle class. It has a more contemporary feel than his other novels, but implies dimensions of history analogous to those of *Vanity Fair* or *Esmond*, and the three together define changing cultural values across a wide span of time. In *The Newcomes* themes of love and marriage, and through them the status of women, are conceived as part of public process, intimately caught up in considerations of money and class.

If the satire exposes false values, his second great theme is nostalgia, not so much in elegiac celebration of the values which have been abandoned, but rather in an intensified disillusionment. He catches this mood pre-eminently in *Henry Esmond* (1852), where the plot enables him also to express a more uncomplicated and directly emotional form of nostalgia through the contrast between Esmond the man and Esmond the boy. Childhood and youth are seen in retrospect to have been a preparation for the chastening vision of maturity in the opening movement of *Philip* (1861-2) as well, though the element of historical nostalgia is not present. Significantly, by turning back to the early eighteenth century in *Esmond* he not only immersed himself in the Augustanism he cherished, but chose a lost cause. Esmond sees the Pretender as a private person, and with the filters of memory and pastiche Thackeray again adjusts the distortions of history, this time more in sorrow than in anger. The escape backwards in time, like the bitter-sweet exile of *The Virginians*, can be seen as a reaction against the materialism of his age. The gesture is rich in his sense of its futility.

To Charlotte Brontë, Thackeray was 'a Titan' but 'never borne away by his own ardour'. The control she admired in him she did not accomplish easily, and the intensely private world she shaped and reshaped in *The Professor, Jane Eyre* and *Villette* defied existing forms. The astonishing story of her family has been often told, but we should remember from it the long apprenticeship in fantasy with her brother and sisters, the consuming mental passion of Angria, the imagined world she created in the writings of her childhood and youth. In all her work, though less in *Shirley*, she enacts a dialectic of fantasy and reason, or release and repression. Thus she forces her last heroine to declare 'I, Lucy Snowe, plead guiltless to that curse, an overheated and discursive imagination.' Her importance, and Emily Brontë's, in the history of the novel, is that they provide a bridge from Richardson and the Romantics to modern psychological literature, to the experiments of James and Lawrence's transcendentalism. It is useless to object of *Jane Eyre* (1847) that the after-dinner conduct of fine ladies is naïvely pictured, or that Rochester is a schoolgirl's sex object. The opening pages demonstrate an incomparable blend of expressionism and discipline. The tableau of the girl in the window-seat, indeed every remembered detail of room and furniture, has disturbing meta-phoric resonance. The tiny wood-engravings Jane peers at command her whole mind and open sensational vistas of icy wastes and empty seas. It is with this sense of utter psychic exposure that we should approach the sufferings she describes at Lowood School, and the straining for a correlative sensationalism of plot. Rochester, French mistress, mad mulatto and all, is nothing to it.

In *Villette* (1853) there are great technical advances, in the sustained dramatic decorum of the narrative persona, and in the cryptic and oblique projection of surrogates for Lucy Snowe (Miss Marchmont, the child Paulina). The supernatural is ruthlessly expunged, and though she insists on facing psychological trauma (compare the ending with that of *Jane Eyre*) in doing so she makes bold use of elipsis, as when she gives only a hectic, figurative account of the loss of parents.

It is unfair to tag Emily Brontë on as if in an aside, but her single novel, an *oeuvre* in itself, is in a way complementary to Charlotte's work. *Wuthering Heights* (1847) is the most purely Romantic novel but, for all that Charlotte was fearful of its abandonment, its energies are held in a dynamic balance by sophisticated technique. Its symbolism is established on a considered, symmetrical structure, its language is pellucid, and the double insulation of those phlegmatic reporters, Lockwood and Nellie Dean, ensures a matter-of-fact rather than a baleful account of its wonders. Together with *Jane Eyre* and *Villette* it accomplishes a late but complete accom-modation of the Romantic impulse to the formal demands of the novel. Though the main actions of these psychodramas take place in the isolation of the moor, or the claustrophobic enclosure of house or pensionnat, the topography and dating are real. Heathcliff is a city foundling, and his exile from Wuthering Heights takes him away to a world we assume we can know. Though Lucy Snowe sees London with a kind of neurotic ceremonial awe, though her inner self moves and her spirit shakes to behold 'a solemn, orbed mass, dark blue and dim — THE DOME', it *is* St Paul's, as Villette is Brussels. And in *Shirley* (1849) Charlotte Brontë takes as a subject industrialism, the topic that exercised so many Victorian novelists.

To understand the difficulties posed by that subject we cannot do better than turn to Charlotte's biographer, Elizabeth Gaskell, but we should first take a wider view. If we assume from the presence

of a later work like *Germinal* an inevitable correlation between
naturalism or social realism and the treatment of industrial life, we
should remember that when the topic was thrust before the
novelists of the 1840s as the core of the Condition-of-England
question there were simply no models of how to write about it.
Disraeli, clearly, felt no technical anxiety. Although he makes
telling use of parliamentary Blue Books to reveal the unthinkable
degradation of workers in *Sybil or the Two Nations*, the novel is a
Hollywood *mélange* of pasteboard gothic and silver-fork romance,
rounded off with Luddites for Indians and the militia for cavalry.
His talent is really exotic-satiric, as in *Coningsby, or the New
Generation* (1844) or the early parts of *Tancred, or the New
Crusade* (1847), befitting his belief in the momentousness of
antechamber intrigue and Young Englandry, and the merchant
banker as charismatic hero. In Dickens too the theme of industrialism is perplexing. On the one hand the ironmaster in *Bleak House*
is the hero as captain of industry, the mythic Saxon resurrected to
challenge the Norman, the candidate for a government of reformist
promise. In him Dickens celebrates a new sense of feudal responsibility, contrasting both with Dedlocked privilege and the rotting
hopelessness of London. In *Hard Times*, however, the point of view
changes. For Rouncewell we have Bounderby, and the enemy is to
be seen indifferently in capitalist, utilitarian and trade-union
agitator. 'Fro' first to last a muddle', and Dickens wishes it would
all go away.

Mrs Gaskell was better placed. She lived in Manchester, where
her husband was a Unitarian minister, and *Mary Barton* and *North
and South* gain direction from an evangelical desire to give an
informative account of things her readers simply did not know. She
attempts this not at a level of political abstraction, nor primarily as
part of a wide structural analysis, but with the closer focus of
reportage, and brings the same skills of sympathetic attention to
the rhythms and rituals of domestic custom she exhibits in *Cranford*
and *Wives and Daughters*. The themes and treatment of the latter
show her affinities with Jane Austen and George Eliot, but in the
industrial novels she was able to concentrate her sense of manners
and sharp ear to observe the newer rhythms of industrial city life.
We do not look to her for the epic urban poetry of Dickens, but she
gives a sufficient documentation of housing, disease, sanitation,

food, and so on, to command the attention and concern of her first readers. By choosing Chartism as a background for *Mary Barton* she meets her subject at its most controversial, risking an encounter with their worst fears and prejudices, and it should not be surprising that romance vies with sensationalism to express the violence of the issue. The Carson murder, however, cannot be entirely put down to melodrama. It seems to be demanded by the forces released in the book. We might compare the profounder ironic symbolism of the scene in *Germinal* where the old miner Bonnemort is galvanized from paralysis by the charitable visit of Cécile Grégoire, the kindly and well-meaning daughter of capitalists, and throttles her.

That set piece of charitable visiting is a succinct means of reference to attitudes and points of connection between the classes. It expresses perfectly the contradictions of concern and condescension, of kindness and exploitation, inherent in paternalism. For Jane Austen Emma can be properly sententious about the humbling lessons of visiting the poor, but the scale of the Victorian novel exposes the increasing inadequacy and irrelevance of the gesture. When the brickmaker in *Bleak House* tells Mrs Pardiggle what to do with her babby's books we feel that the charitable instinct has suffered a mortal wound. But we should in justice remember that for many people, for the class Mrs Gaskell belonged to and addressed, the instinct of concern could not easily find other ways to express itself, and there is no irony in her allowing Margaret Hale to bring to the North those habits of pastoral visiting she learned as a vicar's daughter in the South. More significantly Mrs Gaskell defines differences between these two societies in the absence of ingrained deference. Margaret is struck by the boldness of northern working men, who stare her frankly in the face. Giving and receiving appear as a matter of necessity, a desperate balancing of the scales of boom and slump. Margaret's education in the North does not provide quite the expected contrast between the coherent interdependence of 'natural' rural community and the brash sterility of the new mechanism. She comes to see the social graces of the South as founded on an exhausted subsistence economy. A functional, materialist sense of class takes over from conventional measures. A marriage between Margaret and the manufacturer Thornton is vestigially a union of gentry and trade, become a union of North and South, and the relationship between Thornton and Higgins, for all its idealizing, remains a frank dramatization of master and man, within the cash nexus. In Mrs Gaskell, as so often in the Victorian novel, formal invention has been stimulated by a new sense of social interaction, and we see those paradoxes of sympathy and deep class separation that constitute contemporary consciousness.

'North' and 'South' are temporal rather than spatial metaphors, and the index of social change in time is completed by George Eliot. *Felix Holt the Radical* (1866), her nearest approach to an industrial novel, opens with a stagecoach journey through the central plain of England which is also a journey through economic history — from the ancient world of the buried hamlet which seems to 'lie away from everything but its own patch of earth and sky', through 'the district of clean little market-towns without manufactures, of fat livings, an aristocratic clergy, and low poor-rates'. Then the land 'begins to blackened with coal pits, the rattle of hand-looms to be heard in hamlets and villages', and finally we come to 'a manufacturing town, the scene of riots and trade union meetings'. The time of the novel's main action, like that of *Middlemarch*, is around the Reform Bill of 1832, and in *Silas Marner* and *Adam Bede* she goes back to the turn of the century. Some breaking-back in time was a standard device of the period. Dickens, who was somewhat cavalier about dating and topicality, generally seems to assume about thirty years, to accommodate the action and the projected rewards and punishments of the ending. George Eliot's choice is more pointed, identifying what she called 'pregnant moments in history', when the phasal nature of history conceived by the Positivists was revealed in crisis or transition. (The same motives can be found in Tolstoy.) In *Romola* she elects Savonarola's Florence as a moment of cultural climax and readjustment. Centrally George Eliot is concerned with the social change wrought by the Industrial Revolution, with a focus not on industrialism itself but on those traditional provincial communities, founded on a land economy, where its shock waves are more subtly felt. We should remember that her career in fiction was confined to the years 1856-76 (she began twenty years after Dickens), and her retrospective analyses of village and provincial life were carried out in the light of later social evolutions. We have seen one reactionary use of historical material in Thackeray. George Eliot contains elements of the same, and of the Carlylean 'past and present' rhetoric of contrast, but contrast is less at issue than evolutionary continuity, the growth and working of institutions. In this she is influenced by the German Higher Criticism, and by the historical writings of Niebuhr. It coincides, too, with the positivist creed that there is no aspect of private life which is not importantly determined by public events.

Her farseeing apprehension of these patterns was to demand more and more comprehensive forms of narrative. The expected sentimental functions of pastoral contrast cannot be maintained even in her pictures of Hayslope in *Adam Bede* (1859) and Raveloe in *Silas Marner* (1861), because she inevitably probes processes and structures in a language of tolerant scepticism. Of Marner's Primitive Methodism she says drily, then movingly,

> A weaver who finds hard words in his hymn book knows nothing of abstractions; as a little child knows nothing of parental love, but only knows one face and one lap towards which it stretches it arms for love and nurture.

And with perhaps a touch of atavistic loyalty to her Nonconforming fathers, she contrasts Raveloe,

> orchards looking lazy with neglected plenty; the large church in the wide churchyard, which men gazed at lounging at their own doors in service time ... homesteads ... where women seemed to be laying up a stock of linen for the life to come.
>
> (Chapter 2)

There is a scratch of satire, but also a realization that the linked destinies of Anglicanism and an English village have reached a point of crisis. We might compare young Donnithorne's coming-of-age in *Adam Bede*, or Mrs Poyser's shadow-boxing with the old squire, for their humorous penetration; genre pictures, maybe, but carefully painted to show what it means to be tenant and landlord, descendant of lord or bondman. It is not easy for the reader to be 'sure that Old England was the best of all possible countries'.

Her determinism is vital to her conception of the internal moral growth or corruption of individuals, as well as of the external constraints that hold them. When she describes the small degrees of self-deception that lead Arthur Donnithorne to seduce Hetty, she says 'Our deeds determine us, and we determine our deeds.' It is a brilliantly simple formula, and may stand for her substitution of a scientific, rational ethical imperative for a religious one. From this formula she develops the sombre beauty of dramatic example found, say, in the scenes between Dorothea and Casaubon in *Middlemarch* (1871-2). There, in a famous passage, she speaks of 'that element of tragedy which lies in the very fact of frequency', and suggests that if our sensibility were widened to embrace this realist relocation of the tragic impulse we could not bear it, 'we should die of that roar which lies on the other side of silence'. But some approach to such a sympathy, some attempt to see a way clear through 'the dim lights and tangled circumstance' of modern life, completes her redefinition of a moral imperative, the one thing needful where there is 'no coherent social faith and order which could perform the function of knowledge for the ardently willing soul'. 'Ardent' is a key word in *Middlemarch*, bespeaking a protestant energy which contrasts interestingly with Pater's gemlike flame. His *Leonardo* essay was published in 1869, and the whole Roman episode in *Middlemarch* carries suggestions of a dialogue with the sensibility it expresses. Where Pater might speak of the 'hidden transitions which unite all ages' Dorothea can see only dead civilizations piled on top of one another, in the 'oppressive masquerade of ages'. George Eliot herself seems to imply a maturer synthesis of opposing sensibilities when she speaks of 'the gigantic broken revelations of that Imperial and Papal city'. This is but one example of the incomparable intellectual fullness of *Middlemarch*. Lydgate's interest in epidemic diseases and his training with the physiologist Bichat, who sought the all-unifying tissue, invite metaphoric comparison with the structures of the body politic. Casaubon's futile quest for the Key to all Mythologies (Ladislaw regrets his lack of German) lacks the guiding principles of the Higher Criticism. There is hardly an area of serious discourse not engaged by this novel, but we feel no sense of incongruity between such a commentary and a mere fiction. There is an answering fullness in the dramatic declension of love and marriage, of motive and will, of the fibrous maze of connections which link any act to any other, and a roundness attained by a focus of sympathy constantly shifting. A didacticism which could be overwhelming is

finally transcended by a seemingly unconscious revelation of contra-
dictory impulses. Her view of historical movement seems to partake
of the dominant progressivism of the age, but *Middlemarch* is
disturbingly scattered with images of wounding and truncation, as
if in acknowledgement of the repressive mortifications exacted by
duty. The peroration is remorselessly ambivalent.

> But the effect of her being on those around her was incalcul-
> ably diffusive: for the growing good of the world is partly
> dependent on unhistoric acts; and that things are not so ill
> with you and me as they might have been, is half owing to
> the number who lived faithfully a hidden life, and rest in
> unvisited tombs.

It is important too that Dorothea's expectations of life cannot be
fulfilled in Middlemarch itself (the name connotes both a centre
and a borderland). The typical society has been scrutinized and
found wanting. We might compare this with the turning away from
England to the mythic promise of Zionism in her last novel, *Daniel
Deronda* (1876).

In the late century the attempt to write epically comprehensive
novels of national analysis was abandoned for more specific concerns (James's commentaries of consciousness, Gissing's social
realism, Hardy's regionalism). Trollope, monumentally prolific,
provides the exception. His first, 'Irish', novels were published in
the forties, and by his death in 1882 he had completed sixty-odd
books, which collectively make up the grandest fictional survey of
Victorian society, comparable to Balzac's *Comédie Humaine*. Some
of their groupings invite this collective view, famously *The Chron-
icles of Barsetshire* (1855-67) and the 'Political Novels' (1864-80).
Further, characters and recalled events pass from group to group,
gradually filling in the details of a fictional world superimposed on
the grid of real historical time and place. It is as if he is creating a
single massive plot. This process of accretion and linking recalls in
different ways (besides Balzac) Scott, Zola, Hardy and Faulkner,
though Trollope, we notice, does not share their various gestatory
views of time. His narratives are cursive rather than organic — he
has been cruelly used for confessing to an entirely admirable ability
to write by the clock — and his sharpest talents, of observation,
dramatic deployment and character motivation, are germane to the

comedy of manners or satire. He greatly admired Thackeray, and *The Way We Live Now* (1875), his most ambitious single novel of public life, has the edge and candour of Thackeray's realism. As a market novelist he is prepared to use a full range of sentimental tableaux (*Orley Farm* for example is packed with sophisticated melodrama), but he prefers the well-killed fox to the dying crossing-sweeper. His is the lone true voice of the Tory aesthetic, not Disraelian, but of the shires, gruff.

Meredith's comic spirit also reaches back to Thackeray, in its sense of proportion and the belief that the dispassionate correction of conceit and distorting sentimentality can best be accomplished through the disciplines of wit. His convoluted style is itself a means of holding his characters at cane's length; the voice ambiguously suggests poise and insecurity, the mandarin and the mouthful of marbles. It should be remembered, though, that Meredith was a poet of considerable skill as well as a novelist, and there is poetic depth in his rendering of psychology and sexuality, most freely in his early novel *The Ordeal of Richard Feverel* (1859). He held to a profound, Platonic belief in the equality of the sexes, and in *The Egoist* (1878) with a delicate counterpoint of satire and lyricism he prepared a triumph for Clara Middleton, breaking ground for James's Isabel Archer, and even for the New Woman.

In James we encounter the harbinger of modernism, who achieves a decisive shift of emphasis from subject to form. In a note to *The Portrait of a Lady* (1885) he wrote: 'The whole of anything is never told. You can only take what groups together,' and in his long career he pursued unremittingly the patterns and scrutinies which would reveal the truth of an offered subject, the treasured *donnée*. The transition in the novel from Victorian to modern is complex, and cannot be defined by simple contrasts. The quasi-epistemological concerns of the moderns (James himself, Conrad, Virginia Woolf) develop an impulse we have already seen in Thackeray's reflexive wit and George Eliot's metaphoric probing in *Middlemarch* of the novel's own narrative structures. The quest for narrative autonomy, by annihilating the author as commentator or proposing a dramatic relation between narrator and story, is of course anticipated by Charlotte Brontë and many others. If we recall that the device goes back to Defoe, we see again that the modernist confronts essentially the traditional technical problems of realism. The modernist, it might be said, busies himself with solving the problem the hard way. If this formalist preoccupation can be traced as a continuing process of refinement, it also seems to reflect a loss of confidence in the public register of art, a turning-in on the self as a reaction against the proliferation of social identities.

A famous image in *Middlemarch* shows how a light reflected in a pierglass seems to throw the myriad random scratches on its surface into a pattern. The simile is compared to the distortive forces of egoism, but it may also suggest the possibility that the novelist can find a point of vantage from which to view the hidden patterns of social connection. Trollope apart, the novelists following George Eliot stop short of an inclusive picture of 'the way we live now', and stake out special claims. Even Gissing, who was strongly influenced by both Dickens and Zola, closes down the reference of successive novels to topical focus: socialist careerism (*Demos*, 1886), the means of literary production (*New Grub Street*, 1891), feminism (*The Odd Women*, 1893). He shares with Arthur Morrison the subject of the decayed inner city, with London a dreadful example of the disappointment of reformist hopes. At times, however, the motives he claims for a language of social realism deliberately exclude prescription or political analysis, and seem closer to the late Victorian creeds of art for art's sake.

> I do not dogmatise, remember, my ideas are negative, and on the whole I confine myself to giving pictures of life as it looks to my observation of it ... but without reflecting on its origin.[2]

This brings us back to James's insistence that the artist should not violate the clarity of the subject, which must be allowed to determine its appropriate forms of expression. To emphasize only his formalism, however, is to falsify. He is as substantial a novelist as any High Victorian, but in a new way. His grand persistent themes — of innocence and knowledge, of the morality of art, of betrayal and spiritual corruption — rest on mythic foundations and at the same time are corroborated by specific cultural and historical manifestations. To compare how these themes are treated in

2 April (1891). *Letters of George Gissing to Members of his Family*, ed. A. and E. Gissing, (London, 1931), p.318.

different novels is to see something of James's complexity. The contrast between innocence and corruption is often linked with that between Europe and America. Sometimes the Americans are simply innocent as befits the inhabitants of a new world — a treatment announced in the poised comedy of *The Europeans*, given tragic expression in the case of Milly Theale in *The Wings of the Dove*, and returning to a deeper comedy in *The Ambassadors*. But the most deeply corrupt of Jamesian characters are also Americans — Gilbert Osmond, for instance, in *The Portrait of a Lady*; and in the same novel the sinister polish of Mme Merle turns out to have been born under the stars and stripes. In *The Awkward Age* and *What Maisie Knew* he locates spiritual and sexual decadence in the purposeless *ennui* of a *rentier* society. The dominant example of this layering is the ever-renewed encounter of the innocence of the New World with the corruption of Europe. With Whistler, and later Pound and Eliot, he forms that company of expatriate Americans who mediate between the insular English and a wider cultural experience. In James's case we see the mingling of English, American and European influences. For his explorations of moral psychology he learned from Hawthorne and Flaubert, and also from George Eliot. His use of metaphor in the commentary of consciousness may be seen as a development of her High Victorian patheticism; consider, for example, her recurrent use of motifs of water and drowning in character studies from Maggie Tulliver through to Gwendolen Harleth. His treatment of London, especially in *The Princess Casamassima*, is influenced by Dickens, though, as we have already seen, his characteristic frame of reference is cultural rather than socio-political, and not confined by the traditional bounds of English community. For this wider dimension he could look to the Russians, who in the nineteenth century had perforce to engage a European consciousness which had historically been separate from their own. Here James comes closest to Turgenev, and we find in both the same sense of displacement, with its poignant ambivalencies of discovery and exile. It seems fitting that the meeting place of the two writers should have been Paris.

As a final contrast Hardy's regionalism reasserts the central position in the social novel of traditional English communities. Like Emily Brontë and Lawrence, he sets his study of social relations against a symbolic natural landscape. He lacks their essential romanticism, however, which he qualifies by an instinctive irony and an ambivalent sense of man's relation to natural environment, compounded of Wordsworthian sympathy and a post-Darwinian realization of struggle. His scale of determinism reaches beyond the recognizable time of modern economic change, or the generational time of families, and thus beyond the conventional measures of realism. His Wessex is an ancient place, and yields evidences of Roman and prehistoric civilizations. The choric rustic consciousness provides a mythic redefinition of the past.

> Casterbridge is an old, hoary place o' wickedness by all accounts. 'Tis recorded in history that we rebelled against the king one or two hundred years ago, in the time of the Romans, and that lots of us was hanged on gallows hill and quartered, and our different jints sent about the country like butcher's meat.

The proportions of time and space equally diminish man and induce a grim fatalism. The richness of Hardy's vision resides in a combination of this inherent poeticism, which apprehends the numinous power of Egdon Heath or Maiden Castle (later the landscapes of John Cowper Powys), with a realist address to economic change and the institutional workings of society. *The Mayor of Casterbridge* (1886) blends classical tragedy with themes of changing commercial relations within the community. His last major works, *Tess of the D'Urbevilles* (1891) and *Jude the Obscure* (1896), complete this marriage of tragic and realist forms to produce a revolutionary expressionism, jagged and sombre, which invites comparison with Ibsen. He breaks the moulds of decorum to find a style which is harshly prosaic and transcendental by turns, with a cumulative structure of symbolic episode. It is difficult to realize that the elementalism of *Jude* embraces such mundane topics as divorce and the admission policy of universities.

The end of the century saw the resources of realism pressed into service for a functional literature of entertainment created by the magazine short-story market. The fog of *Bleak House* swirls around the door of 221b Baker Street, and in M.R. James's stories ghosts infest hotel and drawing room. More important are Kipling's technical virtuosity — he too takes part in the transition to modernism — and Wells's directing of the novel to scientific speculation:

Darwinism, eugenics, entropy. The Martians come to the Home Counties, and the Time Traveller sees the sun huge in the sky, and the slow viscous seas which will engulf what once was Jane Austen's England.

2 Poetry

LAURENCE LERNER

Before the nineteenth century, the relationship between poet and poem was simple: the poet was the maker, the poem was the product. If poems were discussed in terms of emotion, this always meant the reader's emotion, not the poet's. After the Romantic movement a new conception appears, that of a poem as the expression of the poet's emotion: a poem is now seen as retaining an umbilical link with its creator. This gives a new twist to the old doctrine of inspiration: the poet who feels uninspired no longer sees himself as out of touch with an external force, but as not in proper touch with his own feelings. And so Coleridge tells us that he cannot write because he has lost his feeling of joy; Wordsworth discovers a 'thought of grief' in himself and writes a poem in order to give 'that thought relief'. This doctrine continues right through the nineteenth century and is still with us. It leads Hopkins to compare the writing of a poem to the conception, carrying and bearing of a child, and Yeats to say that 'out of the quarrel with others we make rhetoric, out of the quarrel with ourselves we make poetry'. Such a contrast between rhetoric and poetry would have seemed incomprehensible to a Renaissance critic: in post-Romantic aesthetics it has become orthodox. The most systematic exposition of this new theory comes in the aesthetic writings of Croce and Collingwood: Collingwood's *Principles of Art* distinguishes between the expression of emotion, which is art, and the arousing of emotion in others, which is craft (or rhetoric). In such a view, the central poetic genre will be the lyrical, and Wordsworth's description of poetry as the spontaneous overflow of powerful feelings provides us with a phrase that can be used as a definition of lyric poetry.

We must begin with the Romantics because Victorian poetry (or at any rate Victorian lyric poetry) is a continuation of the Romantic tradition. We already think of a first Romantic generation (Wordsworth, Coleridge, Lamb, Scott) and a second (Byron, Shelley, Keats). The accident of the Queen's long reign should not conceal from us that Tennyson and Browning are the third Romantic generation, and Rossetti, Morris and Swinburne the fourth. This is not merely to say that Tennyson was soaked in Keats and Browning in Shelley, that Arnold is unimaginable without Wordsworth; but also that there is theoretical continuity. We have to wait for Mallarmé and T.S. Eliot for the doctrine that a poem is an artefact whose existence is independent of the poet's emotions.

The only way to discuss Victorian poetry is to discuss Victorian poems; and so we will look at a number of lyrics before moving out to discuss what conception of poetry they imply. Let us begin with Browning, whose finest lyric is certainly *Two in the Campagna* (1855). The speaker of this, alone with his beloved in the Roman campagna on a hot day of early summer, has been trying to capture a thought that he imagines himself pursuing through the landscape. We are not told directly what the thought is, but it is clearly connected with the longing described in the later stanzas, 'I would that you were all to me'. It is a poem, we realize, on love's imperfection: if the two of them seem to attain perfect union for a moment, 'then the good minute goes'. The last stanza is helpless in its feeling of irrecoverable loss:

> Just when I seemed about to learn!
> Where is the thread now? Off again!
> The old trick! Only I discern —
> Infinite passion and the pain
> Of finite hearts that yearn.

There has been dispute among critics about how far this poem is to be read biographically. Browning had been married eight years when it was written; although the marriage has passed into legend

as one of perfect happiness (the snatching of Elizabeth Barrett from
a sick-bed and a curmudgeonly father have naturally helped the
legend), there have been twentieth-century scholars who have
detected in it a growing series of disagreements, resulting in
tensions and discontent, and who therefore read a personal statement in such lines as:

> I would that you were all to me,
> You that are just so much, no more —
> Nor yours nor mine, — nor slave nor free!
> Where does the fault lie? what the core
> Of the wound, since wound must be?

It is not merely in order to vindicate the Brownings' marital bliss
that it is important to reject such an interpretation. The point is not
simply biographical, but rather involves placing the poem in the
line to which it belongs — that of the Romantic poems of *Welt-
schmerz*, of divine discontent. Shelley's *Ode to a Skylark* is one of
the prototypes of this.

> We look before and after,
> And pine for what is not:
> Our sincerest laughter
> With some pain is fraught,
> Our sweetest songs are those that tell of saddest thought.

The skylark is celebrated as a contrast to the human condition, for
its song is free of the inevitable frustrations of a creature whose
longings are infinite. So sober and rational a man as John Stuart
Mill attacked the reductivism of Benthamite psychology because it
did not sufficiently value that sensitivity which is aware of the
imperfections of happiness. 'It is better to be Socrates dissatisfied
than a fool satisfied,' he wrote in his essay on *Utilitarianism*
(1863). It is not surprising that his taste in poetry was orthodox and
Romantic, that he valued spiritual consolation and Wordsworth's
ability to see into the life of things. *Two in the Campagna*
illustrates Mill's point, and not to realize this is to miss the force of
its most powerful lines. 'Where does the fault lie?' is not a piece of
marital cross-questioning apportioning blame between the two
partners, but a preparation for the helpless accepting of the human
condition on which the poem ends. This is what makes the setting

so marvellously appropriate to the theme: the whole poem is built
on a parallel between a sense experience — the attempt to capture
something elusive that darts about the summer landscape — and
the elusiveness of perfect love. A landscape like this is full of
suggestive analogies — a butterfly, a gossamer thread, an optical
mirage, the play of light. We are in a setting where the natural
scene itself tantalizes and leads on, and in which the theme of the
poem as inevitably belongs as the thistle-ball of the second last
stanza. We misunderstand *Two in the Campagna* unless we read it
as about a happy love: the contrast with, for instance, *By the
Fireside*, in which Browning celebrates unclouded happiness,
should not be exaggerated. *Two in the Campagna* is one of the
central poems of its age: the pain of finite hearts that yearn is
perhaps the underlying theme of all Romantic lyric poetry. It is
found in Arnold's lyrics, many of which are elusively attached to a
shadowy figure known as Marguerite. Marguerite's story, even her
identity, is a harder nut for Arnold's biographers than the well-
documented story of the Browning marriage; and it is at least as
irrelevant to the poetry. The lack of a story suggests that this
unhappy romance survives in the poet's memory not because of
particular problems but because it exemplifies the same infinite
passion and inevitable loss. The finest of all Arnold's Marguerite
poems ('Yes, in the sea of life enisled', 1852) makes no reference to
her except in its title. It too uses an analogy from nature, but in a
very different manner from that of Browning. The isolated mortals
are seen as islands, who in their moments of intensest longing feel
they were once 'parts of a single continent'. This analogy is very like
a conceit: an ingenious and unusual comparison deployed with wit.
The poet does not begin descriptively, placing us literally in a
natural setting that later provides the metaphors, as does *Two in
the Campagna*, as do most nineteenth-century lyrics, including
many of Arnold's: it offers sea and islands purely as analogy. This
could make it into a poem by Donne or Jonson, the sort of poem
Arnold would be ill at ease writing; so it is worth noticing how
strongly Romantic the details are:

> And in their glens, on starry nights,
> The nightingales divinely sing.

This is pure poetic atmosphere, built out of nineteenth-century

materials, sweeping us along with a sense of beauty, not inviting us
to pause and apply the details to the poem's argument: 'divinely',
for instance, is not meant theologically, and means little more than
'beautifully'. And the marvellous last line of the poem, with its
hopeless rhythm, its crushing load of adjectives, invokes the same
infinite pain that Browning's poem ends on, but with less awe,
with more of a bleak despair:

> The unplumb'd, salt, estranging sea.

It is a revealing paradox that Arnold, in some ways the most
personal of Victorian poets, is also the most bookish. Perhaps this
has always been so; that it is certainly so in the nineteenth century
can be in so representative a poem as *Philomela* (1853). This is
quite clearly the work of a classical scholar, who assumes in his
readers a knowledge of the legend. (Philomela, after being raped
and having her tongue cut out by her sister's husband, was changed
into a nightingale; though Arnold seems to be using a variant in
which it is the sister, Procne, who is raped and weaves her story into
a tapestry — or is he just mistaken?) Two themes meet in this
poem: the Romantic theme of infinite yearning, conveyed with
tremendous emotional intensity in the rhythms of the free verse,
and the theme of classical mythology and its survival after so many
centuries. The meeting of the themes enriches some of the most
haunting lines.

> That wild, unquenched, deep-sunken, old-world pain.

This line is quite imaginable in a lyric that is simply about the song
of the nightingale: then 'old-world' would mean 'timeless' — an
assertion that our sweetest songs are (and have always been) those
that tell of saddest thoughts. In this context it also means,
specifically, 'belonging to the old (i.e. ancient) world, where your
legend belongs'. A similar effect comes in

> Here, through the moonlight on this English grass.

It could be a line from *The Scholar Gipsy*, a celebration of the
landscape where Arnold feels at home, hearing the bleating of the
flocks, the cries of reapers, 'all the live murmur of a summer's
day'. But if the nightingale is thought of as Philomela, the English
grass is not dear and familiar, but distant and strange: the

landscape which is normal for the poet is a refuge after many centuries for her.

All this makes Arnold, to use Schiller's invaluable distinction, not a naïve but a sentimental poet: not a poet who is in unreflecting contact with nature, and presents the dry truth, but a poet who strives towards nature and moves us through ideas. For Schiller this is largely a historical contrast: the ancient poets are naïve, the modern on the whole sentimental. The greatest of English sentimental poets is Keats, whose poetry is drenched in longing to return to paganism; and his greatest follower is Tennyson, obviously in his poems to Virgil and to Catullus, in *Ulysses* and *Tithonus*, obliquely in *Maud*. Yet even Keats and Tennyson offer us no more perfect meeting of the literary and the urgently personal than does this poem, unique among Arnold's work.

Romantic melancholy is as central to Tennyson as to Arnold: 'Tears, idle tears' is so mysteriously moving, and so unwilling to tell us what the trouble is, that modern critics have been led to interpret it in terms of depth psychology. But Victorian lyrics are not restricted to one emotional effect, and to raise some other important issues let us look at 'Come down O Maid', from *The Princess* (1847). This poem announces itself as traditional. Its theme is the contrast between valley and mountain: the mountain height symbolizes chastity; the shepherd calls her down to the valley, where love belongs. This is a standard theme of pastoral, and Tennyson the classical scholar has his Theocritus and Virgil in mind, as well as his knowledge of Renaissance poetry: the height-valley contrast comes in Spenser's *Shepherd's Calendar* too. Virgil and Milton lie behind the carefully counterpointed compliment;

> Sweet is every sound,
> Sweeter thy voice, but every sound is sweet,

could be Adam speaking to Eve in Paradise. Yet, for all its traditionalism, this poem, too, is deeply a product of its own age, and shows us that to be contemporary it is not necessary to reject or ignore the past. Several things perhaps make it very Victorian and very Tennysonian. First, there is the fact that the relation to tradition is purely implicit: the reader who does not know his Virgil or even his Spenser will miss nothing essential. Tennyson after all was the great popular poet of the age, and his public varied considerably in level of education. Then there is the descriptive particularity, the rendering of the infinite variety of natural appearances, that Wordsworth announced as the new element waiting to enter poetry, and of which Tennyson is the supreme master. The lines on the 'firths of ice' show this, as do the last three lines — and as does the picture of the waterfall, which then modulates into something else:

> leave
> The monstrous ledges there to slope, and spill
> Their thousand wreaths of dangling water smoke,
> That like a broken purpose waste in air.

'Like a broken purpose': suddenly the picture is imprinted with the feelings of the watcher, and in the middle of some exquisitely meticulous nature poetry a dark voice tells us that the natural world is as ineffectual as we are.

All these aspects of Victorian poetry could have been illustrated — as representatively though less powerfully — from the best of the minor poets, especially Christina Rossetti and William Morris. Towards the end of the century new notes appear, and, though we should not underestimate their distinctiveness, we should also realize that they do not represent the kind of newness that made modern poetry. A.E. Housman's *Shropshire Lad* (1896) combines pithy stanzas, a plainness that is meant to recall the Greek Anthology, with a plangent, even soulful melancholy. James Thomson, who wrote blasphemously witty atheistic essays, expressed a monotonous despair in impressively monotonous verse in *The City of Dreadful Night* (1874). Neither wrote in a style that would have surprised Wordsworth and Coleridge; but Hopkins, of course, did. The violence of his verbal and metrical distortions seems to anticipate T.S. Eliot's claim that the modern poet must be prepared to force, if necessary to dislocate language to fit his meaning.

> Hard as hurdle arms, with a broth of goldish flue
> Breathed round; the rack of ribs; the scooped flank; lank
> Rope-over thigh; knee-nave; and barrelled shank —

Here we seem to hear the twentieth century; and once Hopkins's complete poems were published in 1918, he was fed into the new experimentalism: it is hard to imagine either Auden or Dylan Thomas without the model of Hopkins. Yet, despite the similarities, this is not Eliot's dislocation. These lines do not convey alienation, but the muscular effort of physical work: they joyously accept the world that they so painfully mime. Furthermore the incentive behind the eccentricity is largely linguistic — the alliterations, the delighted use of out-of-the-way words, the flood of metaphors, all reveal a sensibility that loves words and wants to extend the resources of language. Hopkins is pouring new linguistic wine into the old bottle of Victorian nature poetry.

The other new voice is Hardy, perhaps the most difficult of all nineteenth-century poets to sum up, because he wrote so much and in such varied modes. As a nature poet he can write in the Keats-Tennyson manner, though with a new selfconsciousness (as in *Afterwards* (1917)); selfconsciousness carries over into irony both in the innumerable anecdotal poems and in such perfect lyrics as *Heredity* (1916) or 'I look into my Glass' (1898); his ballads (above all the brilliant *Ruined Maid* (1866)) are as much in contact with the broadside as with the folk ballad. Probably his best-loved poems are the series (*Veteris Vestigia Flammae*) that he wrote after the death of his first wife in 1912: they are also his most Romantic, with a tenderness and self-scrutiny that would (surely) have appealed to Wordsworth. Hardy lived to 1928, and most of his poetry was written in the twentieth century. It is not easy to be sure if he was a survival from his own age, or if his work anticipates something important in modernism. His colloquial rhythms and occasionally aggressive linguistic inventiveness seem to make him part of the modern reaction against the 'poetic'; but all his varied metrical experimenting (perhaps no poet since Donne has so wide a range of metrical forms) has something deeply traditional to it.

To say that the new voices of the late nineteenth century do not point towards modernism is not (except on a very whiggish view of literary history) to belittle them. Modern poetry came very largely from France, introduced into English by Pound and Eliot, and its tendency is to emphasize the gap between poetry and other forms of discourse. The directness that makes Hardy so attractive keeps him clear of modernism; and those last representatives of Romantic nature poetry, the Georgians (who do not at all deserve the bad press they have had lately), are capable of a blunt confrontation with experience that is more like Wordsworth than T.S. Eliot.

Narrative poetry

This discussion has so far been about lyric poetry, and so has implicitly accepted the Romantic tendency to equate the lyrical with the essentially poetical. There is a traditional division of poetry, much older than the Romantics, into the three kinds of lyric, narrative and dramatic, and now we shall move to the other two. Since this threefold division leaves out too much Victorian poetry we will add a fourth: those poems whose intellectual content and concern with general issues is so prominent that they no longer have the immediacy of feeling that marks the lyric: these we can class as reflective or meditative poetry. In these other genres we can claim far more of a separate identity for the Victorians than we can in the lyrical: they are more their own men, no longer simply latter-day Romantics. First, then, for narrative.

A famous distinction drawn by Coleridge will be useful here. Describing the plan of *Lyrical Ballads* in chapter 14 of *Biographia Literaria* (1817), he distinguishes two 'cardinal points of poetry', truth to nature and 'the modifying colours of imagination'; and explains that Wordsworth set out to write poems that offered the first, choosing subjects from ordinary life ('such as will be found in every village and its vicinity'), while he was to treat 'persons and characters supernatural or at least romantic'. Apart from Wordsworth, all the great Romantics wrote narratives of this latter kind, and of a power that has never been equalled since, perhaps could not be, once the armies of unalterable law had moved into possession of nature under those redoubted generals Lyell, Darwin and Huxley. No Victorian retellings of myth, legend or folk-tale can be compared to *The Ancient Mariner* or *Lamia*. In Christina Rossetti's *Goblin Market* (1862) the technique of this accomplished versifier moves to something like doggerel, but the psychological content is very powerful — even if the gruesome folk-tale is allowed a rather prim happy ending. Arnold retells a Norse myth in *Balder Dead* (1853) and a Persian legend in *Sohrab and Rustum* (also 1853) and in the latter at least achieves something derivative but impressive. Only in Morris and Swinburne is legend a major concern, but few modern readers now bother with *The Earthly*

Paradise (1868-70) or *Tristram of Lyonesse* (1882). The most famous of all Victorian narratives, the *Idylls of the King* (1859-82), which Tennyson brooded on for years, has a curiously ambivalent relationship to the here and now. It is as if Tennyson can never let himself go into sheer enjoyment of the otherness of the Arthurian story, as Coleridge and Keats had been able to, as Tennyson himself was able to on a smaller scale in *The Lotus Eaters*: the *Idylls of the King*, like Arnold's *Empedocles* (1852), is as much about the contemporary world as about the far past, but the relationship is laboured.

What the Victorians do offer us, however, is a number of uneven but fitfully brilliant narratives of contemporary life. Five in particular are worth singling out. Tennyson's *Princess* (1847) is discussed in Chapter 11. His *Maud* (1855) has always aroused a mixture of admiration and dislike. It contains some of his finest lyric poetry, but contemporaries disliked the hero and disliked the social attitudes it revealed. There is a good deal of militaristic fury and delight in battle-songs, and at the end, when all has gone wrong, the hero sets off to find himself in 'the blood-red blossom of war with a heart of fire'. Tennyson toned down the conclusion slightly, removing the phrase 'the long, long canker of peace'; but the general attitude is clear, and, although it is no more likely to appeal to the twentieth century than the nineteenth, the social point is consistent and (in its way) shrewd. What the hero hates is peace, free trade and commercial values, the Cobden-Bright ideal of progress and benevolent capitalism. He sees his father's enemy, Maud's father, as a crooked member of that world, and his rival, the 'new-made lord', draws his wealth from mines in which 'grimy nakedness drags his trucks'. There is much in common between the protagonist's view of society and Ruskin's (more perhaps than with Tennyson's own!); and at the same time there is a close link between the often frenetic poetry and the hysterical social judgements. Tennyson called the poem 'Maud or the Madness', but this does not mean that he wasn't offering a social critique.

Elizabeth Browning's *Aurora Leigh* appeared in 1856. In general outline the plot belongs to the stereotypes of the Victorian novel: studious intelligent heroine, handsome supercilious cousin who proposes disdainfully, is rejected, and only after long suffering — and blindness — grows to be worthy of her. The triangle is made up by Marian Earle, the lower-class girl rescued from poverty, who does not fit neatly into the stereotype of the rescued harlot. In detail, the poem is often extremely interesting: the fiasco when the girl fails to turn up at church to marry the rich man, or the raped girl's account of morality in class terms, reveal a bluntness that to the modern reader is more attractive than the morally shaped plot.

Clough is the restless outsider among Victorian poets, and *Amours de Voyage* (1858), his best poem, has an ironic diffidence, and none of the moral earnestness we are inclined to think of as the one universal Victorian quality. A young Englishman in Rome sees the 1848 revolution and falls in love; but neither of these two urgent concerns quite gets through to him. The self-deprecating inability to find Rome impressive sounds like an anticipation of the cynicism of Samuel Butler, but Clough's tone is more delicate, his irony subtler, than Butler's. The cautious integrity with which he describes the revolution in terms of what he was actually able to see anticipates much modern journalism (George Orwell, for instance). And when the young man falls in love he finds himself visited by doubts in the very act of expressing his joy. All this makes Clough seem startlingly modern, especially when we add the experimentalism of his versification. Certainly his hexameters have the movement of speech, though we should not overlook the fact that they are based on classical metre: the true anticipator of modern free verse was not Clough but, surprisingly, the more traditional Arnold, as in *The Strayed Reveller* (1849) or *Rugby Chapel* (1867).

And finally Meredith's *Modern Love*, published in 1861. This too could be the story of a novel — a Meredith novel, in fact. It tells (or rather hints at) the story of the break-up of a marriage and the way the couple torture each other, while (ironically) seeming to their friends the picture of domestic bless. But of course a series of sixteen-line poems cannot be like a novel: each poem is self-contained, so each situation can only be rapidly and suggestively sketched. Indeed, those which take most trouble over the narrative are often the clumsiest; and the most powerful tend to be those that move out to a timeless and tragic statement at the end:

> Passions spin the plot.
We are betrayed by what is false within.

Of all these poets, the one who comes closest to the virtues of the novel is, surprisingly, Elizabeth Browning: it is as if too intense a lyric gift, or too markedly personal a style, is a burden the truly narrative poet cannot easily carry. These long narrative poems of contemporary life did not produce such powerful writing as the lyrics, but they are in their way a contribution to the understanding of the age second only to the Victorian novel.

Dramatic poetry

Essentially, dramatic poetry is that in which we are conscious of the speaker. Whereas a lyric invites us to identify speaker and poet (and so easily leads to the Romantic merging of art and life), in dramatic poetry we are aware that they are different. In a play, of course, different speakers interact and each provides a placing of the others. If we extract a single speech — a soliloquy, say — from a play, we are likely still to be aware of what sort of person we are listening to: the clues to this may be implicit in the speech itself. If such a speech is the whole poem, then the poet will take trouble over such clues, carefully implying much that in a play we would learn from what the other characters say.

To a greater or less extent, there has always been such poetry — in Chaucer, in Donne, in some Elizabethan sonneteers, in Dryden and Pope, in Wordsworth — but Browning was the first to practise the mode systematically, and it clearly corresponded to something in his poetic temperament (something he was not always satisfied with). Whether we say that Browning invented the dramatic monologue or that he saw what many poets before him had done is merely a matter of definition. The best way to understand the form will be to examine a particular example; and I have chosen *The Bishop Orders his Tomb at St Praxed's Church* (1845).

The situation is clear. A worldly bishop is dying in sixteenth-century Rome; around his bed are his 'nephews', and he is pleading with them to give him the splendid tomb he has looked forward to for so long. Since the whole poem is spoken by the bishop, Browning has no way of directly conveying the details of the situation, and therefore the first technical problem of the dramatic monologue is to slip the stage directions in as plausibly as possible. The bishop's anxiety over Anselm conveys the information that he is the favourite son; the whole story of his rivalry with Gandolf emerges slowly: the bishop got the girl they were both after, but Gandolf, by dying first, 'snatched' the best spot for his tomb; Gandolf's tomb is inferior, however, both because it is in 'paltry onion stone' and because the Latin is not true Ciceronian. One of our main delights in reading Browning's monologues is the technical skill with which the facts are conveyed; but there are more important qualities too.

The bishop's feelings about his situation provide the poignant dimension of the poem — poignant and ironic together. He does not want to admit that he is pleading, and tries to discuss matters as if all was settled except the details ('And so, about this tomb of mine'), but before long he is scaling down his demand from the presumably more expensive basalt to 'Nay boys ye love me — all of jasper, then.' Hence the irony of the title: he is not 'ordering' his tomb, as he would like to think, but begging.

But the subject is not merely the human interest of the situation: there is a historical dimension too. The bishop's mingling of Christian and pagan is a characteristic of sixteenth-century Romanism; his extraordinarily literal conception of life after death ('And then here I shall lie through centuries / And hear the blessed mutter of the mass') shows just that worldliness (here taken to the point of parody) that fed the indignation of the Reformation. When death is imminent the consciousness of the bishop confuses his two religions with an incongruity that becomes comic ('St Praxed at his sermon on the mount'), just as the nakedness of his envy and malice towards Gandolf reveal how little he is worthy of his calling.

It is clear that the main concern of the poem is to expose the bishop; and our experience as readers is that of getting to know him. This would not be possible without a clear distance between poet and speaker, so that a dramatic monologue is inevitably ironic: we are led to notice things about the subject that he did not intend to convey to us. On the other hand, the speaker will not be simply a figure of fun: if the poem merely exposes him as ridiculous, we are not getting the full richness of dramatic poetry, in which we find ourselves identifying deeply with a character while at the same time being made aware of his limitations. Every successful dramatic monologue offers a complex relationship between the point of view of the speaker and an alternative norm that judges it.

In *The Bishop Orders his Tomb* the positive element in the bishop's character is his love of life. Along with the hypocrisy and unchristian envy goes a sensitivity and responsiveness to this world that is pagan in the best sense. The bishop ought not, of course, to have had a mistress, and his love for her had been purely carnal, but it was a carnal love that praised the richness of the world ('Your tall pale mother with her falling eyes'); his wish to have better Latin on his tombstone than Gandolf did is envy and emulation, but at the same time he does appreciate the style of the Ciceronian.

Browning's speakers often show a richly sensuous delight in the world. Above all this is true of *Caliban upon Setebos* (1864), in which the crude religion of spite cannot prevent Caliban from attracting us with his enormous animal awareness of the pleasures of sense. This is naturally invaluable to the poet, giving him an opportunity to use his verbal powers; at the same time, it may reveal something of Browning's own value-scheme — a moral framework that contains, in suspension as it were, a quite amoral intensity of awareness or an amoral quickwittedness that is shrewder than we care to admit (as in *Mr Sludge the Medium*, 1864). This is particularly important in those monologues whose speaker is morally condemned, but there are other kinds. The speaker may be poignantly self-aware but, at one crucial point, blind (*Cleon*, 1855); or so delicately poised between the sublime and the absurd that the poem almost defiantly invites oversimplified readings (*A Grammarian's Funeral*, 1855); or tormented by his own inner struggles (*Andrea del Sarto*, 1855: in this case the poem need not be ironic at all). The common element is always the coexistence of a delight in the speaker and an awareness of his limitations.

Does Tennyson write dramatic monologues? Some of his poems have named speakers who are clearly distinct from the poet (*Ulysses, Tithonus, St Simeon Stylites*): yet Tennyson is so ineluctably lyrical that his attempts at the dramatic seem halfhearted when compared with Browning's. Suppose for instance we compare *Ulysses* (1842) with *The Bishop Orders his Tomb*. In both cases we learn a good deal about the speaker. Tennyson's Ulysses is not the Ulysses of Homer, but an old man who has kept his longing for adventure, and is about to set out on the voyage from which, according to Dante, he never returned. Browning's effort to imagine himself back in the mind of a Renaissance bishop can be paralleled by Tennyson's adopting the persona of the legendary hero. But there are two differences. In the first place, Tennyson has not been nearly so meticulous over the inserting of stage directions. We know who is standing round the bishop's deathbed, and we learn a great deal of factual information about him — just as we learn that Fra Lippo Lippi has been caught by the watch, and exactly who Bishop Blougram has dined with. Tennyson's Ulysses is speaking to someone certainly, but who? — his subjects? his wife? the reader? The details of scene setting, though of minor importance compared with character revelation, prepare us for the dramatic mode; and the lack of such circumstantial precision in Tennyson weakens the announcement that what is offered is dramatic.

And there is a similar indefiniteness when it comes to distancing. A good deal of what Ulysses says seems to come directly from Tennyson himself. It is Tennyson, surely, who longs

> To follow knowledge like a sinking star
> Beyond the utmost bounds of human thought.

This is so centrally Romantic an aspiration that we can easily imagine it in Shelley (that very undramatic poet). Instead of being invited to notice what sort of person is speaking we are invited to share his aspirations. And if we look at the central paradox of *Ulysses* we can come to the same conclusion: it is a poem of adventure and exploration, a call to 'sail beyond the sunset', and yet its mood is one of deep melancholy. Many explanations of this have been canvassed. Is Ulysses unconsciously guilty at leaving the ancestral hearth? Is it the inevitable melancholy of old age, or Tennyson's own melancholy breaking inevitably through? The one explanation we cannot accept is that it is due to very particular circumstances or attitudes which the poem establishes. We can say this of *St Simeon Stylites* (1842), Tennyson's most Browningesque poem, but not of *Ulysses*, in which Tennyson is at his greatest. By breaking free of the circumstances into a lyric yearning in Romantic vein, Tennyson is truest to his own poetic powers.

Despair, published in 1881, is subtitled 'a dramatic monologue', and an examination of it will teach us much about both Tennyson's limitations and the nature of the form. The headnote tells us: 'A man and his wife, having lost faith in a God, and hope of a life to come, and being utterly miserable in this, resolve to end themselves by drowning. The woman is drowned, but the man rescued by a minister of the sect he had abandoned.' That sounds like a dramatic situation; though once again it is far less specific about establishing the circumstances than Browning would have been. If now we look at the nature of the speaker's despair ('Born of the brainless Nature who knew not that which she bore'), we see that it is the same distress that haunted Tennyson himself from *In Memoriam* (1850) to *Vastness* (1886) ('Swallowed in Vastness, lost in silence, drowned in the deeps of a meaningless Past'). This would not of course prevent *Despair*, when taken in itself, from being a genuinely dramatic poem; it simply suggests that Tennyson's range is narrow, and that he achieves dramatic distancing by expressing and stepping back from his own concerns, rather than seeking out ever new and unusual people and attitudes to write about. But there is another limitation, which suggests that the stepping back is not a particularly skilful act. A certain amount of biographical detail is supplied to explain the speaker's despair:

> Why should I live? one son had forged on his father and fled ...
> And there was a baby girl, that had never looked on the light:
> Happiest she of us all, for she past from the night to the night.

Melodramatic cliché like this is common in Tennyson: in *Locksley Hall* (1842) and even more in *Locksley Hall Sixty Years After* (1886). Both poems have a speaker who is not the author but who speaks with the voice of all the author's prejudices: after the old man's bombast, in the later poem, about Demos, decadence and the abysm, it is a very inadequate placing to make him say 'Patience, let the dying actor mouth his last upon the stage'. In contrast to Browning's fertility of dramatic imagination, Tennyson thinks in clichés and then admits they are clichés. Yet we would be wrong to wish that either was more like the other. If we had the Browning version of, say, *The Lotus Eaters*, it would evoke the situation more vividly but it would not have the verbal magic as the poet loses himself in lyric surrender to the seductiveness of the mood:

> There is sweet music here that softer falls
> Than petals from blown roses on the grass

Or night-dews on still waters between walls
Of shadowy granite in a gleaming pass ...

Among later Victorians, there are elements of the dramatic in Rossetti (*Jenny*, 1870), in Hardy (*The Colonel's Soliloquy*, 1899; *One Ralph Blossom Soliloquises*, 1909; and many of his ballads) and above all in Kipling, many of whose most famous ballads and lyrics, often in dialect, have speakers who are obviously unlike the poet (though he usually sympathizes with them). This is the case in many of the *Barrack-Room Ballads* (1892). The '*Mary Gloster*' (1894) offers an interesting comparison with *The Bishop Orders His Tomb*: it too is spoken by a father on his deathbed, trying to coax or bribe his son to bury him as he wishes, and despite the defiantly unpoetic diction it expresses the growing panic of death with a power that justifies the comparison with Browning. Its more famous companion piece is *M'Andrew's Hymn* (1893), which explores brilliantly the analogies between the Scottish Calvinism of the ship's engineer and his love of his machines ('Predestination in the stride o' yon connecting-rod'): the poem keeps the dramatic persona, while vividly conveying Kipling's own involvement with the material. The same can be said for *Chant-pagan*, one of his most interesting political poems, and probably the best of the *Barrack-Room Ballads of the Boer War*, 1899-1902: the speaker is an English Irregular, discharged, whose experience of fighting has led him to feel he can never take on 'With awful old England again'; and whether his refusal to go on touching his hat to the gentry makes him a revolutionary or a dropout is not easy to settle. The dramatic element often lends an extra dimension to Kipling's poetry, but he is not solely, perhaps not mainly, a dramatic poet; his genius is narrative and even lyrical: one or two of his lyrics ('The Way through the Woods', 'Cities and Thrones and Powers') have a surprising delicacy. Much of Kipling's material is uncongenial to modern readers, but the verbal power of his often vulgar Muse can be irresistible.

Reflective poems: faith and doubt

Of the four kinds of poetry, this is the one most subject to extra-literary influences, and, indeed, this may be the reason it has not received the same acceptance as a kind: the reflective poem is governed less by poetic conventions and more by its subject matter. To discuss such poems in any period is to discuss what worried the men of that time; and what worried the Victorians was above all the problem of belief. The difficulties of Christian belief form the subject of Chapter 8, and this section can be considered a sequel to that chapter, exploring the poetic possibilities opened up by its concerns.

The tensions between science and Christianity are older than Darwin, and what is probably the most famous poetic expression of these, sections 54-6 of *In Memoriam*, dates from the 1840s. Indeed, Tennyson even claimed that the sections preceded Chambers's *Vestiges of Creation* (1844), but there are verbal echoes that make this implausible. It is not difficult to provide an exposition of Tennyson's lines by relating them closely to the issues raised by Chambers, and Lyell's *Principles of Geology*, and subsequently by Darwin: the struggle for existence ('so careless of the single life') and, worse still, the mutability of species as shown in the fossil record. Section 56 asks whether man, 'Nature's last work, who seemed so fair,'

> Who trusted God was love indeed
> And love Creation's final law —
> Though Nature, red in tooth and claw
> With ravine, shrieked against his creed —
>
> Who loved, who suffered countless ills,
> Who battled for the True, the Just,
> Be blown about the desert dust,
> Or sealed within the iron hills?

The concerns are new, and topical. 'Nature, red in tooth and claw' shows us that the idea of the struggle for existence was in the air when Darwin was incorporating it into his theory; and the fear in these lines is of course that the human species will become extinct. But the lines have a traditional ring: the second last line, in particular, could describe the body of Polyneices, unburied by Creon. There is a similar effect in *Vastness*:

> Many a hearth upon our dark globe sighs after many a
>   vanished face,

Many a planet by many a sun may roll with the dust of a
vanished race.

The first line is about individual death, the second about the
extinction of the human race. Tennyson's poems of doubt almost
invariably link these two themes, often with great (though presumably only half-conscious) cunning: this enables him to write on
topical concerns without losing traditional sources of emotional
power. No doubt the dread that individual death leads to annihila-
tion and the dread that the human race will be sealed within the
iron hills as mere fossils, were closely linked in his mind.

Browning too belongs to the poets of the religious debate, most
directly in that oddly grotesque poem on 'how hard it is to be a
Christian', *Easter Day* (1850); but more memorably in his dramatic
poems, many of which are indirect contributions to theological
questions. One of the most knotty and suggestive is *A Death in the
Desert* (1864), in which St John, dying in extreme old age, defends
Christianity against all possible forms of scepticism, including the
doctrines of Renan and Strauss ('was John at all?' and ''Tis mere
projection from man's inmost mind'). Browning's primary motive
in this poem was probably to advance opinions, and the result is
argumentative and, perhaps, not his best work poetically; *Bishop
Blougram's Apology* (1855), on the other hand, is genuinely
dramatic, and though it broaches the issues in which Browning was
interested (that complete disbelief is as hard as complete belief,

> All we have gained then by our unbelief
> Is a life of doubt diversified by faith,
> For one of faith diversified by doubt)

to extract these points as if the poem set out to advance them in
themselves is to ignore the concern with Blougram's character — in
a sense to unwrite the poem. Browning's dramatic genius uses his
theological interests when he is at his best, is used by them when
below his best.

The most celebrated of Victorian agnostics is, perhaps, Matthew
Arnold, who contributed to the debate directly as well as expressing
its impact in his poetry. His two finest poems, *The Scholar Gipsy*
(1853) and *Thyrsis* (1867), are partly reflective and partly lyrical, in
the pastoral tradition: they mingle direct statements about

> This strange disease of modern life
> With its sick hurry, its divided aims,

with symbols that evoke pastoral nostalgia, or attempts to use the now outmoded pastoral tradition, so that the contrast between the modern and the traditional is also a stylistic contrast. In Arnold's more directly introspective poems there is a similar stylistic tension, between traditional imagery and direct statement. The former is sometimes trite, sometimes strangely effective; the latter sometimes ponderous, sometimes powerfully direct. The same poem often seems laboured or embarrassing, then deeply moving. The one completely successful poem is *Dover Beach* (1867), in which the concerns of all his introspective poems find a perfect expression, matter-of-fact without being prosaic. It is almost impossible to say why *Dover Beach* succeeds so wonderfully when very similar poems by Arnold are uneven and often clumsy. Partly it is the scrupulous, quiet description that opens the poem, carefully not making the sea symbolic until it has been established as real. Partly it is the honesty with which Arnold uses the literary reference, showing that the poem has a double subject — on the one hand personal involvement, on the other concern for tradition and the loss of faith (what does the sea say to me? what has it said to men over the centuries?). And partly it is the skill with which the direct lyricism is attached, by explicit discussion, to the intellectual concern, that enables him by the end to use purely abstract language ('nor certitude nor peace nor help from pain') with no diminution of emotional power.

It is not easy to decide if Hopkins is an exception among the poets of the religious crisis. He differs from the others in being a Roman Catholic and an ordained priest: the one who as a man appears to have retained his faith unquestioningly. If we were shown Hopkins's sonnets and told they were contemporary with George Herbert or Bunyan we would of course disbelieve it because of the violent experimentalism of the language, but would it be credible as far as content is concerned? The restless self-questionings, the fear of damnation, the agony of being ignored by God: are these not the traditional dark night of the soul through which the Christian mystic passes before he is born again?

> Wert thou my enemy, O thou my friend,
> How wouldst thou worse, I wonder, than thou dost
> Defeat, thwart me?

God seemed to be thwarting many hundreds in the 1880s simply by
ceasing to exist; and among the poetic reactions to this (the cosmic
irony of Hardy, the aggressive atheism of Swinburne and James
Thomson's essays, the stoicism of Housman, the black despair of
James Thomson's poems) it seems natural to include the fierce
despair of Hopkins, complaining that his cries are

> like dead letters sent
> To dearest him that lives alas! away.

Yet the intensity with which Hopkins rounds on God seems
somehow to be more about a personal relationship that has soured
than about the impersonal problem of belief. Hopkins may despair
but it is not certain that he doubts: his constant fear of damnation
assumes a Christian context. It is not only in style but also, often, in
subject matter that Hopkins is nearer to George Herbert than to any
other English poet.

To relate the Victorian poems of doubt and despair to the
religious crisis of the age is not to reduce them to documents in the
history of ideas. To see what stylistic and rhythmic possibilities,
what use of the dramatic mode, what variations on inherited
tradition, are appropriate to the state of belief being expressed, is to
attain an enriched understanding of poetic form. Ideas matter, and
the poetry of ideas matters, in ways that are related but by no
means the same. Victorian poetry is one way, and an important
one, into the understanding of the Victorian age; it also, being
poetry, has an importance in its own right.

Part II

The society

3 Material development:
the condition of England 1830-1860

BARRY SUPPLE

In 1829 the young Thomas Carlyle published an essay on *Signs of the Times*. Searching for an image with which to characterize the new industrial Britain in its philosophical and moral as well as economic aspects, he hit on the the concept of the machine:

> Were we required to characterise this age of ours by any single epithet, we should be tempted to call it, not an Heroical, Devotional, Philosophical, or Moral Age, but, above all others, the Mechanical Age. It is the Age of Machinery, in every outward and inward sense of that word; the age which, with its whole undivided might, forwards, teaches and practises the great art of adapting means to ends. Nothing is now done directly, or by hand; all is by rule and calculated contrivance. For the simplest operation, some helps and accompaniments, some cunning abbreviating process is in readiness.

Like all metaphors this one needs careful handling, lest the implied analogies are taken too far. Yet in his sense that mechanism and its economic imperatives, together with the rationality and pragmatism that characterized them, were signs of the time, Carlyle dealt imaginatively with what social scientists have arrived at by more prosaic routes — namely, the extent to which the principal determinant of social and moral change, of institutional evolution, in the nineteenth century was to be that complex of changing physical circumstances and relationships that we have come to call the Industrial Revolution.

In this and the next two chapters we shall be considering, in a more or less direct and non-metaphorical way, the evolution of the industrial context of Victorian literature. This was not merely a matter of material change, of getting and spending, wealth and poverty. Industrialization also transmuted the very groupings of Britain, the sort of country and society it was, and the institutions and ideas that shaped and governed it. Such was the context and, indeed, often the content of Victorian literature. Nevertheless, the first sombre impact of industrialism was, almost inevitably, perceived in terms of living standards. Once again, Carlyle provides the touchstone — this time in a famous passage from *Chartism* (1839) which forged an enduring descriptive phrase:

> The condition of the great body of people in a country is the condition of the country itself: this you would say is a truism in all times; a truism rather pressing to get recognised as a truth now, and be acted upon, in these times. Yet read Hansard's Debates, or the Morning Papers, if you have nothing to do! The old grand question, whether A is to be in office or B, with the innumerable subsidiary questions growing out of that, counting paragraphs and suffrages for a blessed solution of that; Canada question, Irish Appropriation question, West-India question, Queen's Bedchamber question; Game Laws, Usury Laws; African Blacks, Hill Coolies, Smithfield cattle, and Dog-carts, — all manner of questions and subjects, except simply this the alpha and omega of all! Surely Honourable Members ought to speak of the Condition-of-England question too.

Carlyle's pleas reflected both a sense that the material degradation of large masses of the population was morally offensive, and a fearful certainty that if the economic and social consequences of industrialization (including the social isolation of the poor) were allowed to proceed without amelioration, then the likely outcome would be catastrophic social unrest and communal violence. It is an appropriate starting point for a consideration of the changing material and social environment of Victorian Britain. This is so not because there was even then any consensus about the effects of industrial growth on the welfare of the poor. That has remained a matter of considerable controversy. Rather, Carlyle's emphasis remains relevant because he concentrated attention on issues that all agreed to be acid tests of the worthwhileness of the economic growth: its effects on personal living standards and the environment; its consequences in terms of new social structures, aspirations and relationships; and its impact on the stability of society and its political framework. 'The Condition-of-England question' was important to Victorian optimists as well as pessimists precisely because it raised all these issues.

Industrial development

A discussion of living standards and social change in early Victorian Britain cannot be divorced from the longer-run economic developments, extending from the late eighteenth to the mid-nineteenth century, associated with the Industrial Revolution. That process involved two striking changes: a decline in the relative significance of traditional (especially agricultural) activity, matched by the increasing importance of manufacturing industry; and an acceleration in the pace of economic change and the growth of output of goods and services. It also coincided with an unprecedented demographic surge, as the British population rose from just over 9 million in 1785 to 21 million in 1851. Taken together, these developments were sufficiently spectacular to invite contemporary comparison with that other upheaval of modern times — the French Revolution.

The drama of industrialization consisted not so much in the increase of total output as in the far-reaching transformation of the economy as a whole: innovations in commodities, techniques and occupations; sweeping shifts in the national balance of economic activity; alterations in the very fabric of people's lives. Moreover, and most important of all in any appreciation of the impact of the Industrial Revolution, industrialization of this sort and on this scale was historically unprecedented. Never before had the world known such a massive application of new techniques and non-human power, such a sustained increase in the level of industrial output, such a growth in the sheer size of manufacturing operations. The changes that took place within a single lifetime covered all areas of economic activity. The production of textiles, coal, iron, machinery, hardware, foodstuffs, clothing, houses, ships and a host of other goods was transformed and increased. Canals, railways and steamships appeared and proliferated. The transition from traditional small workshops to the modern factory concentrated men and capital into huge enterprises which dominated the lives of both managers and employees through the complication of their organization and the discipline of their routine. Industrial sophistication created vast new towns. And in contemplating all this in Britain, contemporaries were experiencing the novel, the unique, the unexpected. Moreover, this experience was geographically uneven. 'Industrial' novels — Dickens's *Hard Times* (1854), for example, or Mrs Gaskell's *North and South* (1854-5), or a host of lesser examples — can be seen not merely as an exploration of new subject matter but as the communication of the character of the industrial culture of the North to the more genteel and traditional South.

Technical change — the application of new inventions — figures very prominently in traditional histories of the Industrial Revolution. And it naturally loomed large in the eyes and minds of contemporaries. The steam engine — although the extent of its adoption by the early nineteenth century has been exaggerated — was perhaps the most spectacular example of the new technology, and it is easy to understand why someone like Carlyle should have taken it as an emblem of the instability of the new society — of what he called 'the blind No-God of Necessity and Mechanism' that held men 'like a hideous World-Steamengine' (*Chartism*) — or why Dickens in *Hard Times* should have struck the keynote of his manufacturing city, Coketown, with the help of the image of the piston of the steam engine working 'monotonously up and down like the head of an elephant in a state of melancholy madness'. Certainly its impact was considerable, as it was extended from the conventional task of pumping water out of mines to a host of other uses, even though it is not until the 1820s and 1830s, when steam power was successfully applied to railway locomotion, that we may accurately speak of the advent of the age of steam (in 1850 the railways used 750,000 horse power as against industry's 500,000 and shipping's 168,000).

Yet the steam engine was merely one example of mechanical

ingenuity, and new machinery was in its turn merely one sort of innovation. Josiah Wedgwood, for example, built a hugely successful pottery/porcelain enterprise on the basis of non-mechanical techniques through the extension of the principles of specialization within his firm. One extreme view holds that the great inventions are better seen as consequences than as causes of the Industrial Revolution. Certainly we can say that they drew their significance from their interaction with methods of organization and with the physical environment. They greatly enhanced the productivity of labour, and did so in integral association with other developments, in ways that transformed the economic environment. Thus the new industrial techniques tended to need much larger equipment and buildings than did less sophisticated methods: factories, engines, complex machinery and gearing, blast furnaces, deeper and bigger mines, railway lines and their massive appurtenances of bridges and viaducts and stations.

The efficiency of the new techniques could often be attained only through large-scale production. By 1815 many substantial cotton mills employed hundreds, the largest well over 1000 workers (the need for out-workers produced huge firms: in 1830 Horrocks of Preston employed 700 spinners in their mills and over 6000 other workers in homes and small workshops); in iron manufacture and coalmining, although the average might be smaller, the larger enterprises also contained workforces to be numbered in hundreds. In mill, factory, ironworks, mine and railway, therefore, the characteristic was an unprecedented massing of the labour force — although, as shown by Disraeli's picture of Woodgate (*Sybil*, 1845), working conditions in a system dominated by small masters could be at least equally oppressive and demeaning. A related development was an increasing specialization of enterprise and of function within the enterprise: workers became exclusively spinners in a mill concentrating on one sort of yarn, or concerned with one small process in the production of standard iron or porcelain products, or one function on a particular railway line. Moreover, the need to maximize output and to coordinate the activities of very large workforces and powered machinery began to impose an unusual discipline — as to duration, intensity and rhythm of work — on the labours of the workforce. 'While the engine runs', wrote one observer, 'the people must work — men, women and children are yoked together with iron and steam.'[1]

The characteristics that were increasingly associated with individual workplaces also came to be associated with industrial groups as a whole. Initially, many factories had been built in rural areas (Charlotte Brontë's *Shirley* (1849) described a remote Yorkshire mill at the time of the Luddite riots in the 1810s). But, especially after being liberated from the need to seek water power in remote rural areas, factories clustered together. Their need for abundant supplies of labour, fuel and raw materials, the importance of commercial, transport and financial services — all tended to concentrate particular industries in particular regions, and within regions in particular towns. Perhaps the most famous example of this trend was the gravitation of the cotton industry to the northwest of England (with a similar if smaller specialization around Glasgow). By 1838, of the 1600 cotton mills in England, some 1200 were in Lancashire — with particularly important groupings in Manchester and in such fast-growing towns as Bolton, Oldham, Blackburn and Preston. There was a similar concentration of the woollen industry (in the West Riding) as well as iron, steel, hardware and the like.

This degree of specialization and concentration helped create a new Britain, in which manufacturing was of much greater significance: the proportion of the labour force in industry rose from 25 to 40 per cent between the 1770s and 1840s, while by 1870 Britain produced a third of the entire world output of manufactures. One concomitant of this was that the centre of economic gravity shifted from the traditionally prosperous agricultural and trading areas of the South to the sources of cotton, coal, iron, steam and engineering in the Midlands, South Wales and (most important of all) the North. This was reflected in the distribution of population; even more in terms of wealth, or at least national output; most of all, perhaps in spirit, for the North was pre-eminently the commercialized, enterprising, practical region. By the same token, to its critics it also presented the social problems of industrialism in their starkest form. In Mrs Gaskell's *North and South*, for example, Margaret Hale rebukes the Manchester mill owner, John Thornton

1 Quoted in J.L. and Barbara Hammond, *The Rise of Modern Industry* (London, 1925), p.208.

(who had referred slightingly to 'the old worn grooves' of southern life with its 'slow days of careless ease'):

> You do not know anything about the South. If there is less adventure or less progress — I suppose I must not say less excitement — from the gambling spirit of trade, which seems requisite to force out these wonderful inventions, there is less suffering also. I see men here going about in the streets who look ground down by some pinching sorrow or care — who are not only sufferers but haters. Now, in the South we have our poor, but there is not that terrible expression in their countenances of a sullen sense of injustice which I see here.
>
> (chapter 10)

Dominating these various changes was the supreme fact of the urbanization of Britain. London was perhaps the most substantial example of this new phenomenon — growing from 1.1 million in 1801 to 2.5 million in 1851. Yet there were others, with equal power to shock. In 1800 London had been the only British town with a population exceeding 100,000. By 1851 there were ten (London, Liverpool, Glasgow, Manchester, Birmingham, Edinburgh, Leeds, Bristol, Sheffield and Bradford). Of even greater symbolic importance was the fact that by 1851 just over half the entire population lived in towns (more than a third lived in large towns of 20,000 or more inhabitants). By the mid-nineteenth century, technology and its associated economic upheavals had transmuted Britain into the world's first urban as well as the world's first industrial nation. Wordsworth's anxieties about 'the increasing accumulation of men in cities' (Preface to the *Lyrical Ballads*, 1800 edition) were to receive a more complex expression in Book VII of *The Prelude*. Although there were many respects in which the industrial transformation of Britain was far from complete by the early 1850s, the early Victorian years witnessed a culmination of economic change and of the more volatile social responses to it. Certainly the processes of capital accumulation and mechanization accelerated in these years: in the cotton industry, for example, the number of spindles doubled and of power looms quadrupled between the early 1830s and the mid-1840s; coal output also doubled between 1830 and 1845; while the most spectacular development of all, the advent of the steam railway after 1825, generated a huge investment and employment boom, particularly in the 1840s. In the peak year 1847 — while Dickens was publishing *Dombey and Son*, with its vivid description of 'the yet unfinished and unopened Railroad' rending Camden Town 'to its centre' — more than a quarter of a million men were involved in construction of railways. At the same time, however, the 1830s and 1840s were years of intensified economic fluctuation, instability and social insecurity.

All this applies particularly strongly to the period before the 1850s. Obviously it would be misleading to assume that after the Great Exhibition of 1851 the turbulence of earlier years abruptly gave way to an age of stability and unflawed progress. Nevertheless, that exhibition, so often used by historians, as it was by contemporaries, as a symbol of Britain's economic achievement, *was* a ceremonial threshold to a new period in which contentment as well as prosperity seemed more widely enjoyed compared with the insecure and often unhappy years of the 1830s and 1840s; and the worst middle-class anxieties about the poor were (at least temporarily) abated.

On the other hand, while by 1851 Britain's industrial and urban development dominated the sort of society that it had become, that society was still heavily influenced by the rural and the traditional. In her introduction to *Felix Holt* (1866) George Eliot had described life in the Midlands at a somewhat earlier date (about 1830). Manufacturing was by then a central feature of social life, but the countryside and its rhythms exerted their own powerful influence: 'The busy scenes of the shuttle and the wheel, of the roaring furnaces, of the shaft and the pulley, seemed to make but crowded nests in the midst of the large-spaced, slow-moving life of homesteads and far-away cottages and oak-sheltered parks.' Similar, if not quite as extensive, contrasts were no doubt still available in 1851, when, of a workforce of just over 9 million, some 2 million were still directly employed on the land and a substantial number supplied the craft and processing and servicing activities associated with agriculture. Moreover, even the non-agricultural population was not predominantly committed to the great staple industries. Some 1.3 million were employed as domestic and personal servants (including almost 40 per cent of working women and girls). It is, indeed, striking that the number employed in domestic service was about the same as that employed in all textiles. Elsewhere there were other parallels to be drawn between new and traditional occupations: the building and construction trades employed about as many people (half a million) as the cotton mills; while against the 219,000 coalminers might be set the 274,000 boot- and shoemakers or the 268,000 milliners and dressmakers. In fact, and in spite of the high drama of industrialization, only a minority of workers were actually engaged in the 'modern', mechanized sectors of industry in Britain in 1851. Yet the statistics of employment only emphasize the enormous and disproportionate influence that those sectors had on the country at large. Employing relatively few people, they were nevertheless the principal centres of high productivity and capital accumulation; prime determinants of the fluctuations as well as the absolute levels of national prosperity; the main stimulants of all sorts of other and more traditional economic activities; shapers of Britain's new urban landscape, and the ever-present objects of a new social consciousness. Employment statistics of this sort also remind us that an industrial society was not (as it is still not) a homogeneous society. This is also relevant to the controversy about living standards during the Industrial Revolution: do we get a truer picture by stressing variegation or by looking at the common experience? We can also ask whether that experience was as wretched and painful as some commentators have suggested.

Living standards

This controversy is concerned exclusively with the condition of the poor. Yet it is as well to remember that people with middling incomes were undoubtedly growing in both numbers and wealth. Far from polarizing society into a growing army of the abysmally poor and a tiny band of the grossly wealthy, industrial development involved a dramatic expansion in the number not merely of capitalist employers in industry (almost 90,000 by 1851) but of traders, managers and administrators, civil servants, engineers, lawyers, schoolteachers and accountants — quite apart from the host of industrial and commercial functionaries, commercial travellers, clerks and shopkeepers with lower-middle-class incomes and life-styles. At a time when the very poor had to subsist on less than 10*s*. per week, and the skilled artisan might earn £1. 10*s*. or slightly more and enjoy a moderate 'prosperity' (a loaf of bread of over 4 lb cost about 9*d*, bacon about 8*d*, and beer 1*d* a pint), a weekly income of £2 could sustain a middle-class lifestyle of sorts and one of £3 could run to the luxury to a servant: the annual wage of a young maid-of-all-work was no more than about £8 or £9 a year plus keep. The Brontë family in 1820, with six children and a curate's income of £200, could afford two maids. On this basis, it might be assumed that an annual income of £100-300 marked the bounds of the modest sufficiency of ordinary middle classes and, although still a small minority, hundreds of thousands lived within this range.

The Victorian urban middle classes — more numerous, more confident and more prosperous than their eighteenth-century predecessors — soon developed their characteristic lifestyle. That style involved an abundance of domestic help, varied and substantial foods, access to personal transport and regular holidays, commodious houses with reasonable sanitary services, and the liberal purchase of culture and education. In contrast, all available stories of working-class budgets confirm that, in the case of a family, an annual income of £50, which was that of the better rather than the worse paid, could only just cover the basic necessities of a limited diet, skimpy clothing, restricted accommodation, and sparse heat and light. It is clear that the number and wealth of the relatively rich increased; there is controversy about the income trends of the relatively poor, but no case has been made for a sharp and sustained increase. It is therefore certain that in this period income inequality was increasing. It has been estimated, for example, that whereas in 1801 the 121,000 incomes over £130 enjoyed about a quarter of the national income, by 1848 the 236,000 incomes (a roughly similar proportion of the population) over £200 had a share of just over one-third.[2] But to acknowledge this is not the same as claiming that 'the poor were getting poorer and the rich richer'. For the rich were also getting more numerous and the poor relatively fewer, while it is at least possible that the poor were *also* getting richer, albeit at a slower rate than the rich. It is, therefore, the more important to assess what was happening to the relatively poor in this period. Were their living standards deteriorating? In terms of the mass of the people, what was the nature of Carlyle's Condition-of-England question? The principal obstacle to any easy answer to this question is the

2 Harold Perkin, *The Origins of Modern English Society 1780-1880* (London, 1969), pp.135-6.

variety of experiences involved: wage *levels* differed according to levels of skills, occupations and even regions (in 1850 agricultural wages in the North, where the pull of industrial development acted as a spur, were almost 40 per cent higher than those in the South). At the same time, the *trends* over time also varied according to the skills, jobs and regions involved. These factors, together with the shortage of reliable statistics, make it very difficult to specify what was happening to 'the' living standards of 'the' working class. We can, however, take an 'average' view by looking at broad movements in prices and wages. Inflation during the Napoleonic Wars pushed prices up by about 75 per cent between the early 1790s and the period 1810-14. This was followed by a fairly rapid fall of about 30 per cent to the early 1820s and a slower downward trend of about 10 per cent — interrupted by slight spurts — to the late 1840s. In practice, price changes were critical for working-class living standards, since wage movements tended to lag behind prices. Thus, during the wars, many, perhaps most, wage earners suffered as prices outpaced wages. In the deflation of the immediate post-war era, however, workers who remained in employment seem certainly to have improved their position quite markedly — by something like 25 per cent in ten years. And in the subsequent generation, from the mid-1820s to the late 1840s, the advance of real wages (again for those in employment, and striking a very rough average of all sorts of experience) was somewhat more halting, with periods of distress looming large, but the general average showing an increase of something under 1 per cent annually in the second quarter of the century.

The aggregate statistics, with all their imperfections, therefore point to a long-run improvement in the material position of the working classes. Why, then, is there such wide disagreement about the impact of industrialization and why does the history of early Victorian Britain, even apart from the impact of short-run crises, offer so many examples of distress and society anxiety?

Before examining these questions in terms of *changes* in working-class living standards, it is as well to emphasize that as far as the overwhelming majority of the population was concerned, we shall be dealing with abysmally low levels of poverty which are difficult for us to grasp. Hence any feasible amelioration amounted to no more than a very small improvement in a very low level of real income. In the early 1840s, for example, only moderately well-paid workers in Accrington cotton mills (say those with over 15*s*. per week) could afford the regular purchase of meat or cheese or butter,[3] while in the spectrum of living standards described by Engels in 1844 the poorest category was not the least numerous:

> the better-paid workers, especially those in whose families every member is able to earn something, have good food as long as this state of things lasts; meat daily, and bacon and cheese for supper. Where wages are less, meat is used only two or three times a week, and the proportion of bread and potatoes increases. Descending gradually, we find the animal food reduced to a small piece of bacon cut up with the potatoes; lower still, even this disappears, and there remains only bread, cheese, porridge and potatoes until, on the lowest rung of the ladder, among the Irish, potatoes form the sole food.[4]

None of this should be so exaggerated as to ignore the fact that contemporary standards *were* different from our own, and that the benefits of industrialization were diffused to the relatively poor, as well as to the rich. Nevertheless, the fact remained that during the early nineteenth century a very large proportion of the population hovered dangerously near some *absolute* subsistence level, and were frequently below the borderline which, by any standards, delineated the possibility of minimum health and moderate comfort.

Turning to the improvements that *did* take place, it is worth emphasizing that the effect of industrialization on working-class living standards was uneven precisely because the pattern of working-class skills and incomes was uneven. Thus, relatively skilled workers — printers, carpenters, building craftsmen, fine spinners, engineering workers, toolmakers, some iron workers, etc. — formed an economic 'aristocracy of labour'. *Their* real incomes undoubtedly tended to rise, and by the end of the period the more prosperous among them enjoyed living standards and even lifestyles which were associated with the respectable lower middle class. Of them, a modern social historian has written: 'These were the workers who ate

3 John Burnett, *Plenty and Want* (London, 1966), p.66.
4 Quoted in ibid. pp.70-1.

meat, vegetables, fruit and dairy produce, lived in the best and newest cottages and filled them with furniture and knick-knacks, bought books and newspapers, supported mechanics' institutes and friendly societies, and paid the heavy subscriptions to the craft unions.'5 Nor was it only these sorts of skills that received better compensation as the industrial society emerged. In the range of wages of town workers, which varied from an abysmal 5*s.* per week to a moderately affluent £2, many factory workers and miners, traditionally associated with the mainstream of industrial development, were among the better paid of the labour force and also among the groups which saw a rise in the purchasing power of their wages.

Compared with skilled workers and the better-placed employees of factories and mines, men and women with skills or occupational commitments unwanted by industrialism or susceptible to the competition of the machine were much less fortunate. Agricultural labourers were under great pressure, as were casual labourers in towns. The latter formed a large part of the subject matter of Henry Mayhew's influential work of social journalism, *London Labour and the London Poor* (1861-2). But the outstanding, and most heart-breaking, example of such casualties was undoubtedly the handloom weavers employed mostly in their own homes. The fierce competition of the power loom, the ease with which non-mechanized weaving could be learned, and the reluctance of handloom workers to leave their jobs resulted in a remorseless squeeze on wages: those of Bolton weavers, for example, after attaining impressively high levels in the early days of industrialization, dropped from 25*s.* per week in 1800 to 14*s.* in 1811, 9*s.* in 1817, 5*s.* 6½*d.* in 1829 and even lower in the 1830s. These were barely subsistence levels. No wonder that a parliamentary committee of inquiry in 1834 (when there were still some 200,000 handloom weavers in cotton alone) found that the sufferings of handloom weavers were 'not only not exaggerated, but they have for years continued to an extent and intensity scarcely to be credited or conceived'. Quite properly, they touched the conscience of even moderately sensitive observers. Someone as imaginative and romantic as Disraeli could not ignore them. In *Sybil* (1845) he described the degradation of a domestic handloom weaver:

5 Perkin, op. cit. p.144.

'Twelve hours of daily labour, at the rate of one penny each hour; and even this labour is mortgaged! How is this to end? Is it rather not ended?' And he looked around him at his chamber without resources: no food, no fuel, no furniture, and four human beings dependent on him, and lying in their wretched beds, because they had no clothes.

There were, of course, other non-mechanized industrial jobs which bore the brunt of the advent of power and superior machinery: the nailers of the Black Country (perhaps as many as 50,000 in 1830), for example, or the silk workers of Spitalfields, or the hosiery knitters of Nottinghamshire and Leicestershire, whose piece-rate wages fell by about a third between 1814 and 1844.

All these examples indicate that behind the misleading clarity of a single measure of real wages lay the varying and contrasting experience of different groups of workers — although, contrary to a general impression, those who experienced the worst material degradation were not those directly involved in the new industrial system, but those whose skills were threatened by the new technology; those trapped in the casual and seasonal labour pools of the teeming cities; and the unskilled labour of town and country. The worst casualties of industrialism were those who resisted, not those who embraced it.

The shifting pattern of occupations during industrialization also raises a second point concerning the condition of England. Irrespective of any improvements in wages, the labour force had to accommodate itself to much more drastic and rapid changes in the very structure of the economy and, therefore, in the material fabric of their lives and day-to-day social relationships. The speed of structural change — the creation of new skills and the abrupt destruction of old, the enforced mobility and uprooting, the sense of insecurity — contrasted with the more settled, if perhaps more deprived, lives in pre-industrial communities. And it was this fact — rather than the simple existence of unchanging poverty — which most preoccupied the imagination of writers concerned with the new lives of the mass of the people. 'The huge demon of Mechanism', wrote Carlyle in 1839, 'Smokes and thunders ... changing his shape like a very Proteus; and infallibly, at every change ... oversetting huge multitudes of work-men ... hurling them asunder ... so that the wisest no longer knows his whereabouts' (*Chartism*). Moreover, the transformation of social relationships, away from the interdependence of status and traditional hierarchy towards the more anonymous connections of an urbanized, commercial society, could in itself be felt (at least by those who lived through it or who had not yet had time to fashion more protective and stabilizing institutions) as a deterioration only very loosely related to real wage rates. At a more prosaic level, the Industrial Revolution also intensified and dramatized economic fluctuations — which had the dual effect of altering both the level of wages and the level of employment. The resulting extremes of unemployment in periods of distress must be taken into any reckoning of the condition of industrial England at this time — or of the imagination of its writers who, like Dickens in *The Old Curiosity Shop* (1840-1), had fearful visions of a night when bands of unemployed labourers paraded the roads, or clustered by torchlight round their leaders, who told them 'in stern languages of their wrongs, and urged them on to frightful cries and threats'.

Finally, we must take account of the fact that the same process of industrialization which increased average incomes also changed the environment within which people worked and lived. It may well be that the hours and the immediate environment of work in domestic industry and in rural areas were no better than in the factory, and that the sanitary arrangements of the countryside left much to be desired. In *Sybil* Disraeli bitingly described the rural town of 'Marney' to whose dilapidated houses, 'open drains full of animal and vegetable refuse', living spaces soaked in 'a concentrated solution of every species of dissolving filth', the disease-ridden 'bold British peasant' returned 'after cultivating the broad fields of merry England'. But the impersonalization of factories, the imposition of a compelling and external discipline, the prolonged activity at the behest of machinery, the sheer problems of mass living in cities, the anonymity of the urban community, the obvious overcrowding in badly built housing devoid of the compensations of the countryside, the unchecked pollution — all these must have amounted to a marked deterioration in the circumstances, and therefore the standards, of life for large numbers of people. In the 1830s, according to the Registrar General of Births, Deaths and Marriages, the mortality among the rural population was 18.2 per 1000; in the towns it was 26.2 per thousand.[6] During that and the next decade amost half the children born in towns died before their fifth birthday. Statistics such as these were undoubtedly related to the poverty of housing, the spread of disease, the atrocious sanitary arrangements, the shortage of wholesome food, clean air, sound water, basic amenities and decent living space. It is, therefore, not unreasonable to view the Condition-of-England question in the early nineteenth century (when cities grew more rapidly than ever before or since) as one that related to the environment of living as much as to the level of real wages. It was a matter of social relations and outlook, personal confidence and self-fulfilment, security and the quality of day-to-day life.

The Condition-of-England question

When Carlyle posed the Condition-of-England question as the most urgent topic for public debate in the late 1830s, he was not only drawing attention to the problems of the poor. He was also contributing to an intellectual and political debate. And even though most participants in that debate came from a restricted range of social classes — the relatively educated and/or wealthy — there was no single, accepted view of poverty, its causes and its cure.

There were, for example, fundamental disagreements about such purely 'factual' matters as the real income of the mass of the population considered in historical perspective. Those who looked enviously back to a preferred past, and deplored the impact of industrialism on the environment and on traditional social relations — men like Carlyle himself, or, less subtly, Robert Southey (in *Sir Thomas More; or, Colloquies on the Progress and Prospects of Society*, 1829) or Disraeli (in *Sybil*, 1845) — also argued that the peasant or artisan of pre-industrial days had been much better-off than the contemporary poor. Even Engels, by no means a sentimentalist, claimed that pre-industrial workers 'vegetated throughout a passably comfortable existence ... their material position was far better than that of their successors' (*The Condition of the Working Class in England in 1844*). On the other hand, robust counter-

6 M.W. Flinn, Introduction to the *Report on the Sanitary Condition of the Labouring Population of Great Britain by Edwin Chadwick*, 1842 (Edinburgh, n.d.), p.13.

arguments were put forward by those, like Macaulay or Samuel Smiles, who had a more sanguine view of the progressive character of industrial development. In 1861 Smiles asserted that recent history exemplified a 'process ... of solid and steady improvement.... The more closely, indeed, that the vaunted "good old times" of the labouring classes are investigated, the more clearly will it appear that they were times of hard work and small pay, of dear food and scanty clothing.' (*Workmen's Earnings, Strikes and Savings.*)

Quite apart from such disagreements, and as the context of the various assertions showed, few people felt that the Condition-of-England question was a simple matter of the changing purchasing power of wages over long periods of time — Carlyle himself was prepared to brush aside the mere bandying of wage and price statistics as inadequate: 'Tables are abstractions, and the object a most concrete one, so difficult to read the essence of. There are innumerable circumstances; and one circumstance left out may be the vital one on which all turned.' (*Chartism.*) Instead, his real anxieties stemmed from the effects of economic and social change on the feelings of the poor, their sense of stability and opportunity, the physical environment, the whole pattern of social and communal relations and the cultural health of society. 'Even with abundance' the labourer's 'discontent, his real misery may be great'. And this was echoed by Dickens who in *Hard Times* (dedicated to Carlyle) referred to the 'unfathomable mystery' in human beings and the need 'to reserve our arithmetic for material objects, and to govern these awful unknown quantities by other means'. Of course, even the environmental argument had an aesthetic and cultural, as well as a physical and sanitary, strand to it. In 1830 Macaulay reviewed Southey's *Colloquies* in the *Edinburgh Review*: the essay has become a classic defence of the material and social benefits of industrialism. He took Southey to task for criticizing the architecture of working-class cottages and for making 'the picturesque the test of political good'. A more sophisticated version of the aesthetic and cultural critique of industrial development emerged later in the writings of men like John Ruskin and Matthew Arnold, who were prepared to treat the presumed material success of industrialism as a secondary matter. In the period under consideration, however, the Condition-of-England question was predominantly a more prosaic matter of the presence (irrespective of any historical comparison) of abject poverty, and its contrast with the affluence of the relatively rich; of the seeming degradation of the physical environment and massing of people into overcrowded cities; and of the apparent worsening of relationships between poor and rich, employed and employer.

Controversy endured, even with respect to the more material aspects of these questions. Those committed to the progressive or optimistic view might well admit to the existence of distress and bad conditions, but nevertheless argue that continued development — of human character as well as economic output — would ultimately have a near-universal effect. Some (although by no means all) economists tended in this more optimistic direction; and Macaulay argued, in the essay on Southey, that in spite of moments of 'great distress' the country 'has been almost constantly becoming richer and richer. Now and then there has been a stoppage ... but as to the general tendency there can be no doubt. A single breaker may recede; but the tide is evidently coming in'. And he was bolstered by more explicit and detailed defenders of industrial development, like the scientist Andrew Ure (*Philosophy of Manufacturers*, 1835) or the statistician George Porter (*The Progress of the Nation*, 1847); and by men like Samuel Smiles, who seemed to argue that one of the main causes of poverty was the failing of the poor, and that those who chose the road to personal improvement could attain at least a modest affluence.

On the other side of the argument, even among those who took a more pessimistic view of material living standards, there was considerable scope for variety of approach as well as conclusions. And there were significant contrasts between the stark, impersonal, but persuasive data compiled by local statistical societies in the new industrial towns, and by zealous administrators like the utilitarian Edwin Chadwick (*Report on the Sanitary Condition of the Labouring Population of Great Britain*, 1842); the evangelical piety of social reformers like Lord Shaftesbury; the energetic condemnation of atrocious living conditions by concerned but pragmatic politicians; or the fierce socialist fervour of Frederick Engels.

Variety, contrast and ambivalence were often present in the great debate on British industrial poverty. For even those who were most outraged or alarmed often acknowledged the achievements of industrialization or at least the two-sided nature of its problems. Thus, Carlyle was violent in his condemnation of the upper, and sympathy for the lower, classes. But even he was obliged to express sympathy for the lower, classes. But even he was obliged to express some admiration of material and practical achievement, and some sense of the origins of poverty in attitudes and social relationships. Hence, more generally with respect to the Condition-of-England question, uncertainty of diagnosis was associated with uncertainty of prescription.

This is an important point because it has its parallel among the novelists who addressed themselves to the economic and social problems of early Victorian Britain. In *Mary Barton* (1848) and *North and South* (1855), for example, Mrs Gaskell deals fearlessly with the appalling poverty and murderous resentment which pervaded the Manchester slums — and yet still saw much that was good in the efforts and potential of industrial capitalism, while perceiving the causes of poverty and social instability in greed, ignorance and human failings which pervaded all social classes. It is, therefore, hardly surprising that her implicit prescription for the eradication of extreme distress involved a change of heart, cooperation between social classes, and occasional emigration. This ambivalence is also marked, albeit in more complex ways, in Dickens, whose deserved reputation as an advocate of social reform and critic of slum conditions and neglect should not conceal his admiration for active men of business and material achievement, nor his commitment to the idea of progress.

Looked at in this way, the larger context within which social novelists perceived the Condition-of-England question was comparable to that which characterized more 'scientific' discussions of social and economic change. Among other observers, too, the *existence* of grinding poverty was accepted as common ground (although there was, of course, considerable division of opinion as to its extent, explanation and likely cure). To those who were directly concerned with a systematic exploration of the Condition-of-England question — economists, philosophers, pamphleteers, reformers, politicians — the most important explanation of poverty was overpopulation. For many, the ideas of Thomas Malthus concerning the tendency of numbers to grow and to place pressure on natural resources was a cause of profound pessimism; it raised the spectre of inevitable poverty for the mass of the people. And the associated theory that the response to temporary improvements in living standards would be population increase and a tendency back to subsistence levels was one reason why classical economics got a reputation as 'the dismal science'. For others, however, the critical role of numbers at least offered the possibility of tackling the problem of poverty by changing habits and therefore population trends. This was related, of course, to the rather crude doctrines of self-help put forward by Samuel Smiles. But a more sophisticated version was directly argued by John Stuart Mill, whose *Autobiography* (1873) referred to Malthus's population theory:

> This great doctrine, originally brought forward as an argument against the indefinite improvability of human affairs, we took up with ardent zeal in the contrary sense, as indicating the sole means of realizing that improvability by securing full employment at high wages to the whole labouring population through a voluntary restriction of the increase of their numbers.

Yet even this 'optimistic' prospect — based as it was on the view that the fundamental causes of poverty were inherent in the behaviour of the poor and could be cured by what Smiles called the 'implanting of better habits' — could have harsh implications. Malthusianism and a firm individualism were powerful forces in the advocacy of a more rigorous system of poor relief so as to encourage the poor to avoid the 'fraud, indolence or improvidence' which the *Poor Law Report* of 1834 saw as the main cause of destitution among the able-bodied.

Of course, many contemporaries were prepared to bypass larger theories and, in the interests of humanitarian ends or mere social stability, to tackle particular problems by charitable work or pragmatic legislation to reform conditions in factories and cities. But the general prescription for poverty almost invariably involved a belief in the long-run efficacy of market forces, combined with a sense of the urgent need to lessen population pressure and improve standards of personal behaviour by direct incentives or more general education. Thus Carlyle, although he condemned *laissez-faire* doctrines and 'Paralytic Radicalism', was not so far from some more 'conventional' opinion when he urged that there were two great practical steps which were dwelling 'in all thinking heads': 'Universal Education is the first great thing we mean; general Emigration is the second' (*Chartism*). And in this sense the resolution of personal problems (Mr Micawber's in *David Copperfield*, or the central problems (Mr Micawber's in *David Copperfield*, or the central characters' of *Yeast* and *Mary Barton*) by emigration was more than a literary convention. Of course, no very large steps were taken in the period under consideration. Nor, on the other hand, was either the apocalyptic view of Carlyle or the optimism of the Macaulay school justified. What happened, rather, was that the turbulence of the 1820s, 1830s and 1840s, compounded of rapid economic and structural change as well as genuinely abject poverty, gave way to a calmer social pattern in the 1850s and 1860s. That calm was misleading: degrading poverty was still present and subsequent decades were to witness both its effects and its rediscovery by the rich. But at mid-century the improvements in real incomes that did take place, the greater stability of the urban environment, and the greater accommodation to industrial society — all produced some respite in the insistence of the Condition-of-England question.

Select bibliography

Burnett, J. *Plenty and Want: A Social History of Diet in England.* London, 1966.

Checkland, S.G. *The Rise of Industrial Society in England, 1815-1885.* London, 1964.

Hammond, J.L. and B. *The Age of the Chartists, 1832-1854.* London, 1930.

Hartwell, R.M. *The Industrial Revolution and Economic Growth.* London, 1971. Part III: 'Social and Economic Consequences'.

Hobsbawm, E.J. *Industry and Empire: An Economic History of Britain since 1750.* London, 1968.

Inglis, B. *Poverty and the Industrial Revolution.* London, 1971.

Mathias, P. *The First Industrial Nation: An Economic History of Britain, 1700-1914.* London, 1969.

Rose, M.E. *The Relief of Poverty, 1834-1914.* London, 1972.

Taylor, A.J. (ed.) *The Standard of Living in Britain in the Industrial Revolution.* London, 1975.

Thompson, E.P. *The Making of the English Working Class.* London, 1963.

Williams, R. *Culture and Society, 1780-1950.* London, 1958.

4 The condition of England 1860-1900

CAROL DYHOUSE

Hippolyte Taine, visiting England in the 1860s, waxed eloquent over the signs of her wealth and the size of her national income. He was amazed both by the number of her prosperous citizens and by the opulence of their style of life. Even writers might live well — Tennyson, he observed tartly, was held to be earning 125,000 francs a year for hardly writing anything at all. But Taine's admiration for all these riches was tempered by a marked distaste for the material and social inequalities which he found to be equally characteristic of British society. France as a country was far less wealthy than England, but he believed that her wealth was distributed more equitably among her citizens. The poor in France he held to be less miserably poor than their counterparts in England, neither did he consider them so degraded as human beings by their poverty.[1]

With a Gross National Product that had more than quadrupled itself (in real terms) in sixty years, it is hardly surprising that the mid-Victorians frequently stood in awe before the material achievements of their own society. Even so, a tendency to self-congratulation which many historians have noticed in the mood of mid-century should not be mistaken for total complacency or a smug satisfaction with the social status quo. It would be equally misleading to chart a simple decline in this mood of national optimism, in

1 H. Taine, *Notes on England, 1860-70*, trans. Edward Hyams (London, 1957), pp.290-2.

the face of the religious uncertainties of the 1860s, the commercial
anxieties of the 1870s, the social tensions of the 1880s, and so forth.
We can point to numerous important observers in late Victorian
Britain, who, right through the years of the 'Great Depression',
continued to marvel at the spectacular gains in wealth and prosperity which industry had brought to the nation. This balance between
optimism and criticism, so widespread in Victorian society, characterized most major novelists too. Dickens, Thackeray, George
Eliot — perhaps even Meredith — all in their way accept the liberal
ethos of progress, yet all have severe criticisms of their society to
offer.

Taine's observations of the 1860s were not without significance,
however, for one of the most important developments of the years
1860-1900 in England was a growing interest in the distribution of
wealth, a striving for more accurate generalizations concerning the
extent to which the material gains of industrialism had brought
benefit to the people. In 1884 a Mr Miller of Edinburgh decided to
devote £1000 to the purpose of inquiring into:

> the best means, consistent with justice and equity, for
> bringing about a more equal division of the daily products of
> industry between Capital and Labour, so that it may become
> possible for all to enjoy a fair share of material comfort and
> intellectual culture, possible for all to lead a dignified life,
> and less difficult for all to lead a good life.[2]

These aims implied an ideal of social justice in advance of most of
his contemporaries. Only a minority of late Victorian social theorists
would have defined a maldistribution of wealth and income as the
major social problem of late Victorian England. From the 1880s on,
however, they generated a small but significant body of literature in
support of this viewpoint. Publications as varied in character and
appeal as Fabian Tracts like *Facts for Socialists* (1886) or *Why are
the Many Poor?* (1884) and Robert Blatchford's *Merrie England*
(1894) expressed the viewpoint clearly; they helped stimulate
debate and the search for accurate data and 'objective fact' so
characteristic of the period as a whole.

2 *The Industrial Remuneration Conference, Report of Proceedings and Papers Read
in Price's Hall, Piccadilly, 28-30 January 1885, under the Presidency of Sir Charles
Dilke* (1885), p.v.

When the body of trustees appointed to administer Mr Miller's fund met in 1884-5 they were all too well aware of how contentious the subject of their inquiry was likely to be. It was decided to form a joint committee with nominees of the Royal Statistical Society, and to organize a conference to which leading representatives of Capital and Labour would be invited. The terms of inquiry which were finally formulated differed slightly but significantly from those quoted above. Instead of *assuming* the maldistribution of wealth, they framed this itself as a question. The final formulation read as follows:

> Is the present system or manner whereby the products of industry are distributed between the various persons and classes of the community satisfactory? Or, if not, are there any means by which that system could be improved?[3]

The 'Industrial Remuneration Conference' opened on 28 January 1885, when Sir Thomas Brassey, the railway magnate, read a paper in which he attempted to answer the question of whether industrial progress had tended most to the benefit of the capitalists or of the working classes. Brassey devoted a short space of time to minimizing the benefits that the growth of industry conferred upon its captains. 'Abstinence from enjoyment', he argued, was 'the only source of capital.' He also tried to demonstrate his conviction that economic forces would always conspire to keep profits down to a minimum. The bulk of his paper, however, represented an attempt to illustrate the solid material gains which had accrued to the working classes over the last thirty years. The researches of Giffen, Mulhall, Rogers and other eminent authorities were cited as providing evidence of this phenomenon.

Brassey's interpretation was indeed derived closely from the work of the leading statisticians of his day — men like Leone Levi or Robert Giffen — who adduced wage data, consumption indices and figures showing mounting deposits in savings banks in support of their contention that the working classes were increasingly finding themselves the beneficiaries of industrial progress. In a paper delivered to the Statistical Society the following year, entitled *Further Notes on the Progress of the Working Classes*, Robert Giffen insisted that

3 Ibid. p.vi.

what has happened to the working classes in the last fifty years is not so much what may properly be called an improvement, as a revolution of the most remarkable description. The new possibilities implied in changes which in 50 years have substituted for millions of people in the United Kingdom who were constantly on the brink of starvation, and who suffered untold privations, new millions of artisans and well-paid labourers, ought indeed to excite the hopes of philanthropists and public men. From being a dependent class without any future or hope, the masses of working men have got into a position from which they may effectively advance to almost any degree of civilisation.... The working men have the game in their own hands. Education and thrift, which they can achieve for themselves, will, if necessary, do all that remains to be done.

In 1886, the year in which Giffen made this speech, Charles Booth embarked upon his monumental study of the *Life and Labour of the People in London*. Booth's studies, and the equally famous researches of Seebohm Rowntree in 1901, showed clearly that substantial numbers — Rowntree suggested as many as 30 per cent of the working people in York — were eking out a miserable existence just on or below what was labelled 'the poverty line'. In Rowntree's study this was defined in terms of an income sufficient to meet 'the minimum necessary expenditure for the maintenance of merely *physical* health'.[4] By any standards, then, Giffen's confident pronouncements in 1886 must appear optimistic.

How solid were the material gains that accrued to the working class between 1850 and 1886? This is a complex question. It has generally been accepted by present-day historians that real wages, after recovering from the 1840s, made modest progress in the 1850s and 1860s, although these slight gains were unevenly distributed between skilled and general labourers. During the years of the 'Great Depression', 1873-96, money wages continued to rise slightly, while prices fell more noticeably, making for fairly substantial (about 40 per cent) overall rises in real wages. Consumption of cheap, imported foodstuffs rose in this period, and better

4 B.S. Rowntree, *Poverty: A Study of Town Life* (London, 1901), p.87.

working conditions, better housing and wider opportunities for education meant that the living standards of the more prosperous sections of the working class improved significantly. A similar improvement in living standards could be seen among the new occupational groups of clerks and white-collar workers whose timid respectability was satirized by George and Weedon Grossmith in *The Diary of a Nobody* (1892). From 1896-1900 to the outbreak of the First World War, however, an upturn in prices effectively checked any further advance in real wages.

These generalizations must be offered with a good deal of caution. In the first place, since the information we have on wages before 1880 is very patchy, any analysis of their general movement is somewhat tenuous. Second, the tendencies described are overall tendencies; they mask both regional variations and also the discrepancies between the remuneration of skilled and unskilled labour. Third, generalizations about overall wage increases present only a limited perspective on the general problem of the economic wellbeing of the working class. They tell us nothing of the percentage of unemployment (which rose from an average of about 5 per cent between 1857 and 1873 to about 7.2 per cent between 1874 and 1895), or of the existence of huge sections of *under-employed* and casual labour throughout the period. Neither do they tell us anything about the more specific forms of chronic poverty common at the time — the poverty of the widowed, the sick or the old. Finally, we are found to remember that, however much average wages are held to have improved during the second half of the nineteenth century, for large sections of the population, even by Booth and Rowntree's standards, they remained disturbingly *low*.

It would be useful to have some measure of the overall distribution of wealth or income in late Victorian society as a clue to the social contrasts that horrified Taine and so many contemporaries. Generalizations of any accuracy are excessively difficult to come by, owing to the numerous problems involved in interpreting the inadequate data available. In 1920 Professor A.L. Bowley attempted to estimate the distribution of the total national income in 1880 among three social groups.[5] The 12.30 million wage earners in the

5   A.L. Bowley, *Change in the Distribution of the National Income, 1880-1913* (Oxford, 1920).

country, he estimated, would probably have received a total of £465 million. Of the rest, those with salaries and incomes amounting to less than £160 p.a. (1.85 million people) might have received £130 million, while those with more than this annual figure (0.62 million people) might be estimated to have been in receipt of a total of £530 million. On this calculation, then, about half the national income was being appropriated by rather less than 5 per cent of the total population.

Late Victorian society generated an enormous amount of interest in its own pathology. It was an era in which despair and optimism were often closely allied. Many individuals, passing through a period of personal crisis engendered by the loss of religious faith, found consolation in a kind of surrogate faith, a fervent belief in social duty. Beatrice Webb, whose autobiographical volume *My Apprenticeship* (1926) provides a wealth of insights into the late Victorian social conscience, describes partly from her own personal experience this 'flight of emotion away from the service of God to the service of man'. In *Robert Elsmere* (1888), a novel which was tremendously successful at the time, Mrs Humphrey Ward presented a fictional dramatization of the same theme. Despair might be transmuted into inspiration: a sense of elation now that man, armed with the tools of rational and scientific progress, was recognized as architect of all social systems, no longer to be seen as immutable or ordained by God.

Beatrice Webb emphasized the way in which a growing awareness of the extent of social and material inequalities in the 1880s inflamed the consciences of many of her generation. She spoke of a new 'collective consciousness of sin' among the upper and middle classes.

> a growing uneasiness, amounting to conviction, that the industrial organisation, which had yielded rent, interest and profits on a stupendous scale, had failed to provide a decent livelihood and tolerable conditions for a majority of the inhabitants of Great Britain.

This in itself could inspire individuals to commit themselves to what they envisaged as a new kind of social service, derived less from charitable intent than from ideals of equity and social justice.

Arnold Toynbee's passionate admission of the guilt he felt as a representative of a privileged class provides the best illustration of this. In a lecture before a working-class audience in London, delivered just before his death in 1883, he confessed:

> We — the middle classes, I mean, not merely the very rich — we have neglected you; instead of justice we have offered you charity, and instead of sympathy we have offered you hard and unreal advice, but I think we are changing. If you would only believe it and trust us, I think that many of us would spend our lives in your service.

The sense of urgency which permeated this and other attempts to rally the consciences of the middle class in the name of a new standard of social justice was rooted in a range of anxieties, one of which was the fear that a growing sense of outrage born of their own sufferings might drive sections of the working class towards revolutionary socialism. Toynbee himself, in the lecture quoted, took pains to impress upon his audience the need for patience, and his conviction that 'without revolution, and without socialism, in the continental sense, we shall be able to do something towards that better distribution of wealth which we all desire to see'.

In her attempt to explain the reasons behind the growing public concern with social conditions in the 1880s Beatrice Webb tended to play down those connected with 'a panic fear of the newly enfranchised democracy'. Even so, it is undeniable that an interest in social reform was sometimes urged upon contemporaries as a timely precaution, an investment in stability and the social status quo. Arnold White, in *The Problems of a Great City* (1898), suggested that 'the premium of insurance paid by property to cover the risk of social earthquake is too low'. Writers of reformist propaganda, of course, whatever their political leanings, were likely to exploit the real or imaginary anxieties of their public. In one of the best-known tracts of the 1880s, *How the Poor Live and Horrible London* (1889), G.R. Sims warned his readers, that 'this mighty mob of famished, diseased and filthy helots is getting dangerous, physically, morally, politically dangerous ... its lawless armies may sally forth and give us a taste of the lesson the mob has tried to teach in Paris, where long years of neglect have done their work'.

However unlikely the spectacle envisaged by Sims may have

been, the image certainly succeeded in arousing public concern. The experience of the Hyde Park riots in 1865 had been sufficient to ruffle the calm of Matthew Arnold's prose when he attacked 'Doing as One Likes' in *Culture and Anarchy* (1869). H.M. Hyndman, leader of the Social Democratic Federation, knew that the threat of revolution was an effective way to bolster demands for specific social reforms: public subscriptions for the relief of the unemployed had increased spectacularly after the scare of the 1886 riots. In an article published in the *Contemporary Review* in July 1886 he warned his readers that the English workers, although basically a peaceful and law-abiding class, 'would not be patient for ever'.

In the closing years of the nineteenth century new kinds of anxieties and uncertainties surfaced in the minds of many politicians and statesmen to produce another surge of interest in social reform. These anxieties were related to the rise of international competition and to imperial tensions abroad. A tendency to interpret international rivalry in terms of a 'Darwinian' struggle in which only the 'fittest' nations might be expected to survive generated an immense amount of interest in 'national efficiency' in turn-of-the-century Britain. The experience of the Boer War was crucial here. The pathetically stunted undernourished and unhealthy bodies of the recruits who came forward convinced many that social reform was a precondition of national, let alone imperial, survival. One result of the revelations concerning the quality of recruits, for instance, was an interdepartmental committee of inquiry which set out, in 1904, to investigate 'the physical deterioration of the people'.

'Efficiency' became one of the catchwords of the early twentieth century, whether prefixed by 'physical', 'social' or 'national'. When Seebohm Rowntree reported on social conditions in York in 1901, he argued that reform was necessary, not only because the kind of poverty he discovered was crippling the lives of large numbers of human beings, but also to ensure Britain's survival as an industrial power:

> Within the last thirty years, Germany, Belgium and even Russia have transformed themselves economically.... We are also face to face with the unprecedented competition of the

United States. The conditions of industrial competition are, therefore, wholly changed and the question of efficiency — mental and physical — has become one of paramount importance.

The most formidable challenge to British industrial power abroad, Rowntree urged, undoubtedly came from across the Atlantic. America was a formidable rival not merely because of her 'gigantic enterprise and almost illimitable resources' but also because 'her workers are better nourished and possess a relatively higher efficiency'.

Social justice, stability, efficiency, survival: all these were ends which motivated late Victorians to take an interest in the social questions of their day.

There is a sense in which a society or culture defines itself through its own definition of social problems. The definition of a social problem is in itself a statement of values. There were certain kinds of extreme position which might be adopted by 'social pathologists' and would-be reformers in late nineteenth-century Britain, and, although only a minority actually adopted such extreme positions, it may be helpful to outline some of their implications here. At one extreme were those who believed that inequalities of wealth or income were in themselves a major social problem, and that industrialism had so far failed to benefit a significant proportion of the population. At another extreme were those who emphasized that the working class as a whole had benefited substantially from industrialism, and had made considerable material and moral progress over the last fifty years. In the conviction that the existing system of social organization had markedly improved the life chances of the majority, these thinkers were inclined to seek the roots of social problems in the lifestyle of a minority — the indigent, the thriftless or the 'undeserving' poor. In this way, then, the poor might be held largely responsible for their own poverty.

The Charity Organization Society (founded in 1809 as 'The Society for Organizing Charitable Relief and Repressing Mendicity') stood squarely for the mid-Victorian virtues of self-help, thrift and individual effort; it tended fairly consistently to construe poverty as the moral failing of the poor. C.S. Loch, the Secretary of the COS, believed that paupers commonly represented the *failures* rather than the *failings* of a civilization. 'Destitution', he argued, 'cannot disappear. Every group of competing men is continually producing it.'[6]

Beatrice Webb has left us a vivid description of the activities of the COS in the 1880s. She recalled in *My Apprenticeship* how on the one hand 'Octavia Hill, C.S. Loch and their immediate followers concentrated their activities on schooling the poor in industry, honesty, thrift and filial piety', while on the other they waged war against that 'indiscriminate charity' held responsible for 'demoralizing' the poor. Yet even the most stringent members of the COS sometimes had to admit that there might be 'exceptional circumstances' — sudden bereavement, acute illness, loss of employment, and so forth — which could precipitate individuals or whole families into crippling poverty. COS policy, then, often centred upon attempts to differentiate between the 'deserving' and the 'undeserving' poor. (Shaw treats the distinction irreverently in his mischievously comic portrayal of Snobby Price in *Major Barbara* (1907).) The 'deserving' poor were usually defined as those deemed to be in possession of sufficient moral and personal resources to enable them, given a modicum of material aid, to pull themselves up to the bottom rung of the ladder of 'respectable' society. In this way, charity organization was seen by its practitioners as a programme of social reclamation.

The inadequacies of this kind of programme as a solution to the problem of poverty became increasingly apparent in the closing decades of the century. Beatrice Webb has described how Samuel and Henrietta Barnett, struggling as social workers against the appalling conditions in the East End, became finally disillusioned with the blinkered assumptions of COS orthodoxy and severed their allegiance with the organization in 1886. Booth's 'Grand Inquest' into the condition of the London populace and Rowntree's survey of York both helped to clarify impressions of the scale and the nature of the problem of want. Both investigations emphasized the intimate connections between hardship and old age, sickness and unemployment. When Mrs Bosanquet criticized Rowntree's

6 Quoted in E. Townshend, *The Case Against the Charity Organisation Society*, Fabian Tract No. 158 (London, 1911), p.12.

methodology in York on the grounds that he had underestimated the extent to which poverty was attributable to deficiencies of 'character and behaviour', Rowntree retorted:

> Nothing can be gained by closing our eyes to the fact that there is in this country a large section of the community whose income is insufficient for the purpose of physical efficiency, and whose lives are *necessarily* stunted. If the men and women in this class possessed as a whole extraordinary energy and perseverance, they might, perhaps, notwithstanding physical feebleness and a depressing environment, raise themselves to a higher level, but it is idle to expect from them, as a class, virtues and powers far in excess of those characterising any other section of the community.[7]

Urbanization was the most spectacular feature of nineteenth-century social change. The 1851 census revealed that, for the first time in history, more people were living in the towns and cities of England and Wales than in the countryside, and it is difficult to exaggerate the impact this made upon the Victorians. The first half of the century had witnessed the rise of the new industrial towns; the second half witnessed their continued expansion in size. Manchester in the 1840s had been the 'shock city of the age': indeed, most of the interest in the social questions of the 1830s and 1840s had involved a focus upon the new factory towns of the industrial North. In the second half of the century, attention shifted back to London, the monster city, which was spawning suburbs in all directions: between 1881 and 1891 four 'towns' with rates of population increase among the highest in Britain (Leyton, Willesden, Tottenham and West Ham) were all suburbs of London. London was also disfigured, in the East End particularly, by some of the largest and ugliest slums in the country.

London loomed huge both in fact and in the minds of contemporaries between 1860 and 1900. Taine had been aghast at its size in the 1860s:

> Three million five hundred thousand inhabitants; it adds up to 12 cities the size of Marseilles, 10 as big as Lyons, two the

7 B.S. Rowntree, *The Poverty Line: A Reply* (London, 1903), p.28.

size of Paris in a single mass. But words on paper are no substitute for the effect on the eyes.

By 1881 the population of London had risen to 4 ½ million, and by 1911 to over 7 million. Taine wrote of London as monstrous, blackened, diabolic. He was horrified by its artificiality, which he saw as reducing nature to something like 'a bad drawing in charcoal on which someone has rubbed his sleeve'. The morbid fascination with the city had great poetic potential — a potential more fully realized in French poetry (particularly by Baudelaire) than in English. James Thomson's nightmare vision of mankind overwhelmed by the city produced *The Doom of a City* (1857) and *The City of Dreadful Night* (1874). An anti-urban tradition was well ingrained in the English mind. In 1891 Rosebery admitted he found

> no thought of pride associated in my mind with London. I am always haunted by the awfulness of London ... sixty years ago, a great Englishman, Cobbett, called it a wen. If it was a wen then, what is it now? A tumour, an elephantiasis sucking into its gorged system half the life and the blood and the bone of the rural districts.[8]

The metaphor was important: in the late nineteenth century the city itself (and especially London) was frequently seen as a consumer of men or, to use the striking image of the poet Verhaeren, a *ville tentaculaire*, sucking the lifeblood from the countryside. There was a common saying that one rarely met a third-generation Londoner, least of all in the East End of London. At the turn of the century Jack London wrote of the area as 'a huge man-killing machine'. As late as 1912 Havelock Ellis, in *The Task of Social Hygiene*, reiterated these fears, inclining to see the city as something pathological, in itself a kind of social disease. (The association of the imagery of disease with the city will be familiar to all readers of Dickens.) Men were attracted to cities, Havelock Ellis argued, like moths to a candleflame, the dangers being similar in each case:

> From our present point of view it is a very significant fact that the equipoise between country-dwellers and town-dwellers

8 Quoted in E. Howard, *Garden Cities of Tomorrow* (London, 1902), p.11.

has been lost; that the towns are gaining at the expense of the country whose surplus population they absorb and destroy. The town population is not only disinclined to propagate, it is probably in some measure unfit to propagate.

The Social-Darwinistic vocabulary of the last sentence quoted here is significant. Havelock Ellis was not of course suggesting that all those who lived in cities were unfit to survive. He was, however, alluding to anxieties that haunted many of his contemporaries at the turn of the century, in particular the spectre of the degeneration of the race. The recruiting experiences of the Boer War period had taught politicians and administrators the difficulties of finding healthy men of good physique in the centres of large cities. The *Contemporary Review* featured an article on this theme by Major-General Sir J.F. Maurice (under the pseudonym 'Miles') entitled 'Where to get Men?' in 1902. The city, it seemed, was sapping the vitality of the people.

In 1901 a pressure group within the Liberal Party under the leadership of C.F.G. Masterman published a collection of essays entitled *The Heart of the Empire*. This was intended as an indictment of the Liberal leaders of the time, who, the contributors believed, were pursuing an unrealistic policy of expansion abroad at the expense of a long-overdue programme of social reform at home. Masterman argued:

> The Centre of Imperialism, as Lord Rosebery is never tired of reiterating, rests in London. With a perpetual lowering of the vitality of the Imperial Race in the great cities of the kingdom through overcrowding in room and in area, no amount of hectic, feverish activity on the confines of Empire will be able to arrest the inevitable decline.

The schemes of social action propounded by those who contributed to this volume ranged widely: none was entirely new. For since the 1880s at least, that 'hectic, feverish activity' which Masterman deplored on the confines of Empire had indeed had its counterpart at home. In 1889 G.B. Shaw had mocked those 'paroxysms of frantic coercion, followed by paroxysms of frantic charity' which he held had mainly distinguished contemporary efforts to find a solution to the social problems of the slum. Like most of Shaw's statements, this was of course an exaggeration, containing at the same time an element of truth. While schemes of reform propounded between 1880 and 1900 were many and varied enough to make nonsense of Shaw's simple formula 'coercion-plus-charity', these schemes were so frequently desperate remedies making little impact on the total problem that the description is not altogether inaccurate.

Of the numerous tracts that served to rivet public attention on the problem of the slums of London in the 1880s, historians have generally emphasized that of the Congregationalist minister Andrew Mearns, entitled *The Bitter Cry of Outcast London* (1883). Appearing at the beginning of a decade of depression fraught with unemployment and social tensions and marked by the revival of socialism, it drew attention to the housing question with fairly direct reference to problems of overcrowding like incest and immorality, which were well calculated to send a thrill of horror through the public conscience. Its impact was spectacular.[9] The interest it generated in the housing question helped bring a Royal Commission on the subject into existence between 1884 and 1885. It also helped to produce a wave of voluntary organizations and effort of all kinds, as well as increasing public interest and support for those institutions that already existed.

It is no easy task to convey effectively the *range* of this effort. Settlements, mission halls, working men's clubs, centres for education, recreation, leisure activities of all kinds, proliferated in the East End, as well as in the slums of all major provincial cities. So did housing organizations, temperance societies, savings clubs and charitable ventures for every conceivable kind of purpose. Contemporaries often wryly commented on the fashion for 'slumming' among various social groups — earnest young men from the universities, middle-class housewives bored by the problems of middle age. Many ardent and energetic reforms of these years, inspired by the idealism of men like Edward Denison, who had pioneered the settlement movement earlier in the century, believed that their very presence in the slum would help to heal that gulf between the social classes they held largely responsible for the existence of the social

9 A. Mearns, *The Bitter Cry of Outcast London*, edited with an introduction by A.S. Wohl (1970).

problem. Others battled for more 'scientific' solutions, evolving increasingly sophisticated methods of administration, inquiry and casework. There were many workers who despaired altogether of reform within what they came to see as the hopeless environment of the slum. Both Charles Booth and the leader of the Salvation Army, General Booth, advocated rescue schemes whereby the most 'degenerate' section of the slum-dwellers, the 'submerged tenth', or the 'residuum', might be transported to the colonies or the countryside. There it was believed they might be 'regenerated' under the moral influences of steady agricultural labour and wholesome rural air. The more disillusioned still endorsed the idea of isolated penal settlements for the totally unregenerate slum-dweller, even the sterilization of the 'unfit' as a precaution against further degeneration of the race.

In the minds of the middle-class observers in late Victorian Britain the slums represented a 'social excrescence', a region *outside* civilization.[10] Slum-dwellers were seen as a heathen and foreign race, inhabiting uncharted continents, or the 'Nether World' of 'Darkest London'. They were frequently described as a predatory species, parasitic and verminous — savage, uncivilized beings. Investigators scandalized the public with tales of violence and immorality, of modes and codes of behaviour which threatened to subvert Respectable Society. Writers as various as Charles Booth, Mrs Bosanquet, Sidney Olivier and Jack London all emphasized the 'dragging down effect' which the slum exerted on the decent or deserving poor who might otherwise have managed to pull them-selves 'out of the abyss'. There seemed little hope for the children reared within its confines. Arthur Morrison's novel, *The Child of the Jago* (1896), is a dramatization of this theme of the slum as self-perpetuating, as a kind of human trap.

C.F.G. Masterman, writing in *The Nineteenth Century* in 1906 about the relationship between the Liberals and the recently founded Labour Party, reassured his readers that the latter was not really a socialist party at all. It had avoided titling itself as such; neither was there anything revolutionary in its immediate policy:

10 G. Stedman Jones, *Outcast London: A Study in the Relationship between Classes in Victorian Society* (Oxford, 1971), Part III, *passim*.

Some of its members do not understand what Socialism means. Some understand Socialism and definitely reject it. Some are Socialists, but reluctant to alarm the mass of the English people with a name which has come to have a technical and unpleasant significance.... The Labour party is a party pledged to evolutionary change.

There was a good deal of truth in these observations. Certainly, those who would have avowed themselves socialists were very much in the minority in that amorphous federation of trade unions and political bodies which had amalgamated in 1900 to form the Labour Representation Committee. Amplifying what he had meant when speaking of the 'unpleasant significance' that attached to the word 'socialism', Masterman argued that in the eyes of 'most of the Middle Class':

> Socialists are men who have bolted with the Municipal funds, or with their neighbours' wives, or if they have not yet done so, would do so on the slightest provocation. Even to the more enlightened, a 'Socialist Party' too often signifies a party pledged to sudden and violent change, involving confiscation, disturbance of the social order, perhaps revolution. It would cut the world into parallelograms, and equalise the thriftless and the laggard.

Popular antipathy towards socialist ideals was a theme in Robert Tressell's satirical novel *The Ragged Trousered Philanthropists* (1914); and to many Englishmen the entire range of socialist opinion tended to be assimilated to the lunatic — and mainly foreign — fringe of the kind depicted by Conrad in *The Secret Agent* (1907).

Masterman's comment would have been even more appropriate in the 1880s, when socialism had been revived as a creed in England, and a number of socialist societies had come into existence, most notably the Social Democratic Federation, the Fabian Society and William Morris's Socialist League. Membership of all three groups was small and mainly middle class. In spite of this and of the constant divisions and conflicts both within and between societies, socialism achieved a large amount of publicity — indeed notoriety — in 1886. The year was one of severe depression, and the SDF had taken the lead in mounting a public demonstration of the unemployed in Trafalgar Square. An episode of stone throwing and looting which followed convinced some sections of the public that socialists were bent on conspiracy and constituted a serious threat to public order. Queen Victoria, in a famous letter to Gladstone, expressed her horror at what she described as a '*momentary* triumph of Socialism and disgrace to the capital'.

This event, and the demonstrations of the unemployed organized by the SDF over the following year, helped to fix the conspiratorial 'daggers and dynamite' image of socialism in the public mind. *Justice*, the SDF newspaper, was banned from 'respectable' bookstalls. Some alarming rumours seem to have circulated at the time — that SDF drilling, for example, in a backyard in Bermondsey, signified preparation for a military coup. Whether or not Hyndman, the leader of the SDF, ever committed himself to the prospect of revolution as serious strategy is in fact doubtful. The events of 1886-7 served to demonstrate the weaknesses of unarmed workers in conflict with soldiers and the police force. William Morris, disillusioned by the experience of these years, abandoned hopes of seeing a socialist order implemented in his own lifetime: in *News From Nowhere* (1890) he envisaged 1952 as the revolutionary year of the future.

G.B. Shaw once argued that in their early days of political naïveté he and other enthusiastic young Fabian socialists had forecast a revolution to coincide with the anniversary of the French model in 1889. The statement should not be taken seriously; it is wholly unlikely that the Fabians ever cherished any belief in either the likelihood or the desirability of revolution. *Fabian Essays*, edited by Shaw and published in 1889, shows them committed to the idea of gradual, evolutionary change. Throughout the late Victorian period one of the main aims of the Fabian Society was to demonstrate the 'respectability' of socialism. Sidney Webb, in his contribution to *Fabian Essays*, reassured his readers that there was nothing to be scared of in socialism; indeed, there had been a good deal of 'unconscious progress' towards socialist goals since mid-century. Socialism, he emphasized, was 'the inevitable outcome' of democracy. Sidney Olivier, in the same collection, argued that socialism would repair and reinforce rather than challenge existing codes of social morality. 'The cardinal virtue of socialism', he asserted, was 'nothing more than commonsense'. Shaw's early plays express a similar view; in *Widowers' Houses* (1892) analysis of the relation between property and morality is followed by the painless removal of abuses through local government. *Fabian Essays* went through several editions and helped to open up discussion among the middle class of socialism as a 'respectable' political creed. The Fabian social and political programme appeared to some contemporaries as being so moderate as to be hardly socialist at all. Paul de Rousiers, a Frenchman visiting Britain in 1896, argued that Fabian ideals were meritocratic, ideals of administrative efficiency rather than of a collectivist character. Sidney Webb's brand of 'collectivism', he assured his readers, would not be recognized as such by any French or German socialist.[11]

Socialism remained very much a minority movement in turn-of-the-century England, dominated by middle-class intellectuals, not all of whom, by any means, were convinced of the need to build up enough support to form a mass political party. Those who did envisage this goal worked energetically to overcome separatism, for better relations with trade unions and with the Labour movement as a whole. Even so, in the early years of this century, the bulk of the Labour movement remained loyal to the Liberal Party, either suspicious of, or actively hostile towards, the theory (or theorists) of socialism. Socialism continued to be seen as a predominantly 'unrespectable', subversive movement by the majority of the public.

Many socialists and radical thinkers did indeed stand for wholesale rebellion against what they saw as the hypocritical social morality and materialist values of the 'respectable' middle class. Respectability might be attacked for its association with hypocrisy and meanness in the individual — as with Samuel Butler in *The Way of All Flesh* (1903). In contrast, Edward Carpenter saw it as the basis of a corrupt social system. In an essay entitled *Defence of Criminals: A Criticism of Morality*, published in *Civilisation: Its Cause and Cure* (1889), he argued:

> Law represents from age to age the code of the dominant or ruling class.... Today the code of the dominant class may

11 P. de Rousiers, *The Labour Question in Britain*, trans. F.L.D. Henderson (London, 1896), p.389.

perhaps best be denoted by the word Respectability ... [which] has to a great extent overwhelmed the codes of the other classes and got the law on its side (so far that in the main it characterises those classes who do not conform to it as the criminal classes).... Respectability is the code of those who have the wealth and the command, and as these have also the fluent pens and tongues, it is the standard of modern literature and the press.

In short, the 'Respectability' of his day, Carpenter concluded, meant 'the Respectability of Property'. 'There was nothing so Respectable as being well-off.'

Socialists often declared themselves frustrated by what they saw as the hollow conventions of 'Respectability': 'Respectable Society' frequently pictured socialism as a threat to the very existence of morality and culture. The old fear of the mob revived in the minds of those who envisaged socialist agitators harnessing the forces of discontent which they imagined to be seething in the slums of cities, riding to power over the ruins of culture and civilization. Two novels published in 1886 provide a range of insights into the kind of insecurities that were generated in this context. George Gissing's *Demos*, intended by its author as 'a savage satire on working class aims and capacities', and Henry James's *The Princess Casamassima* both illustrate contemporary visions of socialism as a primarily destructive force, as a threat to the existence of 'culture'.

In *The Princess Casamassima* the socialist inclinations of the central characters are depicted against a background of vague, conspiratorial, quasi-anarcho-revolutionary activity. A network of dark subterranean plotting is directed by the elusive 'Big Brother' figure Hoffendahl, who (like some kind of Phantom of the Opera) is described by the author as 'a shadowy musician', planning 'a great symphonic massacre'. The imagery Henry James employs throughout the novel is revealing: democracy is repeatedly spoken of as a 'flood', a 'tidal wave' threatening to sweep away culture and refinement. Amid the 'gloom' of radical politics, Christina — symbol of culture, refinement and aristocratic privilege — radiates light. Hyacinth Robinson (whose small hands and feet constitute the traditional trappings of blood, breeding and refinement mis-placed in a plebeian setting) is lured away from politics by the light of art and culture. This process is completed by his journey to

Venice. There he finds himself so overawed by the beauty of the Veronese ceilings that he learns to look with 'a great horror' on 'that kind of invidious jealousy which is at the bottom of redistribution'. Both *Demos* and *The Princess Casamassima* share something of the same moral. 'Culture' depends on the existence of an élite of wealth and sensibility, therefore socialism threatens culture.

It has been argued that between 1910 and 1914 England passed through a period of acute political crisis.[12] Discontent voiced by three of the groups who felt themselves most oppressed or threatened at the time — by women, by sections of the working class and by the Irish people — mounted to a crescendo. Liberal politicians, uncertain of their own values and divided among themselves, were faced with a morass of often conflicting demands from pressure groups, as well as by increasing impatience from the Left, and increasing hostility from the Right. Almost all the elements in this crisis were prefigured in late Victorian Britain. The 1880s and 1890s witnessed outbursts of controversy over the role of the 'New Woman'; social tensions, strikes and unemployment; the rise of socialism and the 'New Unions', demands for home rule from Ireland. All three of these groups — women, workers and Irish — hoped for concessions from the Liberals in Parliament. Altogether the condition of the country did not augur well for the future of a Liberal Party unsure of its role.

Select bibliography

Best, G. *Mid Victorian Britain, 1851-75.* London, 1971.

Briggs, A. *Social Theory and Social Action: A Study of the Work of Seebohm Rowntree, 1871-1954.* London, 1961.

Dyos, H., and Wolff, M. (eds) *The Victorian City: Images and Realities.* 2 vols. London, 1973.

Howe, I. *Politics and the Novel.* London, 1957.

Keating, P. (ed.) *Into Unknown England, 1866-1913: Selections from the Social Explorers.* Manchester, 1976.

Pelling, H. *The Origins of the Labour Party.* Oxford, 1954.

Richter, M. *The Politics of Conscience: T.H. Green and His Age.* London, 1964.

Saul, S.B. *The Myth of the Great Depression.* London, 1969.

Stedman Jones, G. *Outcast London: A Study in the Relationship Between Classes in Victorian Society.* Oxford, 1971.

Williams, R. *The Country and the City.* London, 1973.

12 G. Dangerfield, *The Strange Death of Liberal England* (London, 1935), *passim*.

5 The governing framework: social class and institutional reform in Victorian Britain

BARRY SUPPLE

The point has already been made that Victorian literature cannot be dissociated from the world in which it existed, not merely because of the economic transformation of that world, but because the Industrial Revolution ultimately involved far-reaching changes in the institutions and ideas that governed it. And just as the questioning of established institutions and human relationships can be a vital issue in imaginative literature, so their reform is an important part of its context.

The necessity for reform was indicated by John Stuart Mill in his prescient essays on *The Spirit of the Age* (1831):

> The first of the leading peculiarities of the present age is, that it is an age of transition. Mankind have outgrown old institutions and old doctrines, and have not yet acquired new ones. When we say outgrown, we intend to prejudge nothing. A man may not be either better or happier at six-and-twenty, than he was at six years of age: but the same jacket which fitted him then, will not fit him now.

This was written at the outset of the dramatic and violent campaign which led to the First Reform Act of 1832. Within little more than fifty years Britain's governing framework was to be transformed by sweeping changes in formal mechanisms of government and the great institutions of society. Voting rights were greatly extended and the constituency system adjusted to the new patterns of population distribution created by economic growth. These changes, in turn, helped to create political parties and parliamentary structures in their modern form. At the same time a much more effective system of local government was created, and the structure of and recruitment to the civil service were reorganized. There was also a vitally important series of reforms in education, the army, the church, the law, and so on. Related to all these sorts of institutional reform, the period saw the beginnings of substantial state intervention in the regulation of towns and factories, and a fundamental redirection of the nation's economic and social policies. In effect, then, Mill was correctly anticipating the beginnings of the modernization of British institutions and policy.

The general theme of this chapter is the adaptation of Victorian political and social institutions to the demands and pressures of an industrializing society. It is, of course, true that reform was based upon ideas and theories, many of which antedated the Industrial Revolution. Nevertheless, it is the argument here that those ideas, as with much of contemporary literature, were realized in response to the subtle influence of industrial change and social pressures.

One of the most plausible explanations of contemporary reform was the political emergence of the middle classes and their claims to a larger share of power. In *The Spirit of the Age* Mill had argued that the landed classes no longer had either the qualifications or the exclusive access to the culture and economic influence needed to justify their monopoly of power or the form taken by the institutions which embodied it. Certainly, social change confronted the landed classes with a serious challenge. This was reflected in their apparent loss of function and the emergence of an economically influential and well-educated middle class pressing for a share in political power and social privilege. At the same time, however, change was more than a matter of conceding middle-class claims: the reforming spirit of the age was also a modernizing spirit in the functional sense. Men came to recognize that inherited institutions and policies were generally ill adapted to the needs of an industrial society — that a more representative parliament or better civil servants or more adequate education or more efficient courts or more effective local government were necessary, because the problems with which they dealt had been transformed. Hence it was on grounds not merely of class interest but of humanity, efficiency and

competence that conventional ways of organizing, doing and
looking at things had to be overturned or amended. These twin
themes — class rivalry and the need to modernize and rationalize —
provide, therefore, essential keys to the understanding of reform.

Classes

It is an oversimplification — but a useful one — to envisage
nineteenth-century society as being divided into three important
groupings, each highly stratified within itself. These were: the
upper classes, rich and largely dependent on landed estates for their
wealth and influence, with farmers perhaps considered as appen-
dages to them; the middle classes (business, administrative and
professional), growing in numbers and wealth, and covering many
types of occupation, income and interest; and the working classes,
distinguished by their subordinate position in society and workplace, and by their relative poverty, which nevertheless embraced a
wide range from material desperation to modest sufficiency.

The working classes, during this period, developed a number of
distinctive institutions — friendly societies, cooperative societies,
savings banks, building societies, trade unions. Although these
form an important chapter in the evolution of Victorian society, the
range and depth of their impact were limited. In the first place, the
most influential of them had a restricted membership: they were
primarily associated with the so-called 'aristocracy of labour' — the
skilled workers with material and social aspirations analogous to
those of the lower middle class. They and their families were
heavily — although by no means exclusively — represented in the
'respectable' organizations: friendly societies, whose membership
rose from 1.5 million at mid-century to almost 5 million in 1897;
cooperative societies (1.6 million by 1899); building societies
(640,000 by 1895); and savings banks (9.6 million by 1900).
Second, the nature of working-class institutions encouraged respectability and improvement rather than radicalism and revolt. Admittedly there were critical moments (e.g. in the campaign for
parliamentary reform in 1831-2 or 1866-7) when working-class
protest and unrest, or the fear of it, played an important part in
forcing the government's hand; but throughout the period it was
clear that by itself the working class could do little to change the

society around it, and its apparent successes were hardly ever achieved alone. 'We are apt to forget', wrote Richard Cobden in 1851, 'that the mass of the people, however enthusiastic in favour of universal suffrage, have not the power of carrying that or any other measure, excepting with the aid of the middle class.'[1]

It was this middle class, of course, which was central to Victorianism. The indisputable beneficiaries of economic, social and political change in the nineteenth century, they formed a varied sector of society. The beginnings of their prosperity have already been described in Chapter 3. From mid-century they flowered. Continued industrial, commercial and financial development expanded the salary- and profit-earning class. The development of government outpaced that of the economy as a whole (employment in public administration virtually trebled in the last half of the century to 220,000 in 1901); while the newly significant category of professional men grew very rapidly indeed: between 1841 and 1881, while the total population of England and Wales rose by less than two-thirds, the number of teachers more than trebled, to 170,000, and of other professions quadrupled, to 150,000. In the favourable mid-century years, 1851-71, when the number of occupied males grew by merely 25 per cent, the affluent minority who reported incomes from employment (i.e. excluding profits, interest, dividends) of between £200 and £999 grew by 88 per cent and their aggregate incomes by 90 per cent.

The patterns of middle-class expenditure and lifestyles which had emerged in the first half of the century were extended and solidified with the prosperity, expansion and confidence of the later decades. And much of this expenditure exemplified the extent to which the middle classes valued and could afford domestic and creature comforts. At the same time, however, the sustained growth of savings, investment and insurance bore impressive witness to the habits of thrift and prudence that characterized the middle-class family. And the preoccupation with education (particularly with the growth of private and grammar schools closely modelled on the great public schools of the upper classes) underscored the significance to such families of the acquisition of skills, influence, style and contacts which were the best means of providing unity and

1 John Morley, *The Life of Richard Cobden* (1879), pp.565-6.

coherence to members of a powerful class, and the main way forward for men without large capital resources.

Two subgroups within the middle classes gave them their political and social cutting edges. On the one hand, there were those who were successful and relatively independent in the world of business and its associated professions — the leaders of what Cobden, in 1844, called 'the middle classes — the unprivileged, industrious men who live by our capital and labour'.[2] They were the families that ultimately evolved into a new social type in the late nineteenth century: the upper middle classes with aristocratic pretensions and authority. Beatrice Webb, daughter of a successful timber merchant and a railway promoter, claimed in *My Apprenticeship* (1926) that her sense of social distinctiveness was a consciousness not of riches but of superior power: 'As life unfolded itself [she was born in 1858] I became aware that I belonged to a class of persons who habitually gave orders, but who seldom, if ever, executed the orders of other people', and she went on to describe her many sisters also marrying men who gave orders:

> the country gentleman on his estate and at sessions; the manufacturer in his mill; the shipowner to his fleet of ships on the high seas; the city financier in the money market floating or refusing to float foreign government loans; the Member of Parliament as Financial Secretary to the Treasury; the surgeon and the barrister well on their way to leadership in their respective professions.

On the other hand, there were those whose ranks Beatrice Webb was about to join: the intellectual middle class — professional social scientists, writers, journalists, academics, civil servants, politicians. This subclass is of peculiar importance to us because of its initiative and its ideological contribution to the overhaul of British institutions. Whether as Benthamite radicals, socialists, administrative specialists, painstaking researchers, orthodox theorists, or systematic defenders or critics of existing institutions, their role in reform was vital, and (what was equally important) their position in society secure.

Finally, at the top of the social pyramid were the few thousand families of the aristocracy and the upper or landed classes. In the

2 Ibid. p.305.

early nineteenth century they were still the class 'in possession'. The dominant institutions of the country were 'their' institutions. The men whose wealth and power were based on their landed estates monopolized an unreformed Parliament (before reform it was estimated that 87 peers had the ability to nominate 213 MPs) and a civil service whose senior composition was largely based on patronage; they effectively controlled the composition of the church (the nobility had the presentation of over 7000 out of 11,300 livings), the army, the two English universities and the principal public schools. Through the magistracy, they were masters of local administration and justice in county areas, while exercising considerable influence in the boroughs. When Britain was well launched on its Industrial Revolution, its institutions still reflected the pre-industrial significance of landed wealth, and continued to provide coherence, selfconsciousness and confident purpose to a traditional upper class.

This sweeping control of the nation's political and social institutions excited a good deal of criticism in the early nineteenth century, and fundamental reforms in its middle decades. Yet there was more to the upper classes than a narrow exclusiveness of outlook and economic role. Their land was, of course, of supreme importance; and strict land and inheritance laws enabled them to maintain the great concentrations of estates; in 1876 just over 500 noblemen between them owned about 15 million acres, or close on half the country. But they did not stay exclusively on the land. It was, indeed, precisely the concentration of estates in the hands of eldest sons that obliged them to seek positions for younger sons in the army, the church, the civil service, the law, politics, and even carefully selected parts of the business world. Thus the aristocracy and gentry joined the boards of joint-stock companies and financial institutions in the City. This was partly a matter of prestige, and Trollope, in *The Way We Live Now* (1874-5), was concerned to criticize what he considered the ignoble sale of noble names to bolster shady corporate enterprises. Yet it was not merely a matter of prestige. In terms of corporate work, and even more in the development of the resources of their own estates (mineral deposits, transport enterprises, urban development, etc.), there is every reason to believe that noblemen and gentry made an active contribution to the industrial society.

In the last resort, however, there is no denying that we are dealing with a *landed* upper class, and one which exercised its considerable power through its control of non-commercial institutions. In practice, of course, their power was based on deference and influence as much as coercion, and was accompanied by the assumption that they would exercise it responsibly. Hence, perhaps the most penetrating social criticism in the early nineteenth century was that the landed classes were neglecting their obligations as privileged rulers, and were treating the institutions of state like a species of private property. The upper classes, wrote John Stuart Mill in 1831, 'do not love England as one loves human beings, but as a man loves his house or his garden.' In *Sybil* (1845) Disraeli described the 'meridian splendour' of aristocratic life in the 1820s: 'Then the world was not only made for a few, but for a very few.... A schoolboy's ideas of the Church then were fat livings, and of the State rotten boroughs. To do nothing and get something formed a boy's ideal of a manly career.' And in *Chartism* (1839) Carlyle bitterly attacked the upper classes for failing the poor: 'For this is now our sad lot, that we must find a *real* Aristocracy, that an apparent Aristocracy, however plausible soever, has become inadequate for us.'

Yet if the upper classes were thought to be neglecting their responsibilities, that presumed neglect only threw into high relief two other powerful motives for reform: the sense that the problems with which Britain's governing institutions had to deal had changed so drastically that, in their traditional form, these institutions could no longer cope with them, and a feeling (albeit not a universal one) that other social groups now not merely deserved but were qualified to participate in the governing framework. For some, it had become a matter of national necessity and wellbeing that political power should be shared. This was Macaulay's central argument to Parliament in 1831: 'I do not conceive that, in a country like this, the happiness of the people can be promoted by a form of government in which the middle classes place no confidence, and which exists only because the middle classes have no organ by which to make their sentiments known.' The sense that the newly important middle classes were sufficiently worthy to share political power and social prestige was exemplified not only by writers on politics and society, but also in such fictional characters as the industrialists Mr Thornton (*North and South*) or Robert Moore (*Shirley*).

The reform of government

Parliamentary reform was the outcome of a prolonged campaign and of many forces. These were well exemplified in the 1832 Reform Act, which, like many first steps towards institutional change, although not the most extreme, was the most difficult and keenly contested. The bitter opposition and dreadful fears of the Tory Party and much of the aristocracy were balanced by the vehemence of the proponents of reform, who included not merely radicals of various hues — George Eliot's *Felix Holt* (1866), set in 1832, sketches some of this variety — but quite moderate and even conservative members of the middle classes, anxious to share power with and reduce the dominance of the landed interest in Britain's government. Yet it is important to bear in mind that reform was based not merely on middle-class desires or rational political theories but also on the pressure from many sections of the working classes, eager for fundamental constitutional change. That change, therefore, came about partly because of the need to contain the violent expressions of public opinion which seemed to threaten revolution. And in later years novel after novel dramatized the anxieties about popular disturbances which conditioned the reactions of writers as sympathetic to the working classes as Charles Kingsley (*Yeast*), Mrs Gaskell (*Mary Barton*) and Charlotte Brontë (*Shirley*). In 1831-2 this fear had been a profound force making for the acceptance of reform. In the middle of the struggle the Prime Minister had referred to 'middle classes who form the real and efficient mass of public opinion, and without whom the power of the gentry is nothing'.[3] But to Macaulay, fearful of 'the wreck of laws, the confusion of ranks, the spoliation of property, and the dissolution of public order', reform was 'a practical question'. Addressing the House of Commons in 1831, he said:

> I support this plan, because I am sure that it is our best security against revolution.... I support this bill because it will improve our institutions; but I support it also because it tends to preserve them. That we may exclude those whom it is necessary to exclude, we must admit those whom it may be safe to admit.... We say, and we say justly, that it is not

3 Quoted in N. Gash, *Politics in the Age of Peel* (London, 1953), p.15.

by mere numbers, but by property and intelligence, that the nation ought to be governed. Yet, saying this, we exclude from all share in the government great masses of property and intelligence, great numbers of those who are most interested in preserving tranquillity, and who know best how to preserve it.

In this sort of context, it is not surprising that the Reform Act of 1832 was not as extreme in its immediate effects as most of its opponents had feared. The extension of voting rights to a wider range of property holders only increased the electorate by about 217,000 (from 435,000), although population and economic growth increased this by a further 400,000 by 1867; over 150 seats were redistributed from relatively unimportant constituencies to new centres of population, but there were still 115 MPs from boroughs with under 500 electors; and influence and patronage were still strong. Nor was there any revolution in the social composition of the House of Commons: in 1833 some 500 MPs, and in 1865 some 400, were members of the landed interest, and well over 40 per cent of this number at each date were the sons of peers or baronets. Clearly, much remained to be done before the contemporary anticipation of a great political and constitutional upheaval could be justified, and Macaulay's impassioned plea was subsequently reflected in the wry comment of *The Poor Man's Guardian* that the Reform Act was passed 'not with a view to subvert, or even remodel our aristocratic institutions, but to consolidate them by a re-inforcement of sub-aristocracy from the middle classes.'[4]

Nevertheless, new social classes and new industrial areas now had increased representation in Parliament (Huddersfield, Rochdale, Bradford and Stoke-on-Trent being represented for the first time). A process had begun which was soon seen to have profoundly changed the balance of the constitution, away from what Walter Bagehot referred to as the 'dignified' elements (i.e. the Crown and the Lords) and towards the 'efficient' elements (i.e. the Commons and the government responsible to it). Moreover, even the modest changes in the electorate and constituencies of 1832 put in motion a

4 Asa Briggs, *The Age of Improvement* (London, 1959), p.258.

process which, after two more rounds of reform in the 1860s and 1880s, was to flower into the modern system of parties, bureaucratic electioneering and a well-disciplined parliamentary structure. In these indirect consequences we can see a further adaptation of government to the needs of an industrial society.

The door of parliamentary reform, which had been eased ajar in 1832, was thrown open with a rush a generation or so later — a burst of parliamentary reform which led George Eliot to reiterate her doubts about the desirability of a radical extension of the working-class franchise (*Felix Holt's Address to Working Men*) and Thomas Carlyle, now elderly and on the verge of hysteria, to compare the 'inexpressibly delirious' reform movement to the most foolhardy of adventures (*Shooting Niagara*). Yet these were uninfluential voices. Indeed, it was a Tory government, led by Lord Derby and Disraeli, which took the 'leap in the dark' of 1867. Responding to public demonstrations in favour of reform, to the dictates of political opportunism, and to the tide of sentiment in favour of bringing more (male) groups within 'the pale of the constitution', it gave the vote to the urban working class. Household suffrage was granted to about 2 million, and in towns the working-class voters were in a clear majority. The redistribution of seats again largely favoured the new industrial and urban centres. With the precedents so well established, modernization and democratization proceeded rapidly. In 1872 the introduction of the secret ballot virtually eliminated intimidation of voters by social or political superiors; in 1883 strict controls were instituted to check corruption and excess electoral expenditure; in 1884 a further broad extension of the male suffrage enfranchised the agricultural working class, thus inflicting a blow to the landed classes in their very own stronghold; and in 1885 there was another instalment of constituency redistribution. These developments also had enormous effects on the political system. For with the need to woo a large and complex electorate, party organization had to be improved, campaigning became more professionalized, voters had to be mobilized, parties within Parliament had to be better disciplined, electoral promises and programmes became more important, and Cabinet control of the Commons began to assume its modern significance.

Yet the result, in terms of the end products of political action, was nowhere as radical as the sceptics feared. The traditionalism and urbanity of the political system, its remoteness from any deep commitment to genuine ideological confrontation, continued almost untouched — encapsulated in Trollope's political novels of the 1870s (*Phineas Redux*, for example, or *The Prime Minister*). Nevertheless, by the 1880s the basic appearance, perhaps even the mechanics, of the constitutional and political system which had existed in the early stages of industrialism had been shattered and, with it, the aristocratic monopoly of power. In part this embodied an adjustment of social classes. But it also reflected a basic institutional adjustment: the new needs of policy, the tasks of government and the new problems of industrialism could not be approached through the mechanism of a pre-industrial Parliament, whose main representation was of the landed interest. The governing framework had to be made consistent with the social and economic framework. And this necessity was exemplified at the level of local government and public administration.

Reform of urban government was an inevitable concomitant of parliamentary reform in 1832, and followed within three years. The unanswerable case for change lay in the fact that many of the municipal corporations were corrupt, neglectful and oligarchic, with little initiative or imagination; that, in general, and in spite of the efforts of improvement commissioners, their powers were almost irrelevant to the problems of urban growth and industrial change; and that there was hardly any organized government in the *new* industrial towns, where the problems of rapid population growth made the need for good administration more striking. The desire for improvement, honesty and efficiency in local administration joined with the powerful drive to assert effective middle-class influence in the determination of their own interests and environment. In 1835 the reformed Parliament suppressed almost 200 corporations in England and Wales (Scottish municipalities had been reformed in 1833) and replaced them with councils elected by rate-paying householders of three years' standing. Soon after, the Act was extended to towns which had not previously had corporations, so that vitally important cities like Manchester and Birmingham, themselves the product of industrial development, got their first modern municipal governments in 1838. (London's complex problems postponed a similar solution until 1888, although a first step was taken in 1858, with the creation of the metropolitan Board of Works.)

Initially, the powers of municipal councils were limited, but their creation laid the basis for the accretion of more and more authority and responsibility in matters affecting the environment, health and public services. Indeed, with a franchise more democratic than Parliament's in the middle years of the century, operating in a much more decentralized society than the twentieth century is accustomed to, close to people's interests, and susceptible to middle-class influence, the municipalities in the 1830s and the 1840s were perhaps more accurate indicators of the drive and power of the new middle classes than was even the reformed Parliament — just as the local community was a more vibrant and significant setting than was the metropolis, for novels of general significance.

The same cannot be said for local government in rural areas, where the landed classes were very firmly entrenched, controlling not only the land but also (as lords-lieutenant and justices of the peace) administration. Yet such a governmental structure appeared increasingly anomalous in the face of pressure from other interest groups and the ineffectiveness of an unwieldy, part-time system. Once again, parliamentary reform exposed local deficiencies. Following the overhaul of the rural franchise and of constituency arrangements in 1884-5, county government was restructured in 1888. Separate county councils with substantial administrative powers were established for the shires, or distinct parts of very large counties, and for boroughs exceeding 50,000 population. In London, the massive London County Council was formed. The councils proved both more appropriate instruments for representative government and more effective bodies for the complex tasks of administration and regulation in late nineteenth-century Britain.

In the case of the civil service we are once again dealing with an institution which, in its traditional form, was enmeshed in an increasingly unsatisfactory system of patronage, deriving from a close control by the landed upper classes. Referring, as often was the case, to scandals which were in the process of reform while he was lampooning them, Dickens personified this problem of parasitism in the aristocratic Barnacle family in *Little Dorritt* (1855-7). The Barnacles, claiming 'vested rights' in the slothful Circumlocution Office, perpetuated the doctrine of 'how not to do it' and ensured that 'wherever there was a square yard of ground in British occupation under the sun or moon, with a public post upon it, sticking to that post was a Barnacle.' In fact, condition varied from department to department, and the system was by no means completely ineffective. In any case the formal, permanent bureaucracy was supplemented by a breed of energetic and dedicated, administrative reformers — men like Edwin Chadwick or Southwood Smith — who based their public activities on strong private views. They were very influential in achieving the 'revolution in government' of the 1830s, 1840s and 1850s, which extended central government activity into increasing regulation of the Poor Law, public health and safety, factory conditions, commercial matters, the new railway system, etc. Nevertheless, the basic and traditional structure of the civil service was seen to be both too exclusive in terms of middle-class aspirations and (even more important) ill suited to Britain's administrative needs in mid-century.

Dissatisfaction with the civil service came to a head as a result of unease over maladministration during the Crimean War, the consequent establishment of a private Administrative Reform Association (1855), and the Report of the official commission of investigation (of Sir Stafford Northcote and Sir Charles Trevelyan). The last, emphasizing that the civil service suffered from excessive departmentalization and was too often considered to be an appropriate employment for 'the unambitious, and the indolent and incapable', recommended its overhaul and modernization: the creation of a unified service under a commission, the selection of civil servants in the higher grades by examinations (based on the literary and liberal curriculum of the older universities), and the distinction between work of a routine character and that needing higher qualifications. Haltingly, these proposals were adopted, although even such a reasonable man and efficient civil servant as Anthony Trollope criticized examinations in *The Three Clerks* (1858) and in his *Autobiography* (1883) referred to 'the dangerous optimism of competitive choice' and the advantages of giving 'berths in the Civil Service ... exclusively to gentlemen'. Finally, in 1870, examination became compulsory in the Home Civil Service (the Foreign Office held out until 1919). Taken together with improvements in the internal structure and efficiency of the civil service, these steps marked a new era in public administration. Yet the ethos of the service remained strongly marked by a preference for gentlemanly authority rather than 'mere' technical competence or intellect; and the type of examination protected those fortunate enough to have access to the older universities or expensive private education.

The effect of reform on the social composition of government was not, therefore, very simple. And the fears of the aristocratic clergyman in *Felix Holt* — that 'the ignorant multitude' would be 'judges of the largest question', the fear of 'letting the windlass run down after men have been turning it painfully for generations' (chapter XXIII) — little of this came to pass. In the House of Commons the landed classes were in the majority until the late 1880s, and even then continued to dominate late Victorian governments (the aristocracy by birth provided 60 per cent of Cabinet members in 1867-84 and 58 per cent in 1885-1905); the landed influence in country administration was still powerful even after delayed reform had come in 1888; and the civil service was largely an upper-class preserve throughout the period. On the other hand, there was a sense in which the rule of the upper classes was on suffrance — dependent on carrying out reforms and policy innovations and on a sensitive responsiveness to public opinion, particularly middle-class opinion. 'No government can long have a majority in this House', said John Bright to the Commons, 'which does not sympathise with the great middle class of this country.'[5] In effect, reform meant power-sharing, and the new role of the middle class and the maintenance of aristocratic influence and privilege went hand in hand.

An important reason for this compromise was the fact that the rising middle classes, represented and distorted in so many Victorian novels, often based their reforming zeal on an objection not so much to the aristocracy as to the *exclusive* character of aristocratic privileges. In fact, success in the maturing industrial society was frequently associated with conventional aspirations — to send children to aristocratic schools, for example, or to invest business profits in landed estates. Indeed, it was characteristic and significant that the conventional governing classes and institutions welcomed the

5 Quoted in *The Times*, 7 January 1975.

new wealth. In Dickens's *Little Dorritt*, for example, when 'Treasury', 'Bishop', 'Horseguards' and 'Bar' gather at Merdle's house to celebrate the parvenu's astounding financial success, 'Treasury' tries to persuade him to enter Parliament, and 'Bar' urges him to buy a large estate then going cheap: 'Such a purchase would involve not only great legitimate political influence, but some half-dozen church presentations of considerable annual value.' (Book I, ch. 21.) And as the century progressed it became easier to cap the acquisition of education and estates by the acquisition of a title: of the 200 new peerages granted between 1886 and 1914, about 70 were granted to businessmen (of whom about 20 had inherited landed status from fathers who had purchased estates).[6] To a shrewd observer like Thomas Escott in the 1870s, it seemed clear that 'the increase in the wealth of the middle classes, and their intermarriage with their social superiors, have caused them to assimilate the tastes and prejudices of their new connections.... It is the aristocratic principle which dominates our political as it dominates our social system.'[7]

In measure as the traditional élite accommodated infusions of new wealth, so government continued in the hands of men who had at least the appurtenances of a leisured class of gentlemen. And this process of legitimization reflected the prejudices of the country at large, where, in Gladstone's words, there was a 'distinct popular preference for a man who is a lord over a man who is not'.[8] This sort of deference, as wise politicians recognized, was an important fact of political life. In 1845, for example, when Richard Cobden was urging on the landed interest in Parliament that it should abandon the very ark of its covenant by accepting the abolition of protection on imported grainstuffs, he based his argument on this point:

> This is a new era. It is the age of improvement, it is the age of social advancement.... The English people look to the gentry and aristocracy of their country as their leaders. I, who

6 F.M.L. Thompson, *English Landed Society in the Nineteenth Century* (London, 1963), p.294.
7 J.F.C. Harrison (ed.), *Society and Politics in England, 1780-1960* (New York, 1965), p.282.
8 Quoted in Thomas Arnold, 'Democracy': Introduction to *The Popular Education of France* (1861).

am not one of you, have no hesitation in telling you, that there is a deep-rooted, and hereditary prejudice ... in your favour in this country. But you never got it, and you will not keep it, by obstructing the spirit of the age.[9]

Although the House of Lords was occasionally guilty of just such an obstruction, on the whole the landed interest represented in the Commons did manage to adjust fairly smoothly to the spirit of the age — whether embodied in the pressure for institutional reform or in the impetus to major alterations of policy. That is why it is perhaps truer to say that the middle class came to share, than that they appropriated, political power in Victorian Britain: in the last resort their challenge was not resisted, but accommodated.

The uses of government: the reform of institutions

The forces which were altering the balance and workings of the Victorian constitution and destroying the exclusive nature of aristocratic privilege — the pressure of powerful classes to participate in the membership of institutions and the need to adapt those institutions to the new and pressing needs of an industrial society — were felt just as keenly in other areas. They manifested themselves, for example, in the overhaul of the great institutional bulwarks: the law, the church, the army and education. These will be considered in this section. In addition, those forces produced a redirection of basic economic and social policies; and this will be considered in the following section. In both instances, it is worth emphasizing that the prior reform of government set up a momentum and created the mechanisms which made it easier to pursue radical change in other areas.

In the case of the English legal system, the radical, reforming instinct had been at work long before parliamentary reform (in his *Autobiography* John Stuart Mill referred to his father's 'abhorrence of the chaos of barbarism called English Law'). Indeed, from the 1820s there was effective organizational change and oversight of prisons and police, some reform of the jury system and the method

9 Quoted in D. Read, *The English Provinces, c. 1760-1960: A Study in Influence* (London, 1964), p.145.

of paying judges, and a reduction of the number of offences involving the death penalty. Nevertheless, the eradication of the abuses and inefficiencies inherent in the extraordinary structure of courts and the process of justice — the creaking, fog-bound system described by Dickens in *Bleak House* — was not adequately tackled until 1873, when the administration of the three common law courts was amalgamated with that of Chancery, and provision was made for the more orderly arrangement of courts, judges and appeals.

Understandably perhaps, the Church of England was even more resistant to the thrust for change than was the English legal system. Yet even here the age of reform saw some significant erosion of its privileges and of the exclusive access of its members to positions of power and prestige. Thus the constitutional revolution that we associate with the 1832 Reform Act was really begun in 1828 and 1829 with the repeal of legislation which had hitherto banned Nonconformists from serving in municipal corporations and Crown offices, and with the awarding of similar rights, as well as the right to vote for and sit in Parliament, to the Catholics. Further, in 1830s, particularly after the reform of municipal government, which gave them a much more prominent role in political society, the Dissenters began that pressure for the elimination of other civil disabilities which finally led to the legitimization of marriages outside the Anglican Church (1836), the permitting of non-Anglicans to enter Oxford or take degrees at Cambridge (1854-6), the abolition of obligatory Church Rates (1868) and the abolition of the Anglican monopoly of fellowships and university offices at Oxford and Cambridge (1871). Meanwhile, again during the great reforming decade of the 1830s, the internal structure of the church was itself brought more up to date with the creation of a permanent Ecclesiastical Commission (1836), which was awarded powers to redistribute bishops' incomes, and thereby mitigate the gross disparities of episcopal wealth. Cathedral chapters were also reformed and the abuses of excessive pluralism curbed. As with reforms in other, and much more secular, institutions, ecclesiastic changes involved a much greater degree of centralization (with a growing power for bishops) and a rationalization of structure. Here as elsewhere, of course, reform gave rise to ambiguous responses, even among pragmatic men. Thus Trollope's attitude can be seen in *The Warden* (1855-6): he reluctantly recognizes the inevitability of church reform, but prefers the humane Mr Harding to the energetic Mr Bold.

Comparable — but even slower — reform overtook the army, in which the power of the upper classes was preserved by the system of purchasing commissions, the extensive use of patronage, the *de facto* independence from civilian authority, and the general institutionalization of snobbery. Much of this went on relatively unquestioned as long as the memory of Waterloo was unclouded by any major wars which might expose the inefficiency of the military system. But the growing claims of non-landed classes to be treated as rulers and, even more, the disasters of the Crimean campaign, which exposed both the incompetence of senior officers and the hopeless inefficiency of the army, produced some keen criticisms of the aristocratic ethos and an outcry in favour of reform. Even so, as with other institutions, entrenched interests and attitudes managed to postpone change. Finally, during Gladstone's great reforming Ministry of 1868-74, the situation of the ordinary soldier was improved; the main administrative departments of the army were brought under the direct control of the Secretary of State for War; the regimental structure was reorganized on more rational and controllable lines, and in 1871 the purchase of commissions was abolished. Of course, none of these steps made the Army a middle-class, let alone a democratic, institution. Tradition, influence, snobbery and the sheer cost of being an officer still ensured that it embodied an upper-class ideal. But there had been a shift in the definition of the upper class involved, and in general the military machine was moved on to lines which were rational and responsible and more appropriate for Britain's purposes in an industrial world.

The sorts of issues which were made explicit in the consideration of reform in the civil service and the army — that is, the access of new groups to membership and authority, and the adaptation of structure as well as membership to render the institution more effective — were also powerfully exemplified in educational institutions.

Only very modest changes took place at the level of basic education for the mass of the population — even though popular education was the most commonly proffered long-term solution to the problems of the poor. (Felix Holt wanted the miners to organize school for their children on the grounds that until 'they can show there's something they love better than swilling themselves with ale, extension of the suffrage can never mean anything for them but extension of boozing'.) Nevertheless, *something* was achieved. The state gradually moved to circumvent the effects of the sectarian jealousies of Anglicans and Dissenters, to compensate for what were seen as the deficiencies of private elementary education. A system of small grants and an inspectorate was established in the 1830s. In 1846 the special committee of the Privy Council with educational responsibilities took an important step towards improving the status and skills of teachers by subsidizing their salaries and stimulating a system of apprenticeship, training colleges and retirement pensions. In 1862 the government subsidy to teachers' salaries was related to their pupils' success in formal examinations in basic skills. And in 1870 the Education Act provided for the creation of School Boards and state schools. Although attendance at school was not made compulsory until 1880 (and then only until the age of ten) nor free until 1891, the principal step towards a state system of education had been taken in 1870. That step was taken in response to the mounting anxieties about the relevance or adequacy of basic education for the needs of an industrial society or (perhaps of equal or greater importance) the political stability of an emerging democracy. It was, indeed, no accident that the Education Act should follow so closely on the enfranchisement of the urban working classes in 1867 — when Robert Lowe had urged that Parliament 'should prevail on our future masters to learn their letters'. Yet Lowe had also stipulated that education should not 'raise children above their station and business in life ... but fit them for that business.' And, broadly speaking, that was the most that was achieved: educational provision remained heavily class-based, and the educational opportunities for the children of the very poor remained extremely limited, while the content of instruction tended to be neither truly liberal nor adequately vocational, but merely tried to provide the very barest literate and numerate skills appropriate for the simplest routines of life in industrial society.

In the case of the upper and middle-classes, the critical stratum of education was that of secondary schooling, which was provided in institutions ranging from venerable public schools (which in the early nineteenth century concentrated on a severely classical curriculum taught in a bleak and often brutal environment) to dissenting academies, old-established but frequently decrepit grammar schools, and private day or boarding schools for those who could afford them. Here, the main stimulus to educational reform came privately — notably (but not exclusively) from a few headmasters at public schools: men like Thomas Arnold at Rugby (1828-42), who sensed the inappropriateness of the older system and the potentialities of secondary schools as training grounds for leadership in the new environment. This might involve the introduction of mathematics, modern languages and history. But changes in the social environment and expectations of the school were even more important, for 'character', discrimination and self-confidence were judged to be more relevant than mere scholarship to attainment and leadership in the fields of imperial, military, administrative, business or professional endeavours. Moreover, the example of public schools was also important because it was followed by a host of 'lesser' schools catering for the broad mass of the middle classes. The state of secondary education still left much to be desired, but growth and internal change had ensured that it could fulfil a broad range of new social functions for the relatively rich with relative ease.

The reform of English universities was more explicitly a matter for the state, because of their position as chartered bodies. (Scottish universities were less affected by vested interest, more open socially, and enjoyed high academic reputations.) Initially, as we have seen, criticism concentrated on the Anglican exclusiveness of Oxford and Cambridge. But their archaic administrative structures, limited curriculum and neglect of research also provoked attention and criticism — and some modest internal change. In 1877 the Oxford and Cambridge Act strengthened the universities as against the constituent colleges and facilitated the use of the latter's wealth to improve the curriculum. Meanwhile the expansion of the university sector proceeded in response to intellectual and practical needs. In 1828 the metropolitan liberal and radical middle class had established a non-sectarian 'University of London' (later University College), which prompted the establishment of the Anglican King's College in 1831, and led to the creation of the present University of London in 1836. Provincial centres like Durham,

Manchester, Liverpool, Birmingham, Leeds, Sheffield, Aberyst-
wyth, Cardiff and Swansea developed their own university institutions or medical schools. And in 1889 Parliament began to make a
small annual grant to university colleges.

Clearly, educational reform in the nineteenth century served a
variety of needs — including class interests. But there was one
theme — refracted and distorted as it might be — that ran through
most changes in educational institutions: a purposeful attempt to
improve both their relevance to the changing society around them
and the competence of those who attended them. In this respect
educational institutions had to respond to the same forces which
had transmuted the civil service, the army and the Constitution
itself, even though it responded very little to that larger and more
generous impulse which had moved writers like Mill or Carlyle or
Matthew Arnold or John Ruskin to feel that in a genuine and
profound provision of education lay the best hope for the improvement of the working classes. 'The rich not only refuse food to the
poor,' wrote Ruskin in *Unto this Last* (1862), 'they refuse wisdom;
they refuse virtue; they refuse salvation.'

The uses of government: the reform of policy

The reform of government and the use of a reformed government
to transform and enlarge access to social institutions went hand in
hand with redirections of economic and social policy. And, as with
institutional change, this both depended on the prior adjustment
of the governing framework and reflected an amalgam of class
interest, altruism, pragmatism and theory.

The free-trade movement — the pressure to eliminate duties on
imported goods and exclusive restrictions on commercial arrangements — drew together these various strands, for it reflected the
laissez-faire theories of classical economics, the outlook and ambi-
tions of Britain's thriving entrepreneurs, and the logic of British
productivity and industrial supremacy. The process of reducing
duties and abolishing restrictions (e.g. on the use of non-British
ships in British or colonial trades or on the export of machinery) began
in the 1820s. But the most substantial advance came in Peel's budgets
of 1842 and 1854, which eliminated the duties on over 600
items, reduced those on most of the others, and introduced an

income tax to compensate in part for the loss of revenue, which was in any case partly made up by the increased consumption of the cheaper goods.

The repeal of the Corn Laws in 1846, although the most spectacular victory of the free-trade movement and the industrial middle classes, was a somewhat different matter precisely because the laws (i.e. protective duties on the import of grainstuffs) reflected the traditional power and vested interests of the landed classes. The attack on them was therefore an overt confrontation of classes: 'the fervour and efficiency' of the Anti-Corn-Law League — Manchester-based and led by Richard Cobden and John Bright at the head of the manufacturing and commercial interest — was seen by Cobden as reflecting 'a middle-class agitation'. Cheap food, an abundant trade and (some cynics said) low wages were the principal motives of the supporters of the abolition of the 'tax on bread'. But, at a more general level, their campaign was consistent with the expansionist needs of an industrial Britain, trading freely and successfully on a world scale. Yet the proximate cause of the repeal was the impact of high food prices and famine in Ireland: a sufficient number of representatives of the landed interest realized that it would have been intolerable to maintain a tax on imported food while people were dying from the consequences of food shortages. As with constitutional change, a combination of ideology and special interests provided the mounting pressure, political pragmatism the immediate occasion, for a reform which brought structures more into line with the changing needs they served.

With the Corn Laws out of the way, most of the remaining issues involved in the freeing of trade were more straightforwardly economic in character. And with Britain's growing industrial maturity Gladstone, as Chancellor of the Exchequer, made an almost clean sweep of import duties and restrictive trade legislation in the late 1850s and early 1860s. Moreover, Britain's new economic policy also entailed other sorts of liberalization (laws to facilitate the formation of joint-stock companies and the rational investment of capital, for example, or the abolition of stamp duties on news-papers and the freeing of communication). Only towards the end of the period, with the advent of economic pessimism, increased govern-ment expenditure, and a keener perception of social inequality, were there rumblings in the field of fiscal policy which anticipated the more restrictive commercial policies and the more progressive taxation burdens of the twentieth century.

The problem of poverty overlapped with the question of the liberalization of the capitalist economy, because distress and its relief were relevant considerations in the repeal of the Corn Laws. And it would be wrong to dismiss the view that the pressure for free trade was bound up in part with the expectation that prosperity would eliminate misery. At the same time, however, until late in the century the prevailing doctrines not merely of the governing classes but of many schools of radical thought were sceptical of the ability of the state to tackle the problem of poverty directly, or to interfere with those market or moral forces which were held to lie at the root of low wages and material distress. The orthodox political economist W.R. Greg, reviewing *Mary Barton* in the *Edinburgh Review* in 1849, proposed the following as 'the language which every true friend to the working-man would use':

> Trust to no external source for your prosperity in life; work out your own welfare; work it out with the tools you have. The charter may be a desirable object, the franchise may be worth obtaining; but your happiness, your position in life, will depend neither on the franchise nor the charter, neither on what parliament does, nor on what your employer neglects to do; but simply and solely upon the use you make of the fifteen or thirty shillings which you earn each week, and upon the circumstances whether you marry at twenty or at twenty-eight, and whether you marry a sluggard and a slattern or a prudent and industrious woman.

Not surprisingly, he disapproved strongly of Elizabeth Gaskell's hero, the Chartist and trade-unionist John Barton. Yet, in so far as poverty was seen as the outcome of overpopulation and the mismanagement of private lives, there was some scope for government activity, whether direct or oblique, to foster beneficial habits of self-help among the poor.

The system of poor relief inherited from the eighteenth century was based upon individual parishes, and consisted mainly of direct payments to the very poor ('outdoor relief') and the subsidy of agricultural wages, both graded according to the size of the pauper family and the cost of living. As this system evolved in the first thirty years of the nineteenth century, it was criticized on the grounds that outdoor relief encouraged idleness, poverty and excessive population growth; was extravagant of public resources; and lent itself to inefficiency and maladministration. The most influential critics of the old Poor Law were the reforming utilitarians, strongly influenced by Malthusian population theory, and they exercised a very powerful influence on the Royal Commission which investigated the situation in 1832-4, and on the subsequent legislation of 1834, which closely followed the Commission's somewhat biased report. It was recommended that the able-bodied poor should no longer receive allowances in aid of wages (although this was left to the discretion of the Commissioners who were to administer the new system). Instead, they would receive help only in workhouses. And in order to inculcate a sense of moral responsibility among workers and prevent abuse of the system, the Commission propounded the principle of 'less eligibility': workhouse conditions for the able-bodied were not to be preferable to the living standards of the low-paid; the situation of the pauper 'must cease to be really or apparently so eligible as the situation of the independent labourer of the lowest class'. In addition, control of the relief system was to be orderly, efficient and centralized: the national Poor Law Commission laid down guidelines, and local management and administration and financing was to be handled by grouped parishes (Unions) under Boards of Guardians.

The basic system, which in effect lasted for the rest of the century, quickly earned a bad reputation, and was certainly characterized by some harsh practices and a patently inhumane logic. It augmented those deep-felt attitudes that Dickens echoed so well in *Great Expectations* or in the story of Betty Higden in *Our Mutual Friend*. On the other hand, the extent of application and the success of the princples that lay behind the New Poor Law must not be exaggerated. A variety of policies, including extensive outdoor relief, continued; local resistance to its enforcement was frequently successful; some of the worst potential rigours were soon mitigated. Above all, although the law is often interpreted as an adjustment of social policy to the harsh rigours of industrial capitalism, it was in fact precisely in industrial areas, where the main cause of poverty might be intermittent unemployment, that it proved impossible to apply the full rigour of the law, in part because it was physically impossible to move armies of workers in and out of workhouses in line with the fluctuations of employment levels.

If the basis of the New Poor Law was the belief that poverty for the able-bodied was largely the result of individual behaviour (profligate expenditure, laziness, excessively early marriage or large families, etc.), then it followed that poverty might be greatly eased by the spread of what had become middle-class values: thrift, self-help, prudence, hard work, sobriety, ambition. This provided considerable scope for writers like Samuel Smiles to preach the doctrines of individualism and prudence to the working as well as middle classes. 'Misery', Smiles argued in a *Quarterly Review* article on workman's earnings in 1860, 'is the offspring of individual improvidence and vice; and it is to be cured, not so much by conferring greater rights, as by implanting better habits.'

It also left some scope for government action, since the role of formal institutions in the encouragement of thrift and prudence meant that the state could find a role in fostering the better instincts of Victorian mankind. Accordingly, in the early and middle decades of the century laws were passed to facilitate the incorporation and offer legal protection to the funds of friendly societies (which insured their working-class members against sickness, death and old age), savings banks, building societies, cooperative societies and even trade unions (which, it was argued by some of their supporters, had important insurance roles through their various benefits). And in 1861 the government established the Post Office Savings Bank, which was an immediate success, with almost 6 million accounts and £83 million deposits by the early 1890s.

Of course, none of this 'solved' the problem of poverty, but for many members of the working class (admittedly, mostly those already slightly better-off than their fellows) it helped change the social and institutional environment, and was one more indication that the reform of the governing framework had implications, and by no means deleterious ones, extending well beyond the classes which had worked directly for that reform.

This point is also relevant to the last category of policy changes to be considered: factory reform and sanitary improvement. The atrocious working conditions in many factories and mines were patently abuses which only the most determined of ideologues could have ignored — especially as they involved women and children, i.e. categories that were exceptions to the theory that individuals would do best for themselves when left to themselves. In the event, the opponents of state intervention were defeated by a movement which cut right across established political and some class lines. Under the leadership of Lord Shaftesbury, an aristocrat and evangelical, a combination of middle-class liberals, humanitarians and working-class pressure groups set out to control child labour and factory hours. Once again a reformed Parliament made the difference: earlier unsatisfactory attempts were followed in 1833 by the first effective Factory Act, which resulted from one of those committees of inquiry whose persistent bluntness served to administer intermittent shocks to the nineteenth-century conscience. The Act applied to most textile factories. Children under nine were excluded from them, and the hours of work of children limited. In a significant departure, inspectors were appointed to ensure the enforcement of the Act (and also, it turned out, to be a focus of initiative and channel of information for future state action). In 1842, again following a startling report, women and girls were excluded from employment in mines and limits placed on the lower age of boys. At last, in 1847, after years of agitation, a most important victory was won: a ten-hour day was introduced for women and children, which, when subsequently tightened up, ensured that most men also had a limited working week: by then, ten and a half hours on weekdays and seven and a half hours on Saturdays. These early developments in the field of factory and mine regulation were followed in the subsequent decades by extension of the scope of legislation with regard to type of workplace and object of regulation (i.e. safety features). By the last decade of the century such 'interference' had become an accepted and institutionalized part of the state's function.

The urban environment in the early nineteenth century was possibly more of a scandal, certainly much more visible and a more obvious threat to the wellbeing of *all* classes, than were conditions in factories. And in this case the reform movement, largely in relation to direct threats to public health, was the outcome of three main strands of activity. First, the concern of local inhabitants (often middle-class and professional men) led in the second quarter of the century to voluminous exposures of local housing and health conditions, based on painstaking statistical investigation. Second, investigation, in the utilitarian tradition, by the Poor Law Commissioners, led to Edwin Chadwick's seminal *Report on the Sanitary Condition of the Labouring Population of Great Britain* (1842), which emphasized the relationship between poverty, disease and the appalling sanitary conditions. This, in turn, stimulated a renewed public concern with the problem and, more critically, an official parliamentary inquiry which exposed gross deficiencies and impurities of water supply and sanitary arrangements in general. The outcome was the Public Health Act of 1848. The third factor was the actual threat of disease. A cholera epidemic in 1831-3 led to the temporary establishment of central and local boards of health, and its renewed onslaught in 1847-8 gave a final boost to the campaign to pass the Public Health Act. That Act established a central Board of Health along the lines of the Poor Law Board, and provided for the creation of local boards, if local inhabitants wished or if the death rate exceeded 23 per 1000.

Administratively, the new measure was not a success, and it encountered increasing opposition from critics of centralization. In 1858 the Board's duties were dispersed to various government departments. At this time local boards of health were not very numerous, but the return of the dreaded cholera in 1865-6 once again produced action and legislation: local authorities were compelled to appoint sanitary inspectors, and central government for the first time was empowered to enforce the removal of nuisances, the provision of sewers and a good water supply. After a strong royal commission (1869-71) had specified the basic sanitary requisites of a civilized life (adequate water, drainage, housing, food inspection, proper provision for burials and suppression of nuisances and the causes of disease), the Local Government Board was established to coordinate the services relating to the protection of public health. In 1875, that *annus mirabilis* of domestic legislation, Disraeli fulfilled his promises of social reforms to the new electorate of 1867. Among the new statutes were: the Artisans' Dwelling Act, which tackled, however imperfectly, the housing problem by extending powers over slum clearance and housing from a few cities to all towns; the Sale of Food and Drugs Act, the first substantial measure to mitigate adulteration and protect quality; and the great Public Health Act, enacting the recommendations of the earlier

Royal Commission (itself appointed by Disraeli) which consolidated a vast amount of legislation and established the framework of British sanitary legislation into the twentieth century.

Obviously, even this spate of activity, spread over some fifty years, could not completely transform the environment of the mass of the people. The problems that had given rise to legislation continued to harrass the relatively poor for the remaining quarter century of Victoria's reign — and beyond. Nevertheless, we must not underestimate the legislative achievement in the context of the problems of an industrial and urban society. In principle and practice there had been huge strides forward. And their very extent meant that their implication had yet to be worked out. Yet, although there was little new social legislation of a fundamental sort for the balance of the century, by the last quarter of the nineteenth century the 'new Britain' created by the Industrial Revolution was strikingly visible. Within a lifetime the most profound changes had transformed almost every institution of the 'governing framework'. These changes had necessitated the use of the state power as a guiding, interventionist element in what was now an urban, industrial society. But that power could coexist with an ostensibly individualistic ideology precisely because it was not distinct from, but a reflection of, the structural patterns, political stresses and economic necessities of that society.

Armed with vastly more information and better machinery than before, and confronted with problems of a much more spectacular urgency and danger, the governing framework from the 1830s set about a series of fundamental reorientations of British economic and social policy. Although by the early 1850s the initial impetus seemed to have waned, the apparent 'equipoise' did not last very long. Insistent political, social and economic problems again manifested themselves, and a further measure of constitutional reform (in 1867) gave another push to the process of state action. In an extraordinary bout of legislation from 1869 to 1875 there was an impressive overhaul of major institutions (the church, the law, trade unions, the army, the universities, the civil service) by the Liberals, and then a sweeping series of new social policies by the Tories.

The fact that both the main political parties were concerned with this major series of institutional and policy reforms is an indication not merely of the degree of political consensus that underlay much superficial disagreement on such topics, but also of the extent to which reform was — in the last resort — more a matter of necessity than of ideological choice. This was a point well made by Trollope in one of his political novels, *The Prime Minister* (1875-6). Admittedly, the spate of social legislation seemed to slacken after the mid-1870s. As had been the case in the 1850s, this was due in part to the fact that some of the more pressing problems now seemed less urgent — to some extent because of the legislation that had been enacted. Even so, again as had happened earlier, things did not stand still. On the one hand, the 1880s and 1890s witnessed very substantial reforms of central and local government, and important consequential changes in political organization and behaviour. On the other, within the existing framework of legislation, state activity broadened and became more effective. Thus the Board of Agriculture (1889) and the Board of Education (1899) were established; and the responsibilities of the Home Office, the Board of Trade and the Local Government Board were extended in such areas as factory inspection, labour matters and the coordination of the new local government units. Indeed, this periodicity — institutional reform, followed by policy innovations, followed by a period of absorption in which the implications of new institutions and policies were worked out — had an obvious logic. And it was to continue into the new century, when a new mood and a new perception of Britain's social problems once more necessitated far-reaching changes in institutions and policies. This rhythm, enduring through varying patterns and with uneven timing, perhaps marks a fundamental response to industrialism. To this extent, such modernization is a never-ending process. Yet it had a beginning; and Victorian Britain was where it began. The Eminent Victorians were the first of the moderns.

Select bibliography

Briggs, A. *The Age of Improvement, 1783-1867.* London, 1959.
Brinton, C.C. *British Political Thought in the Nineteenth Century.* New York, 1949.
Bruce, M. *The Coming of the Welfare State.* London, 1961.
Clark, G. Kitson. *The Making of Victorian England.* London, 1962.
Cole, G.D.H. *Studies in Class Structure.* London, 1955.
Ensor, R.C.K. *England, 1870-1914.* Oxford, 1936.
Parris, H. *Constitutional Bureaucracy: The Development of British Central Administration since the Eighteenth Century.* London, 1969.
Perkin, H. *The Origins of Modern English Society, 1780-1880.* London, 1969.
Roberts, D. *Victorian Origins of the British Welfare State.* New Haven, Connecticut, 1960.
Smellie, K.B. *A Hundred Years of English Government.* London, 1950.
Taylor, A.J. *Laissez-Faire and State Intervention in Nineteenth Century Britain.* London, 1975.
Thompson, F.M.L. *English Landed Society in the Nineteenth Century.* London, 1963.
Webb, R.K. *Modern England from the 18th Century to the Present.* London, 1969.
Woodward, E.L. *The Age of Reform, 1815-1870.* Oxford, 1938.

6 The sense of the past

J. W. BURROW

Evidence of what William Morris mildly called his century's 'tendency to retrospection' lies, of course, all around us: as Victorian Early English, Decorated or French Gothic Churches, as Venetian Gothic museums and schools, Grecian clubs, markets and concert halls, French Renaissance station hotels, Scottish baronial villas, Queen Anne flats and a Perpendicular Parliament. But a qualification is needed, for surely the list should also include such things as Moorish public baths or music halls? What looks at first like a copious testimony to a sense of the past begins to dissolve into a eclecticism in which an uninhibited enjoyment of the associative qualities of things could be satisfied as readily by the merely picturesque or exotic as by anything which could more properly be called historical.

The same thoughts apply with perhaps even greater force to the use of 'historical' subjects in painting. Not that the past was not sometimes preferred as a setting for reasons which we have to recognize as serious, even if it was often an ideal rather than anything like an actual past. The Pre-Raphaelites sufficiently demonstrate the possibility of an earnest escapism. Nevertheless, we can safely presume that the manufacturers of costume paintings were not actuated by any profound sense of the abiding significance of the past in choosing themes like those listed by Jeremy Maas: 'besotted cavaliers, laughing monks, lecherous highwaymen ogling at serving wenches ... and Napoleon in various attitudes of post-Waterloo discomfiture'. The public's apparently insatiable appetite for conversation pieces in historical costume is an interesting subject in the sociology of taste, but it is not the subject of this chapter. Its existence does, however, help to remind us how the notion of a 'sense of the past' can range from a casual taste for fancy dress to earnestly held and vehemently propounded social, moral and aesthetic preferences.

Moreover, though stylistic eclecticism and revivals were a characteristic Victorian phenomenon, they were not a new one. Even putting aside the fact that, for example, almost all European architecture from the Renaissance to the present century has been in some sense a revival, the battle between Greek and Gothic architectural styles had been joined long before the Victorian era began. What the Victorians added, apart from an extra dimension of seriousness and scholarliness in the treatment of Gothic, was further ingredients, still more revivals, until the confusion of styles became, as one of the leading Goths, A.W.N. Pugin, put it, 'the carnival of architecture'.[1]

It is tempting, then, to attempt simply to draw a line between seriousness and frivolity, between architects, painters and authors to whom some period or aspect of the past presented itself in full seriousness as a cherished heritage, a spiritual home for the modern world, or an unanswerable condemnation of it, and those who merely used the past as a source for an archaic and hence exotic vocabulary for their trade: the knights and cavaliers who trotted warily or cavalierly across page or canvas, and the spirelet half-heartedly mumbling the enchantments of the Middle Ages from the new school roof. But this distinction cannot be pressed too far. The sense of history fostered by Walter Scott's novels obviously included far more than the outward and circumstantial, but it characteristically included these also, as well as the superficial charm of archaic words and things, in a way that was not alien even to the most serious Victorians. Ruskin, for example, who denounced the casually incongruous applications of Gothic motifs to building, admitted the charm exercised for him by such words as 'vault', 'arch', 'spire', 'pinnacle', 'battlement'.[2] In Victorian

1 J. Gloag, *Victorian Taste* (London, 1962), p.34.
2 Ibid. p.79.

attitudes to history, the influence of Romanticism can be seen, in part, as a stress on the potential significance of the concrete and particular, on the visible, tangible surface, as well as on the distinctive inward spirit. In *Past and Present* (1843) Carlyle laments the limitations of the chronicler's description of King John, when he visited his abbey: 'what did he say, what did he do; how looked he, lived he; at the very lowest what coat and breeches had he on?' Carlyle tries to do it for him, imagining John as 'a blustering, dissipated human figure with a kind of blackguard quality air, in cramoisy velvet, or other uncertain texture, uncertain cut, with much plumage and fringing'.

Carlyle here seems to be wishing that his chronicler, Jocelin, had been Walter Scott. He is lamenting the loss, not of the tinsel and fustian of the past, but of individualizing sensory detail. Thackeray has much the same thought, expressed in an only superficially contrary fashion, when he calls, at the beginning of *Henry Esmond* (1852), for history to 'pull off her periwig'. It is not that he does not want visual immediacy, but it must be the real surface, not the contrived one. Carlyle's attempt to recover a sense of the homeliness and palpable humanity of history in place of the dummies of conventional pageantry is essential to the moral lesson of the Jocelin parts of *Past and Present*. But this too, vital to the imaginative enterprise of understanding the past, obviously has its own form of triviality; something like its counterpart in painting is seen in the transition from the grandiose historical scenes of Benjamin West or Benjamin Haydon in the early years of the century to the more sentimental and domestic treatment of historical subjects, as in Millais's *The Boyhood of Raleigh* or Yeames's famous *When did you last see your Father?*

It is hardly surprising, in fact, if, just as the line between sympathy and sentimentality is necessarily sometimes a fine one, so is that between a decorative antiquarianism or a contrived informality, and the attempt to re-create the past in something like its full singularity and ceaseless humble eventfulness. But if the distinction between serious and trivial often rests on qualities as uncertain and individual as taste, talent, imagination and feeling, it is also possible to make a cruder and more confident distinction between the decorative and occasional use of the past and what we may call its ideological uses, provided we bear in mind that the distinction does not correspond to one between artefact and written word. There were costume novels as well as costume paintings, and architecture was often, and even typically, in the Victorian period, an intensely ideological art.

For of course ideological positions and public debate could rarely be separated altogether from some view of the past or even from versions of some specific part of English history. It was, after all, only relatively recently that most political and cultural debate had been conducted in the historical mode, in terms of references to the examples of classical antiquity, to English constitutional and legal precedent and even sometimes to Magna Carta. Again, English institutions had changed at an uneven rate: the universities, for example, with their religious exclusiveness, their rules of celibacy (until 1871), and what the eighteenth century called their 'monkish style of architecture', seemed to their detractors as offensively medieval as to their defenders they sometimes seemed enchantingly so. The validity and claims of important English institutions derived originally from specific historical events; thus, the status of the Church of England clergy, relative both to the Roman church which to some nervous early and mid-Victorians seemed about to reabsorb them, and to the Dissenters, was bound up with a particular view of the early Christian church and of the religious and political history of England from the fifteenth to the seventeenth century.

If only because of this, if one knew what a mid-Victorian thought of Charles I and Cromwell one would have more than an inkling of whether he voted Liberal or Conservative. Cavalier and Puritan, High Church and Dissent, were still two cultures, confronting each other across a table in Yeames's picture. As the historian Lecky said, 'We are Cavaliers or Roundheads before we are Liberals or Conservatives', and the great medieval historian Bishop Stubbs thought the seventeenth century unsuitable for university history teaching because it was too topical. Some of these sensitive areas in the past actually acquired an increased significance in the nineteenth century. An Age of Reform, often contemptuously indifferent to precedent and ancient rights, was obviously one for looking out one's title deeds, if they could still avail, as the Oxford Tractarians attempted to do in the 1830s for the Anglican church.

The articulate traditionalism and social nostalgia — there is a vital difference here to which we shall have to return later — which are such marked features of early and mid-Victorian thought and sensibility were in a large measure a response to the three immense upheavals which had preceded and ushered in the Victorian era: the French Revolution, the Industrial Revolution, and the remarkable reconstruction of many fundamental English institutions which had taken place in the 1820s and 1830s, largely under the intellectual guidance of the utilitarian school of Jeremy Bentham and James Mill and their close allies, the political economists.

Of these, the French Revolution was the most remote, both in time and place, though the more recent revolutions of 1830 and 1848 and the Chartist agitation in England were uncomfortable reminders, as was the Paris Commune of 1871. To English eyes it had generally worn two aspects, not incompatible, though the emphasis could be varied at will. First, as the destruction of a corrupt and frivolous ruling class, lacking a sense of social responsibility — which could be taken as either a warning to the English or a vindication of their superior qualities — and as the release of demonic forces, normally contained by respect for law, in the terrible form of the revolutionary mob. In either guise it largely replaced the fall of the Roman Empire as history's sternest and most dramatic moral lesson. The impression it made on Victorian imaginations is impossible to gauge in extent, but clearly it was sometimes profound, particularly in the 1830s and 1840s. We see it, of course, in Carlyle, whose *French Revolution* (1837) gave it classic form for his contemporaries, in Dickens, and in Kingsley who had witnessed the Reform riots in Bristol in 1831; it also helps to explain how Matthew Arnold could take the trampling down of the Hyde Park railings and flowerbeds in 1866 as a symptom and symbol of anarchy.

The second relevant 'lesson' of the French Revolution was taken to be its failure in construction, marked by the ephemerality of its 'paper constitutions' and the subsequent instability of French political life and institutions, which were frequently ascribed to the revolutionaries' deliberate destruction of tradition. All this seemed, particularly under the tutelage of Edmund Burke's *Reflections on the Revolution in France* (1790), to provide an exemplary reinforcement of the essentially romantic distrust of 'machinery' — the abhorrence of Carlyle and Arnold — seen as something rationally designed but lifeless and lacking roots in the past. A corollary was a conviction that changes should be gradual and 'organic'; the central metaphor of Burke's conservatism, that of house repairs and improvements, with the building retaining its essential identity and continuity, was one which had many Victorian echoes. Another was the belief, so marked in Carlyle and Arnold, and emphasized also by George Eliot, most explicitly in *Felix Holt* (1866) and by Kingsley in *Alton Locke* (1849), that an inner self-discipline or self-regeneration rather than formulae such as the People's Charter or the Ballot, was the one thing necessary. Christian tradition coincided here with a romantic insistence on an inner principle of vitality and growth, and a supposed lesson of the French Revolution.

More immediately important, however, to the formation of an articulate traditionalism or an idealization of some aspect of the past, was the provocation provided by the reforms of the 1820s and 1830s, and the anti-traditional doctrines of utilitarianism and political economy. With a different epistemology, the utilitarians were as contemptuous of tradition as the French revolutionaries. What the Revolution and the ideas of the eighteenth-century *philosophes* had been for an earlier generation, utilitarianism and political economy became for the early Victorians, a test of modernity, to be accepted, repudiated or somehow transcended. This critique of institutions was essentially a-historical or even anti-historical; to the utilitarian, precedent, prescriptive right, ancient privilege, the pieties induced by habit and time, were no argument, or were even a negative argument: 'the wisdom of our ancestors' was Bentham's particular abhorrence. This attitude can be found even among those whom we think of as hostile to utilitarianism: Dickens, for instance, whose Mr Gradgrind (*Hard Times*, 1855) is probably the best-known utilitarian in fiction, enjoyed himself by naming the dummy books on his shelves 'The Wisdom of our Ancestors', and subtitling them 'Ignorance. Superstition. The Block. The Stake. The Rack. Dirt. Disease.'

Neither traditionalism nor a medievalist social nostalgia was new in the early Victorian period; Burke was the chief sponsor of the former, which was really only making explicit and 'philosophical' one of the most powerful strains in English intellectual and political history; William Cobbett had already propounded many of the themes of medievalist social nostalgia. Nevertheless, the 1830s were in many respects a turning point. For one thing, the reforming impulse had made traditional English institutions — as Macaulay, for example, had argued in 1832 that it would — more defensible, by removing their worst abuses; in its own terms 'machinery' works. The question from the 1840s onwards was not whether to reverse the reform legislation — that was hardly an issue — but whether what was now needed was more of the same, further extensions of the franchise, the ballot, church disestablishment, or something quite different. Second, the doctrinaire nature of utilitarianism and the apparently far-reaching claims of political economy, so that they seemed to offer not only a guide to government action or inaction but a whole code of social behaviour, provoked an equally articulate response. This had already begun in the earlier period, notably in writings of Coleridge and Southey, and had been comically dramatized by Peacock, but in the 1830s and 1840s the evidence of a reaction was unmistakable: its landmarks are Keble's sermon on 'National Apostasy' in 1833, which makes a convenient starting point for the Oxford Movement in the church; the appearance of Pugin's *Contrasts* in 1836, with its juxtaposition of a gentle, harmonious, beautiful medieval world and an abhorred, callous, hideous, modern commercial one; in 1843 Carlyle's *Past and Present*; and Disraeli's *Coningsby* (1844), which was to be the basic text for the Young England Toryism of the 1840s.

It was in the 1830s and 1840s, too, that the Gothic revival in architecture became serious, scholarly and fiercely ideological. There had been a frivolous eighteenth-century rococo Gothic in stucco and even papier mâché; the early nineteenth century had seen a romantically 'horrid' Gothic, of which Fonthill Abbey had been the archetype; now the time had come for an earnest, pedantic, doctrinaire Gothic revival, proclaiming Gothic as the only truly Christian, 'natural' and English architecture, and anxiously concerned to find and impose the 'correct' period of Gothic style. This last aspiration was particularly associated with the Cambridge Camden Society, founded in 1839, and its journal the *Ecclesiologist*, which fixed on the Decorated period as the model for new church building and 'restoration'. In its own way, of course, this was as absolute and a-temporal a standard as the utilitarians' 'greatest happiness' principle, even though it was one embodied in and derived from a past period. One of the founders of the Camden Society, J.M. Neale, declared that he would gladly see Peterborough Cathedral demolished if it could be rebuilt in the approved Decorated style;[3] the Society's activities in 'restoration' leave no doubt that he meant it.

Such a remark, in fact, brings us back to a necessary distinction between traditionalism and nostalgia or reaction, even if the lines are often blurred and few cases are so clear as this. There was nothing traditionalist in this position; it involved a condemnation of the whole history of English church architecture since the fourteenth century. Reaction could be very radical. Consider, however, a more complex case: the theological position of the Oxford Tractarians. It was, in theory, strongly traditionalist, in that its central inspiration was the claim of the Church of England to an unbroken inheritance of the Catholic apostolic succession, and to belong to what Newman, in a phrase Disraeli might have envied, called 'the royal dynasty of the apostles'. Unfortunately their Anglican forebears had not always taken the same high view of their church as the Tractarians did, nor, so long as they remained Anglicans, could the latter accept the whole of Roman Catholic tradition. Inevitably they were driven to pick and choose, to ask, as Ruskin was to do in architecture, at what point the 'authentic' tradition had lost its purity: the fourth century? the later Middle Ages? Or did it, as Newman was ultimately to accept, still survive in the modern Catholic church? Only when he had shed his Anglicanism was Newman able to write a fully traditionalist work, his *Essay on the Development of Christian Doctrine* (1845). Even for Catholics, however, the solution was not always simple. Pugin, for example, was a Catholic convert whose architecture and writings were in essence a campaign to re-Catholicize his country. But it was essentially medieval Catholicism that he wished to see reintroduced and his faith was shaken by a visit to Rome — not, as might perhaps have been expected, by what Victorian visitors often thought of as the unedifying spectacle of the Papal court or the squalor of the Papal capital, but because of his detestation of the Renaissance and the Baroque. Papal Rome and the English Middle Ages were in a sense competitors for the English Catholics'

3 Reginald Turnor, *Nineteenth Century Architecture in Britain* (1950), p.68.

allegiance. Cardinal Wiseman, for example, rejoiced that his 'Early Christian' novel *Fabiola* (1855) 'is undoing some of the medieval frostwork which late years have deposited round English Catholic affections to the forgetfulness of Rome and its primeval glories'.[4]

As an example of an acceptance of the national past entirely untouched by any tendency to reaction or any serious temptation to nostalgia, we may take Macaulay. He enthusiastically welcomed the reforms of the 1820s and 1830s, but he regarded them not as a repudiation but as a consummation of English constitutional history. He accepted political economy also, and notoriously delighted in demonstrations of material and intellectual progress, but he rejected utilitarianism for what he regarded as its neglect of experience and its contempt for the past. Typical of his own triumphalist version of English history is a passage like this from his essay on Sir James Mackintosh (1835):

> To us, we will own, nothing is so interesting and delightful as to contemplate the steps by which the England of Domesday Book, the England of the Curfew and the Forest Laws, the England of crusaders, monks, schoolmen, astrologers, serfs, outlaws, became the England we know and love, the classic ground of liberty and philosophy, the school of all knowledge, the mart of all trade. The Charter of Henry Beauclerk, the Great Charter, the first assembling of the House of Commons, the extinction of personal slavery, the separation from the See of Rome, the Petition of Right, the Habeas Corpus Act, the Revolution, the establishment of the liberty of unlicensed printing, the abolition of religious disabilities, the reform of the representative system, all these seem to me to be the successive stages of one great revolution.

Later in the century there were to be other, more systematic and cosmopolitan statements of the idea of progress, as in the Comtean version of intellectual and scientific development through necessary stages, or the deterministic neo-Darwinian versions, allegedly though loosely based on the theory of evolution. Macaulay evinces here a satisfaction and confidence which has probably more often

4 David Mathew, *Lord Acton and his Times* (London, 1968), p.37. Cf. Brian Fothergill, *Nicholas Wiseman* (London, 1963), pp.135-7.

figured in imaginative literature as caricature than with full authorial approval; the classic instance is of course Dickens's Podsnap in *Our Mutual Friend*. But Macaulay, in his combination of antiquarian and libertarian sentiment, of national pride and respect for tradition with enthusiastic endorsement of material and intellectual progress, very probably expressed the feelings of more of his contemporaries than any other author mentioned in this chapter.

It is natural to turn from an optimistic fusion of progress and tradition like Macaulay's to its antitheses in the extremes of neo-medievalist nostalgia. Of course 'nostalgia' is not a wholly adequate term: one has only to think of Coningsby's symbolic marriage to Edith Millbank, the manufacturer's daughter, or of Carlyle's call to the captains of industry in *Past and Present*. Nevertheless, it is worth considering why the nostalgia does often seem so extreme. To sense degradation and to regret the good old days is common in all societies, and particularly understandable in a period of rapid and unsettling social and economic change. What may at first seem surprising about the nostalgia of early Victorian England is the remoteness of the period it chose above all to idealize. Of course, the location of many mid-Victorian novels in a fairly recent past has often been noted. Clearly nostalgia was not altogether absent for older simplicities and formalities, and particularly for the coaching age which preceded the coming of the railways: 'Alas! we shall never hear the horn ring at midnight, or see the pike gates fly open any more' (*Vanity Fair*, 1848).

But though the railways obviously did mark the end of an era, if not quite so dramatically as Thackeray jocularly contended in the *Cornhill*, with modernity on one side of the track and everything from Ancient Britons to highwaymen on the other,[5] there was little tendency to idealize the Regency or the eighteenth century as such, and much explicit condemnation. The critics of the recent past, evangelical, utilitarian and romantic, had done their work too well, and it would not be hard to build up a Victorian stereotype of the eighteenth century as brutal, cold-hearted, raffish, irreligious, indecorous and unfeelingly neoclassical, a fit setting for aristocratic

5 Kathleen Tillotson, *Novels of the Eighteen Forties* (Oxford, 1954), paperback ed., p.105.

seducers, cynical dowagers, uncouth drunken squires, hunting parsons and out-at-elbows men of letters. Thackeray and Macaulay, of the great mid-Victorians, cherished the Augustan age, but essentially it was only when standards had changed towards the end of the Victorian period that the eighteenth century could come to stand, uncensured, for wit and elegant artifice, as in Aubrey Beardsley, or the essay called 'A Defence of Cosmetics' which Max Beerbohm wrote for the first number of *The Yellow Book* (1894). In the reaction against industrialism and utilitarianism, it was not the pre-industrial world of Augustan England the Victorians idealized, and in this, whatever the awkwardness and frequent defiance of historical fact in their medievalism, Victorian social critics showed a sound historical judgement, recognizing that much of what they hated was rooted in an earlier, capitalist-commercial revolution, and had not sprung abruptly into life with Adam Smith, Richard Arkwright and Jeremy Bentham. Of course, for Catholics and Anglo-Catholics — to use the term that became current later in the century — the Reformation was an obvious and distressing historical fracture. Catholicism was often accompanied or even inspired by enthusiasm for the Middle Ages, though there were Catholics, of whom Newman was one, to whom they meant little. In any case, it was not only Catholics who regarded the sixteenth century, and sometimes the fifteenth also, as the scene of a second Fall. Ruskin, for example, was clearly embarrassed by the Romanism of his favourite period, while William Morris virtually ignored it.

In some cases, particularly in matters of aesthetics, Romantic archaism and hostility to the cosmopolitan neoclassicism of what Ruskin called 'the foul torrent of the Renaissance' played a major part. But there were other reasons why the fifteenth and sixteenth centuries should be seen as the watershed, and particularly the Dissolution of the Monasteries. The crucial issue here was poor relief — the supposed contrast, which Cobbett had vehemently posed, between the meagre and degrading relief grudgingly doled out to modern paupers and the kindly charity, asked for as a right and freely dispensed, from the buttery hatch of the monastery. The outcry against the workhouse 'Bastilles' of the New Poor Law of 1834 naturally intensified these feelings. One of Pugin's most telling illustrations in *Contrasts*, added for the 1841 edition, was the representation of medieval and modern relief of the poor, and it was also a significant element in Disraeli's social criticism. Eustace Lyle, the young Catholic aristocrat in *Coningsby*, has revived the practice of almsgiving as a weekly ritual. The lord's hall, with the noble family eating, though at a higher table, with their dependants, as described in *Ivanhoe* (1819), and comically in Peacock's *Crotchet Castle* (1831), was also a powerful image both of rude plenty, which had an obvious appeal in the years of acute distress in the first half of the century, and of the bonds between master and man in a patriarchal social order, eroded in later times by aristocratic exclusiveness and the cash nexus. Trollope's Miss Thorne in *Barchester Towers* (1857) managed only an approximation to the idea: she and Mr Thorne dined in their hall, but tête-à-tête, and on the day of the rustic sports degree was preserved; the orders ate separately.

The vision of a shared and ordered social life, contrasting with commercial greed and the anarchy of uncontrolled competition, is common in virtually all nineteenth-century neomedievalism, but in other respects there was a shift of emphasis around the mid-century, reflecting the relatively easier times of the fifties and sixties after the bitterness over the New Poor Law and the acute poverty and distress of 'the hungry forties'. The formation of the Pre-Raphaelite Brotherhood in 1848, and the publication of Ruskin's *Seven Lamps of Architecture* in the following year, can be taken as convenient marking points for the transition, though Pugin's work had already anticipated it to some extent. The emphasis on charity and rough plenty, and the concern with 'how it came about that this land of roast beef was changed all of a sudden, into a land of dry bread or oatmeal porridge' (so ran Cobbett's gloriously unhistorical formulation), was increasingly replaced by a marked anti-industrialism not shared by Disraeli or Carlyle, by a stress on the ugliness of modern life, the lack of joy in work, and the impoverishment of the spirit by the division of labour and machine production. If the festive great hall, the groaning board, and the monastery, glowing, as Carlyle says of St Edmundsbury, 'ruddy through the night', were the presiding symbols in the first half of the nineteenth century, later Victorians preferred the cathedral and the workshop, and their hero was not the patriarchal lord or abbot but the anonymous stone-carver.

The culminating works of the earlier period are Carlyle's *Past and Present* and Disraeli's *Coningsby* and *Sybil* (1845). Disraeli's work qualifies as such because, despite the undeniably tinsel and in many ways perfunctory quality of his view of the Middle Ages, and despite the fact that relatively little of it was original, he does present the most coherent diagnosis of how the medieval paradise had been lost: a parvenu Whig aristocracy, regardless of the social responsibilities recognized under feudalism, had risen to wealth on the plunder of the monasteries and to power on the ruins of the Stuart monarchy. As history it was a schematic travesty, but it was consistent and reasonably specific.

Past and Present offers no such clear diagnosis. It is even rather doubtful whether it should be classed as a medievalist work at all. Carlyle had no particular interest in or affinity for the Middle Ages as such; his own historical interests were in later periods. He was above all a Puritan, and Martin Luther was perhaps the greatest of his heroes. He detested the cult of the picturesque, which had been one of the sources of the Gothic Revival, and he had no aesthetic sympathy with medievalism; he thought Bath the prettiest town in England and once distressed William Morris by referring approvingly, on a public occasion, to St Paul's Cathedral, whose building (*vide Past and Present*) epitomized for him the concept of a mighty work (or rather Work). No writer was more aware of what hunger might mean, but he had none of the English early Victorian delight in groaning tables, baronial or otherwise. He seems to have come upon the twelfth-century chronicle of Jocelin of Brakelond with its account of his hero, Abbot Samson, more or less by accident.

Carlyle's concern is unmistakably with 1843, with the poor men sitting, as though frozen by enchantment, in front of St Ives workhouse. St Edmund's Abbey under Samson is a pattern for him only in the loosest sense; his view of it entirely lacks the painfully literal, prescriptive character of Pugin's or even Ruskin's view of the Middle Ages. Constantly he emphasizes the remoteness of his subject: the crabbed, monkish Latin of Jocelin, the near-unimaginability of his life. The Abbey is compared to a Mastodon, its ruins 'like an old osseous fragment, a broken blackened shin-bone of the old dead Ages', reminding us, and perhaps Carlyle's first readers, of Tennyson's 'nature brings not back the Mastodon' (*Morte d'Arthur*, 1842). The remoteness is the point; it is overcome in quick glints of common humanity in the story of Samson and his world. If, the rhetoric insists, through the alien forms we can discern the inner spirit, why can we not re-create, not the form, but the spirit? We possess it in some sense, or we could not recognize it, though in us it is stifled by the various modern 'isms' of Carlyle's allegorical demonology. To use the past as Carlyle does here is in effect to transcend the categories of 'a sense of the past', but his book is inescapable in this discussion because it is by far the most rhetorically and imaginatively powerful, as well as perhaps the most widely influential, treatment of a medieval theme in the literature of social criticism.

Past and Present, then, resists classification, but more than anywhere else it belongs with what has been called the 'two cities' model: Bury and Manchester are like juxtaposed images in Pugin's *Contrasts* or Ruskin's comparison of Giorgione's Venice with the London in which Turner grew up.[6] But though this was a form medievalist criticism inevitably took, with the Middle Ages functioning, in the cruder versions, as a kind of timeless model, or even utopia, as a foil to the present, there was sometimes more than a simple dichotomy. In Ruskin and Morris, for example, the utopian strain is balanced by an awareness of tradition, and even by a kind of baffled traditionalism which has a poignancy that one does not find in a more revolutionary sensibility like Carlyle's. Consider the chapter on 'The Lamp of Memory' in Ruskin's *Seven Lamps of Architecture*, in which he celebrates the effects of time and historic association. He begins by remembering a scene in the Jura, and then imagines it as 'a scene in some aboriginal forest of the New Continent'.

> The flowers in an instant lost their light, the river its music; the hills became oppressively desolate; a weariness in the boughs of the darkened forest showed how much of their former power had been dependent upon a life which was not theirs, how much of the glory of the imperishable, or continually renewed, creation, is reflected from things more precious in their memories than it, in its renewing. Those ever springing flowers and ever flowing streams had been

6 See John D. Rosenberg, *The Darkening Glass: A Portrait of Ruskin's Genius* (New York, 1961), p.52.

dyed by the deep colours of human endurance, valour and
virtue: and the crests of the sable hills that rose against the
evening sky received a deeper worship because their far
shadows fell eastward over the iron wall of Joux and the four-
square keep of Granson.

This looks, not back to Carlyle, though Carlyle had his own sense of
landscape as the handiwork of man and hence a product of history,
but forward to Proust.

Ruskin goes on to apply the thought to architecture:

For indeed the greatest glory of a building is not in its stones,
nor in its gold. Its glory is in its Age, and in the deep sense
of voicefulness of stern watching, of mysterious sympathy,
nay even of reproach or condemnation which we feel in walls
that have long been washed by the passing waves of humanity.

With intense earnestness Ruskin is here employing concepts drawn
from the eighteenth-century aesthetic of the picturesque in defence
of a doctrine of reverence for antiquity and continuity through
time, which matches and recalls the solemnity of Burke's rhetoric in
defence of the historic Constitution. Fittingly, Ruskin concludes
with a denunciation of 'restoration', a condemnation of modern
stylistic eclecticism, and a call for the adoption of a single agreed
architectural language: his contention that the agreed language
should be Gothic is logically only secondary.

Ruskin felt acutely the disaster of a broken stylistic continuity,
and the lack of a living tradition. The radicalism, in one sense of
the word, which this predicament evoked from those who felt it
most strongly, is often striking. Perhaps the most famous instance is
the recently married William Morris's discovery when setting up
house, that, as his biographer J.W. Mackail put it, 'Not a chair, or
table, or bed; not a cloth or paper hanging for the walls; nor tiles to
line fireplaces or passages; not a curtain or a candlestick; nor a jug
to hold wine or a glass to drink it out of, but had to be re-invented,
one might almost say, to escape the flat ugliness of the current
article.'[7] But in Ruskin's and Morris's notions of art, though not in
their social ideas, the radicalism was accompanied by a feeling not
just for medieval models but for continuity and the effects of time.

7 J.W. Mackail, *The Life of William Morris* (London, 1899), Vol. I, p.143.

Both were implacable enemies of the architectural 'restorers'. Morris, in the manifesto he wrote for the Society for the Protection of Ancient Buildings, founded in 1877, diagnosed the ailment: 'The civilised world of the nineteenth century has no style of its own amidst its wide knowledge of the styles of other centuries. From this lack and this gain arose in men's minds the strange idea of the Restoration of ancient buildings.' A 'restored' building was a kind of forgery of which no earlier age would have been guilty. In the past,

> if repairs were needed, if ambition or piety pricked on to change, that change was of necessity wrought in the unmistakeable fashion of the time ... but every change, whatever history it destroyed, left history in the gap, and was alive with the spirit of the deeds done amidst its fashioning.

In architecture and design, the problem was seen as the corruption and subsequent rupture of a tradition. The consequences, as Ruskin and Morris saw them, were on the one hand well-intentioned destruction, and inert forgery substituted for a living past, and on the other a monstrous stylistic promiscuity. Yet in other contexts it was possible to think of tradition in a more comprehensive and optimistic fashion, and actually to welcome, albeit anxiously, the eclecticism offered by taking history rather than dogma as one's guide. This was essentially what Walter Pater pointed to when he wrote, in *Plato and Platonism* (1893), that 'modern thought is distinguished from ancient by its cultivation of the relative spirit in place of the absolute'. It was exemplified, within a Christian context, by Frederick Temple in his contribution to *Essays and Reviews* (1860), the controversial manifesto of liberal Anglicanism, when he wrote that the Bible, being a history, 'is hindered by its form from exercising a despotism over the human spirit', and by J.A. Froude when, in a sympathetic account of the church in the high Middle Ages, he took comfort that the clergy had been neither perfect nor all-powerful: 'It would not have been well if they had been. The business of human beings in this planet is not summed up in the most excellent of priestly catechisms.'[8]

8 J.A. Froude, 'Times of Erasmus and Luther', in *Short Studies on Great Subjects* (London, 1898), Vol. I, pp.52-3.

The best-known exponent of the idea is Tennyson's dying Arthur:

And God fulfils himself in many ways,
Lest one good custom should corrupt the world.

All cultures, institutions and creeds are ultimately liable to petrify into formulae and must then be cast off; the body dies so that the spirit may renew itself. It is Carlyle's 'clothes philosophy' in *Sartor Resartus* (1838), though Carlyle's acrid strenuousness excludes the gentler cultural eclecticism this idea could sometimes contain. Nevertheless, the pressure to some kind of synthesis was almost always present in some form. The nineteenth century offered a scene of immense cultural variety compared with earlier periods; partly it arose from a more extensive, exact and inward understanding of the past and of alien cultures; partly from the increasing heterogeneity of a complex and mobile industrial society — the same complexity which offered such a rich field of social observation to the Victorian novelists. There was not one code or two, but many: a code of honour and snobbery; a code of utility, self-help and getting on; a code of Christian morality in its various guises, sometimes in the form of a Calvinistic strenuousness growing increasingly secular, and even a Romantic and aesthetic cult of self-expression or self-realization. To devise names for these varieties was a serious and attractive exercise. Carlyle's personifications, Mammonism, Dandyism, Dilletanteism, and the rest, are an exercise in cultural dramaturgy and analysis; so, less vigorously, are Matthew Arnold's Barbarians and Philistines and the antitheses of Hebrew and Hellene in *Culture and Anarchy* (1869). And very often these conflicts of culture and attitude found their appropriate historical correlatives. In an age of waning faith, a particular interest attached to the confrontation of paganism and early Christianity in the ancient world. Two cardinals, Wiseman (*Fabiola*) and Newman (*Callista*, 1856), wrote novels on this theme, as did Kingsley in *Hypatia* (1853) and Pater in *Marius the Epicurean* (1885). Swinburne's *Atalanta in Calydon* (1865) presented the same conflict seen from the perspective of a Dionysian Hellenism. Similarly, the seventeenth century offered ample scope for displaying one's preference for chivalric cavalier virtues or sternly Hebraic ones.

Such cultural diversity suggested both the difficulty and the possibility of a comprehensive assimilation; it is not surprising that the Faust or Wandering Jew figure is an important nineteenth-century image. Disraeli's Sidonia, though not ageless, is of the type: 'Sidonia had exhausted all the sources of human knowledge: he was master of the learning of every nation, of all tongues, dead or living, of every literature, Western or Oriental.' In properly mythical fashion, the price of his omniscience seems to be that he has renounced love. Disraeli's character, who appears in both *Coningsby* and *Tancred* (1847), is a Byronic man of mystery, with cousins in the Gothic novel, in a way which assigns him to the imaginative world of the first half of the century. Matthew Arnold's *The Strayed Reveller* (1849) strikes the same chord more soberly, but the later, more philosophically and aesthetically pondered incarnation is really Pater's Mona Lisa, a summation of the world's experience, and understandably a little weary (*The Renaissance*, 1873). For Pater the idea of cultural summation touched divinity. The figure of Christ worshipped by the Christians in *Marius the Epicurean* 'seemed to have absorbed, like some rich tincture in his garment, all that was deep-felt and impassioned in the experiences of the past'. The Mona Lisa's fatigue is understandable: the nineteenth-century sense of the past would tax any powers of assimilation, and collapse into eclecticism was all too easy, reminding one of the taste in interior decoration caught by Tennyson in *The Princess* (1847): the Greek busts and

> Carved stones of the Abbey-ruin in the park,
> Huge Ammonites, and the first bones of Time;
> And on the tables every clime and age
> Jumbled together.

In an intellectual world menaced by the sheer copiousness and variety of its own cultural bric-a-brac, it could well seem vital to retain some reassurance of an underlying direction and coherence in history, or even some possibility of synthesis. A dawning sense that no such reassurance may be available, though it begins well before the end of the century, is a not inappropriate mark of the shift from a distinctively Victorian to a distinctively modern sensibility.

Select bibliography

Chadwick, O. (ed.) *The Mind of the Oxford Movement*. London, 1960.
Chandler, A. *A Dream of Order: The Medieval Ideal in Nineteenth Century English Literature*. London, 1971.
Clark, K. *The Gothic Revival*. London, 1950.
Gloag, J. *Victorian Taste*. London, 1962.
Hunt, J.D. *The Pre-Raphaelite Imagination 1848-1900*. London, 1968.
Maas, J. *Victorian Painters*. London, 1969.
Mackail, J.W. *The Life of William Morris*. 2 vols. London, 1899.
Rosenberg, J.D. *The Darkening Glass: A Portrait of Ruskin's Genius*. New York, 1961.

7 Painting and illustration

GEOFFREY HEMSTEDT

The art critics, who told us sixty years ago that the Victorians were
no good, have brought their pictures out of attics and museum
basements, blown the dust into our eyes, and reproached us for
neglecting them. By good fortune they have carried off this witty
effect at a time of increased interest in Victorian history and culture
generally, and the art of the period has been made widely available
in reproduction and exhibitions. It is invaluable to the student of
literature as evidence not just of things seen but of ways of seeing.
We may look to Frith's *Ramsgate Sands* or Tissot or Orchardson for
dramatic illustration, seeking an aid to historical imagination, and
we recognize that their habits of arrangement and interpretation
are different from ours, in selection and sentiment. We may
approach the work of a particular painter by trying to relate it to
developments in art history, and we can identify processes of
influence and reaction among the great variety of styles in the
period, famously, for example, in the work of the Pre-Raphaelites
or Whistler. But we quickly discover too a broad area of external
interactions: between art and patronage; literature, painting and
illustration; markets and techniques of reproduction; painting and
photography; art and manufacture; and so forth.

The dominant mode of Victorian art was realism, and nearly all
the important artists of the age can be seen either as trying to fulfil
what they saw to be its demands (often trying to redefine them) or
as challenging its constraints. That realism which seems

characteristically Victorian must be related to a shift in taste, from the academic and allusive idioms favoured by aristocratic patronage, to the bourgeois desire for art which is accessible and which explains itself. In the forties and fifties especially, a strongly middle-class patronage gave heavy impetus to narrative painting, and we may detect in the relation in such work of treatment and subjects the same congruence between formal realism and the investigation of social identities which we find in the development of the novel. For example Frith's *Derby Day* (1856), with its related dramatic episodes, invites the viewer to measure the status and fortunes of groups and individual figures. The treatment combines reportage with sentiment and suggestions of satire, and the crowds who first went to see the picture would have known readily how to 'read off' its incidents. Will the countryman in a smock let himself be fleeced by sharpers, or will his girl persuade him to hang on to his money? The boy acrobat is hungry, poor child. That fellow with a mourning band will come to no good, and so on. The painting is filled in with a mass of detail, and a careful argument of costume.

It would be misleading, however, to associate realism with the selection of subject alone, or to trace the evolution of Victorian painting along a line of narrative which moved from Wilkie through Frith to Fildes and Herkomer, in a required progress towards social realism. The technical preoccupations of the age go far beyond this, and with confusing effect. To take one instance: it happened that the emphasis on narrative in the early and mid-Victorian period coincided with the placing of high critical value on careful finish and clarity of depiction in paint. For this, various influences have been suggested, the most important being photography and German painting. The first cannot be overestimated, and it is difficult for us to re-create imaginatively the revelation offered by the photograph, and the sense it gave that there was an authoritative image. From the Germans, English painters took techniques of laying clear pigment on a light ground, effects of bright distinct colouring and clean contour, and hard surface. We might associate this second influence with the initial shock of Pre-Raphaelitism, in such a picture as Holman Hunt's *The Hireling Shepherd* (1851). We could identify the uncompromising vividness of colour with Hunt's revolutionary impulse, and with his revision, through insistent religious symbolism, of conventional expectations of genre and landscape. When the painting is categorized as a Pre-Raphaelite work in this way we are encouraged to recognize specific motives, rather than conditions of current influence, as the occasion for its technique. These motives are found in the ideals shared, in the years following 1848, by a group of young men (centrally Hunt, Millais and Rossetti), who, inspired so the story goes by a book of engravings of the frescoes in the Campo Santo at Pisa, wished to emulate painters earlier than Raphael. Photography, certainly, seems a long way from this, and if we seek a fuller context for the Pre-Raphaelites we shall probably find it in the Romantic strain that links them to Keats, in their medievalism, and in the later work of Burne-Jones, Morris and the Decadents. We should then encounter a familiar polarity in Victorian culture, or at least in interpretations of it, which opposes aestheticism to materialism. But if we look again at Hunt's picture, and imagine him working on it in the year of the Great Exhibition which celebrated the marriage of art and technology, the camera and the die press as painter and sculptor, the polarity seems not so absolute. We recognize that Hunt's intense and undiscriminating concentration on every square inch of canvas, his high degree of technical anxiety, produce an effect much closer to the spirit of his own age than to that of the age before Raphael.

To pursue this point a little further, we might consider Millais's *Mariana*, painted in the same year (1851), taking a subject glimpsed by Tennyson in a line of Shakespeare. It was exhibited at the Royal Academy without title, but with the refrain from Tennyson's poem.

She only said, 'My life is dreary —
He cometh not' she said;
She said, 'I am aweary, aweary,
I would that I were dead.'

The designed contrasts of light and dark give varied emphasis and relief lacking in Hunt's picture, and allow the deliberately awkward pose of the figure, with its brilliant deep blue, to dominate, expressing dramatically the yearning and langour of the poetry. But Millais accompanies this with a scrutinizing attention to detail and texture, in his painting of drapery, leaves, stained glass, metal, wood, and so forth, and it is not surprising to learn that he painted the stained glass from windows in Merton College Chapel, the scene through the window from a friend's garden, and carefully bought velvets and other fabrics to model the draperies. That the picture should have been at first ill received may, as in the case of *The Hireling Shepherd*, be put down to its quality of exposure, of frankness and sharp focus; but the virtuoso draughtsmanship, the meticulous empirical modelling, the resourceful looting around for a subject (and its popular literary connotations), the reconstruction of an imagined past — all of these are to be found in the mainstream of Victorian narrative painting, and all offer the accessibility and ready coherence which might attract a bourgeois buyer. (*Mariana* was in fact sold to a dealer for the considerable sum of £150.) Millais was to become a widely popular painter and make a lot of money. His canvases got bigger, his paint looser, his narratives more sentimental, and it is all too easy to compare his soap advertisement *Bubbles* of 1886 with the brave and perilous Mannerism of *Isabella* or *Christ in the House of His Parents*, both painted, amazingly, when he was only twenty. We should also recognize that the motives he shared with Hunt, the confident willingness to enforce new images for the age, a historicism which was at once liberating and empirical, far from being the special preserve of angry young men, were very much in the air.

In other contexts the effect can be disconcerting. Today, the Catalogue of the Great Exhibition of the Works of Industry of All Nations, with its Gothic water-closets and Anglo-Catholic billiard tables, may seem at times like a grotesque spoof concocted by Marcel Duchamp and Heath Robinson. But these things were the wonders of the age, and attracted six million visitors to Paxton's great iron and glass prefab in Hyde Park. The bizarre contents of the Crystal Palace expressed the early prime of industrialism, its brashness and pride in making things. Like much Victorian art, the exhibition blended solemnity with a touch of hysteria. Its objects are solid and rich, outward signs of success and prosperity. At the same time their decoration is often wildly fanciful, with a cavalier promiscuity of revived styles. Again, behind all this is the spirit of the new patronage, especially in the innocence of a sense of decorum, and the looked-for triumph of the inappropriate.

To make a final comparison with the Pre-Raphaelites, consider Hunt's *A Converted British Family Sheltering a Christian*

Missionary from the Persecution of the Druids (1850). The title's thick prose appropriately introduces the programmatic earnestness of the picture. The subject would not have been merely quaint at the time, but would rather have invited an oblique reference to current sectarian crises, and we may recall that the Pre-Raphaelites were suspected of Roman Catholic sympathies. Hunt took every care with historical accuracy. The shelter is properly primitive, the fabrics, we are sure, are such as might have been woven on simple looms, sandals and pottery innocent of mechanical process. But the flesh on Hunt's models has been rounded on a diet of pork pies and well-grilled chops, and it is raw, pink and British as flesh should be which has been protected from sun and rain by the fashions of mid-century. The work is earnest, meticulous, technically impressive; it is also very awkward, to the point of ugliness. It could not have been different. In looking at the conscious reconstructions of Victorian historical painting we necessarily encounter a double perspective, the chosen subject exposed in idioms which have become unfamiliar. To make sense of the *Druids*, as of the gear of the exhibition, we have to come to terms with a unique context of newness; the contending impulses of art and technology, of poetry and realism.

The early dominance of narrative may also be seen as exploiting the watering down of Romantic themes and images to a rhetoric of sentiment. Turner lived on until the end of the exhibition year, and Ruskin had published the first volume of *Modern Painters* in 1843, in an attempt to establish the supremacy of his style of painting. But that supremacy is more a matter of cumulative recognition than of an effect immediate at the time. We might as well look to John Martin, master of the debased sublime, for an example of the popular communication of the Romantic style. In the year of Turner's death Martin began work on the lurid *Judgement* paintings, having first negotiated terms for their mass reproduction in engraving. Landscape, however, had lost the absolute centrality that Constable and Turner had given to it as the medium of Romantic avowal. The thirties had seen the decline of the Norwich School, following the deaths of Crome and J.S. Cotman, and the last fading of the great period of English watercolour painting which reached back well into the eighteenth century. Of course, the Victorians produced important works of landscape, from the philosophic and religious allegories of Dyce and the precocious impressionism of David Cox, to the work of Henry Moore, Wilson Steer and MacTaggart, and inevitably the painting of landscape continued to be a major preoccupation throughout the period. But there were a set of characteristic *uses* of landscape which may be contrasted with Constable or Turner as Tennyson may be contrasted with Wordsworth. Roughly speaking, the articulation of feeling through the portrayal of nature became more schematic, with a more deliberate sense of local arrangement, of foregrounds and backgrounds. At worst it became merely atmospheric, as in those countless dank paintings of huddled cattle, Highland by preference, dimly seen through a blur of mist and cracking varnish. In some cases there was a coincidence between a more precise patheticism and the favoured precisions of technique we have already considered in the Pre-Raphaelites and contemporary narrative paintings. We might here compare Tennyson's sense of nature on a small scale (the Romantic turned botanist) with the sharply detailed, and pointedly chosen, flora in the work of Arthur Hughes, or the well-known *Broken Vows* by P.H. Calderon, or Bowler's *The Doubt; Can These Dry Bones Live?* Most striking is Millais. In his *Ophelia*, landscape has become a bowering enclosure of greenery, an effect emphasized by the curving top of the frame. It is curiously like looking into one of those glassed recesses in natural history museums which recreate the 'natural setting' for the stuffed coyote or dabchick, and these little scenes indeed have a very Victorian quality, with the creatures frozen for ever in dramatic attitudes of purpose or repose. The device may be better seen in Millais's *The Blind Girl*, where a genre subject, the beautiful beggar girl, is posed against a landscape lit into contrasts of brilliant yellow-green and sombre blue-purple as a storm ends and a rainbow appears in the sky. A younger sister has sheltered under the blind girl's cloak, and is seen as if in the act of covering her eyes and uncovering them again to discover what it must be like to be blind. More impressive still is the same painter's *Autumn Leaves*, where the iconography of detail has been completely abandoned, and instead the artist composes a sombre statement purely of figure arrangement, colour and natural symbolism.

This increasing consciousness of design will find many echoes in the period. The student of literature may encounter it in the changing styles of illustration of novels and poetry. The illustrators of the thirties and forties worked in a tradition of robust and distortive graphic humour which reached back through Gillray and Rowlandson to Hogarth. Cruikshank, illustrating *Sketches by Boz* and *Oliver Twist*, was able to employ a popular satiric technique which adapted freely to the energy of the texts, and he had the advantage of a journeyman's knowledge of the appropriate media of reproduction. His sense of design was clear and decorous. His figures have at their best the suppleness and confidence of the grotesque, and his sense of space is contained in the free vignette definition of the borders of the plates. He fails when confronted with purely sentimental subjects (the happy-ending tableaux at the end of *Oliver Twist* for example), because the style simply will not adapt to a pretty or idealized image. In contrast Hablôt Browne ('Phiz'), who illustrated most of Dickens's books in the forties and fifties, took to crowding his plates with comment pictures and significant detail, and gradually moved away from the cruder line found in his wood-block work (for example his contributions to the *Master Humphrey's Clock* novels) to a less controversial, blander style for the etched plates of the monthly serials, as if in conformity to the taste of the period. It is as well to describe briefly some conventions of publication. Dickens's early weekly serials were illustrated by woodcuts 'dropped into the text', and could exploit an immediate relevance to the content of the letterpress. The plates for the monthly serials were printed by intaglio process, separately from the letterpress, and bound into the numbers, two for each episode, immediately before the text. In the serial, therefore, they can be regarded as having the function of a film trailer. It is likely that the reader glanced at them and guessed at what was coming, and Dickens, who instructed Browne closely, seems to have been aware of this. When the serial issue was complete the publishers would provide a binding service for 1s. 6d., and the plates would be bound in at an appropriate point of the text. This practice encouraged dramatic tableau, and anyway it was not within the scope of Browne's talent to approach in illustration the landscape or the symbolic elements of Dickens's writing. He did, however, especially in *Bleak House* and *Little Dorrit*, draw for plates which had been machine-ruled, to give a dark ground for night subjects, and there are some city subjects among them.

Thackeray, who illustrated some of his own work, admired
Cruikshank and the earlier satiric manner, and he happened to be
an indifferent draughtsman. *Vanity Fair* and *Pendennis* were
illustrated with full-page intaglio plates and woodcuts both, the
latter including decorative capitals and occasional tailpieces. In
keeping with his narrative style, and appropriately to his manner of
drawing, he tended to avoid sentimental subjects in the full plates,
or to drop them into the background. (For example the long-
awaited reunion of Dobbin and Amelia is so treated, the fore-
ground figures being merely the lookers-on.) Instead he busied
himself with free decoration and witty allegory in the woodcuts,
recalling Cruikshank's graphic puns or the old political satires
against Napoleon or the Prince Regent.

Satire, however, was out of favour, and the regard for photo-
graphic realism increasingly infected illustration as it did painting.
When the freer manner of graphic satire tried to adapt to the
demands of conscientious sentimental realism there was an impasse
in style, and Browne is as good an example of this as any. These
problems were brilliantly resolved in the sixties. Then we find
Moxon's *Tennyson* illustrated by Creswick, Millais, Hunt, Horsley,
Rossetti, Stanfield, Mulready and Maclise, in a single volume.
Painters of the first rank had turned to illustration, tempted by
money and encouraged by the high technical skills of servicing
wood-engravers. The speculative publication of anthologies and
'galleries' boomed, often promoted by master engravers like the
brothers Dalziel, who themselves chose the subjects to be illustrated
and commissioned the artists. The wide experience by so many of
the discipline of drawing for engraving, with its pressures to
simplify and concentrate design, can be seen as a transitional
influence from the detail and exactitude of the early Victorian
period to the formal experiments of the late century, though the
precision of the engravers' technique served the sharp line as well.
The achievement can be seen at its best in the Moxon *Tennyson*, in
the sombre and deliberate studies for the Dalziels' *Bible Gallery*, or
in the single plates for set-piece narrative poems in magazines like
Good Words or *Once A Week*. Illustration was frankly the *raison
d'être* for many of these ventures, and the artists delighted in a
range of opportunity, with none of the pliancy Dickens would have
demanded of Browne, but seeking their own interpretation of the

subject. Here is Rossetti, writing to William Allingham in 1855, considering illustrations for the *Tennyson*.

> I have not begun even designing for them yet, but I fancy I shall try The Vision of Sin and The Palace of Art, etc. ... those where one can allegorise off one's own hook on the subject of the poem, without killing for oneself and everyone a distinct idea of the poet's.

Two examples will give an idea of the new earnestness in novel illustration. George Eliot, visiting Florence in 1860, decided to write an Italian story. She went back there a year later, and, with Lewes, read extensively in the Maglabecchian Library to research background for a novel about Savonarola's Florence, *Romola*. She made long lists of the names of prominent political figures, painters, sculptors and scholars, and took notes about subjects as diverse as prices, salaries, localities and costume. She investigated the sumptuary laws, and transcribed from family archives all the items of a wedding trousseau. The minuteness of detail recalls the Pre-Raphaelites; the eagerness of rediscovery and historical projection suggests Browning. Clearly such a novel would require an unusually qualified illustrator, and she found him in Frederic Leighton, who had travelled on the Continent from his boyhood, and had a special regard for Florence, where he had studied at the Accademia delle Belle Arte when he was fourteen. His first completed canvas (1850) was *Cimabue finding Giotto in the Fields of Florence*, and in 1851 he painted *The Death of Brunelleschi*. His most famous Italian subject picture had been *Cimabue's Celebrated Madonna is Carried in Procession through the Streets of Florence*, which had been a sensation at the Royal Academy in 1855, and was bought by the Queen. His was the graver style of art arising with the new connoisseurship of the fifties, and it is interesting to note that Ruskin's critical acclaim (in *Academy Notes*, 1855) blends a regard for narrative and detail with scholarship and a sense of the historic aptness of styles. He is describing a connoisseur's realism when he remarks that the procession is

> painted on the purest principles of Venetian art ... that is to say, on the calm acceptance of the whole of nature, small and great, as, in its place, deserving of faithful rendering.

Everything is done as well as it *can* be done. Thus, in the
picture before us, in the background is the church of San
Miniato, strictly accurate in every detail; on the top of the
wall are oleanders and pinks, as carefully painted as the
church; the architecture of the shrine on the wall is well
studied from thirteenth-century Gothic, and painted with as
much care…: The features of the boys are carefully studied,
and are indeed what, from the existing portraits of him, we
know those of Giotto must have been in his youth.

He is also describing a very Victorian picture, which, though he
feels able to compare it favourably with Veronese, remains to later
eyes a pastiche.

The *Romola* illustrations are placed interestingly between these
early historical narratives and Leighton's achievement as leader of a
movement of High Art which carried through the sixties to the
eighties, a movement of academic revival, concentrating on Hellen-
istic figure study. The best work in this mode was by Leighton
himself, Olympian compositions of brilliant colour and related
space and volume, and by Albert Moore, harmonious and lyrical.
But the memories of the fifties stuck fast, and the lithe young
women in the pictures of Alma-Tadema and Poynter, for ever in
and out of pools and apodypteria, have a faintly suburban air, and
might be transposed, decently robed, to the different waters of
Cheltenham or Leamington Spa. Tadema girls whisper together
and read letters from young men rather as keepsake beauties had
done in narrative pictures thirty years before. In Leighton there is
none of this. A single illustration from *Romola* shows how he makes
a narrative subject the occasion for expression through pure design.
The plate 'Coming Home' shows Romola waiting to greet her
husband, after a long absence, and it explores ideas of sexuality,
menace, weakness and will, which are themes of the narrative; thus
it both illustrates (taking a particular moment from the text) and
interprets. It merits unusually full attention, because it suggests a
central point of balance in Victorian art. The narrative impulse is
both contained and transcended as Leighton explores a scheme of
significances derived from expressive line and tone. Romola stands
at the head of a flight of stairs, as Tito climbs towards her. The
horizontal plane of the perspective is at a level with her ankles, and

1 *Derby Day* by W. P. Frith (The Tate Gallery, London)

2 *The Hireling Shepherd* by W. Holman Hunt
(reproduced by permission of the City of Manchester Art Gallery)

3 *Mariana* by Sir John Everett Millais
(reproduced by kind permission of the owner)

4   *Early Britons Sheltering a Missionary from the Druids* by W. Holman Hunt
    (Ashmolean Museum, Oxford)

5   'The Last Chance' by George Cruikshank (illustration to *Oliver Twist*)

6 'My Child-Wife's Old Companion' by Hablôt Browne ('Phiz')
(illustration to *David Copperfield*)

8 'Please Ma'am, Cook says, can we have the peas to shell' by Sir John Everett Millais (illustration to *The Small House at Allington*)

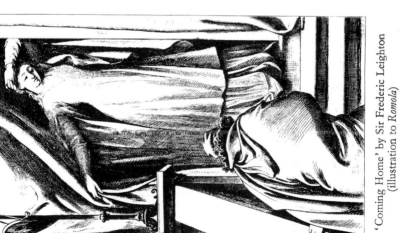

7 'Coming Home' by Sir Frederic Leighton (illustration to *Romola*)

9 *The Beguiling of Merlin* by Sir Edward Burne-Jones
(reproduced by permission of the Trustees of Lady Lever Art Gallery)

her full-length figure dominates. The vertical lines of a metal sconce and a straight-falling curtain to either side of her increase the sense of height, and of her eminence. Tito's half-figure in comparison, seen from below, is huddled in a cloak as if with an arm twisted behind the back. He seems at once to threaten her from below (his momentum as he climbs the stairs) and to cower before her (the spatial relation of the two figures). Romola is shown in an attitude of great weariness, her head drooping towards her left shoulder and her left hand cast across her forehead, palm outwards. With her right hand she seems to part the curtains that surround her and to clutch as if for support, and the double swirl of her robe adds to the sense of uncertain balance, of weariness and feminine weakness. The design is based on the contrast of straight and fluid line. The coping on which Tito rests his hand and the stairs he climbs are shaded in a dark hatching against a clear white, emphasizing their hard angularity. The shading of the lower area is more extreme than the rest, and the drapery around Romola, costume and curtains, flows and swirls gracefully. The contrast is marked at the point where the hem of her dress breaks over the top step, and the motif is taken up with lighter emphasis in the curling supports and branches of the straight sconce rod rising from the coping. We see from this that meanings are conveyed not by significant objects but by their forms.

The second example of sixties' novel illustration is taken from Millais's work from Trollope. Millais avoids both Browne's programmatic detail and use of dramatic conventions, and Leighton's High Art. He cues many illustrations with a line of dialogue ('May I give him your love?' or 'I wish you would be in earnest with me'), and assumes that the reader will look to the writing for narrative explication. If the picture is thus simply a visual projection of what has already been described, he need not impose a scheme of significances on a casual image, and the way is open to simplification and subtlety. His choice of subject is free: no need for crisis or tableau, but a random image from the undistinguishing flow of social intercourse; and these images can be assembled to give an accumulating interpretation of character rather than incident. In *The Small House at Allington* Trollope describes the tightly circumscribed life of the widow Dale, her loneliness, and the thousand small sacrifices of self-effacement she must make to give her daughters some measure of freedom and opportunity. Trollope dramatizes these feelings through a delicate domestic realism. The peas she has picked from her kitchen garden will not be eaten because her daughters are to dine at the Great House.

> Let her daughters eat from her brother's table and drink of his cup. They were made welcome to do so from the heart. For her there was no such welcome as that from the Great House ... nor at any other house, or any other table!
> 'Mamma will stay at home to eat the peas.'
> And then she repeated to herself the words which Lily had spoken, sitting there, leaning with her elbow on her knees, and her head on her hand.
> 'Please, Ma'am, cook says, can we have the peas to shell?' and then her reverie was broken.

This is the subject for illustration, and the title simply repeats the maid's speech. Artist and writer are committed to a decorum of plain record, a regard for the eloquence of mundane circumstance. We might compare George Eliot's emphasis on the uniqueness of what appears ordinary. We are also reminded that the whole area of fiction which concerns itself with the commentary of consciousness is finally inaccessible to the illustrator, and that the tentative quality of Millais's work here, though it discovers new ways of relating naturally and unemphatically to the text, confesses a peripheral function. Novel illustration survived until the end of the century, but there was not again the serious attention to formal questions found in the sixties. The heavy livid plates illustrating Hardy in *The Graphic*, or the Household edition of Dickens, are distracting, and have only a commercial justification.

The late century may be seen in terms of both contrast and continuity. For example the high seriousness of G.F. Watts is famously associated with sombre allegories like *Hope* (1886), but he was almost seventy when he painted it, and had been a prize-winner in the competitions to decorate the new Houses of Parliament in 1843 and 1847. Thus he carried through the century the allegorical history-painting tradition associated with Haydon. He was also the true portraitist for the age, and his well-known studies of Carlyle and Gladstone are painted with controlled energy and psychological penetration. His art seems to demand public or national status, with the claim of consistent gravity. Throughout the reign institutional patronage provided varying stimulus to art, nationally and provincially, and we can trace in it both an honest pride of acquisition and a hunger for culture. For men like Eastlake and Poynter the calling of the artist was subordinated to the responsibilities of administration, and their labours, together with those of countless scholars, officials and patrons, created a legacy of great public collections. To reconcile the poles of past and present was a persistent motive for the age; it is found in voracious imitation, in history painting, in architecture, in literature, and in the rich variety assembled in proliferating galleries and museums. The union of art and science in South Kensington remains its characteristic monument; you could find there the fossilized remains of lost species, or a plaster cast of Michelangelo's *David* (or even of Trajan's Column, though it was cut in half to fit in), together with contemporary art and technology.

There were elements of reaction. In the aesthetic movement there is a strong instinct to free art from functional ties (this especially in the writings of Pater), or to reassert natural balances of use and beauty, as in William Morris and the arts and crafts movement, with their attempts to get back behind industrial time. Like Burne-Jones, Morris was initially inspired by Pre-Raphaelitism, but whereas Morris's medievalism is put to Carlylean uses (the utopian mutuality of *News From Nowhere*), in Burne-Jones the sense of art for art's sake begins to take over. His delicate decorative skills are central to the development of art nouveau, but he is also a bridge between Rossetti's heavy sex and the morbidity of the Symbolists and Decadents. All these possibilities are conjoined in *The Beguiling of Merlin* (1873-7), with its sinuously combined themes of trance and sexuality, its suggestion of androgyny and necrophilia, its delicate, but intense and enclosing, colour system.

The strongest reaction against the dominance of subject came from Whistler, who helped bring to English artists the different influences of the French (Courbet and, later, Manet) and of Japanese art. His use in titles of musical terms like Symphony, Nocturne and Arrangement emphasized considerations of form, the inherent values of space and colour. He sought free textural effects in his use of paint, denying any expectation of careful finish. He provided a focus for a younger generation of artists, including

Wilson Steer and Sickert, who in 1885 formed the New English Art Club as a collective exhibiting body to challenge what they saw as the authoritarian and insular complacency of the Royal Academy.

Through all this, narrative painting survived, and indeed it rivals landscape as providing the essential occasion for continuity in English painting from the eighteenth century into the twentieth. The narrative of sentiment and social description, authoritatively set forth by Wilkie in the twenties and thirties, was developed on a broad front: in rustic or Scottish subjects (Webster, Faed), in melodramatic 'progresses' or tableaux (Egg, Elmore), in grand composition (Madox Brown's *Work*, Frith's *Derby Day*), or in complex moral allegory (Hunt's *The Awakening Conscience*). In the late century Fildes, Herkomer and others pressed towards social-realist subjects (*Applicants for Admission to the Casual Ward, Eventide in the Westminster Workhouse, On Strike*), but they could really only adapt what the painters of the previous generation had done already, and along with Tissot and Orchardson they still turned to the traditional favourite set pieces — courtship and marriage, separation and homecoming, sickness and death. The true appeal of sentiment can be seen in thousands of oleographs and chromolithographs, which were sold for pennies or given away with soap or almanacs. Dogs, descended from Landseer's, guard the hearth or rescue infants from the millstream. Nelson (or Wellington or Raleigh) has his boyhood or glorious manhood. Soldiers enlist, leave wives and sweethearts, massacre heathens, come home as grizzled veterans, take children on their knees. Young girls have their first dance, or kiss, or fall; they are too early, too late, under the sycamores, on the brink. This is the art of the music sheet or the penny weekly, of popular song and melodrama, but it touched sooner or later every point of what we see as serious Victorian art. Leighton's goddesses looked nice in the parlour, and that Arrangement in Grey and Black *was* Whistler's mother, and you couldn't help wondering if she was thinking of her boy.

8 Faith, doubt and unbelief

J. W. BURROW

There is much intellectual history of Victorian England in its notable apostasies. Among the first, and to his contemporaries the most deeply disturbing, was the reception of J.H. Newman into the Roman church in 1845; a series of Oxford clerics and fellows of colleges similarly defected in the ensuing decade. But already, in the late 1840s, another kind of apostate had appeared, lost not to a rival faith but to a scepticism which earlier generations had robustly called 'infidelity' and which later Victorians, adopting the term coined by T.H. Huxley, were to call 'agnosticism'.

These defections from the established church were symptoms of a crisis which, during the middle years of the century, called in question both its doctrines and its institutional identity. Earnest Anglicans were obliged to take a stand, which often proved uncomfortably precarious, on two central issues. First, could the Church of England be both an established church, subject to Parliament, and a spiritual body, a branch of the universal Catholic church founded by Christ, defining its own doctrines and enforcing them on its members? Second, could or should Anglican doctrine be broadened to accommodate itself to the findings of modern biblical scholarship and modern science? To the Tractarian leaders of the Oxford Movement — Edward Pusey, Hurrell Froude, John Keble and Newman — the first was a vehemently proclaimed necessity, the second an abhorrence. To their liberal opponents, the so-called Broad Churchmen, the latter seemed the task to which their generation was peculiarly called, so that the Church of England might become a truly national church, encompassing all shades of Christian opinion. To them, the authoritarian claims the Tractarians made for the Church of England as part of the Catholic church descended from the Apostles seemed at best an irrelevance and at worst detestable. But if the Tractarian High Church position came, after Newman's defection, to look uncomfortably like a staging post on the road to Rome, the liberal one could seem alarmingly like a bridge optimistically suspended over an abyss of doubt. Both positions required intellectual poise and flexibility — opponents were apt to call it dishonesty — and it is hardly surprising if for some they proved in the long run impossible to sustain.

It is perhaps as hard now to understand as it is difficult to overestimate the intensity of feeling which these defections produced. Families and friendships were rent as though by civil war. The Roman church was regarded, even among the highly educated, with a fearful hostility nourished through generations by Protestant horror stories of idolatory and superstition, of priestly tyranny, persecution and vice, and sinister Jesuit plots. The new converts to Rome were popularly called 'perverts' rather than converts, and anti-Catholic feeling ran high in the 1850s. Gladstone, himself a High Churchman, whose sister Helen was one such convert, referred to the newspaper report of the event as 'the record of our shame' and urged his father to expel Helen from the family home.[1] Three of the four sons of the great Evangelican Christian William Wilberforce became Roman Catholics; the remaining Anglican, Samuel Wilberforce, Bishop of Oxford, wrote of his brother Henry's defection: 'I heartily wish he might settle abroad: but having him here after this dreadful fall seems to me beyond measure miserable; and his broken vows and violated faith weigh heavily on my soul. May God forgive him.'[2]

The unbeliever was regarded with much the same kind of horror as the Jesuit, as a subverter of society. Unbelief was still commonly thought of as sinful in itself, a consequence and almost certainly a cause of moral weakness. When J.A. Froude resigned his fellowship

1 S.G. Checkland, *The Gladstones: A Family Biography 1764-1851* (Cambridge, 1971), p.330.
2 David Newsome, *The Parting of Friends: A Study of the Wilberforces and Henry Manning* (London, 1966), p.360.

at Exeter College, Oxford, in 1849, after the publication of his 'infidel' novel *The Nemesis of Faith* (1848) which was burned in the College Hall by the Sub-Rector, his father was pitied as though for a son's death. It marks a notable shift of opinion when, from the 1860s onwards, in the numerous second- and third-rate religious novels of the period, the unbeliever began to be presented as a victim to be reclaimed, preferably by the love of a good woman, rather than as an ogre.[3] Doubt had become too pervasive simply to be confounded with individual wickedness, though it is a tale as late as 1872 which gives us this description of 'the peculiar cast of an atheist's face — the brow devoid of all grandeur, the fixed and soulless expression of the eye, the look of stern calculation, the intense materialism of his creed pervading all.'[4]

Apostasy did not affect only the peace of mind of individuals and the harmony of families. In early and mid-Victorian England a far higher proportion of educated men were in clerical orders than was to be the case later as professional opportunities expanded. Education was still largely in clerical hands, and religious tests were in force at the universities until 1871. The clergyman was the mentor of youth; together with the squire he was the focus of rural life. In such a society conversion to Roman Catholicism or the onset of unbelief could mean social and financial disaster. Resignations and ejections from fellowships and chairs, renunciations of clerical orders and livings, suspensions and prosecutions of clergy for heresy, often represented personal crises whose distress and notoriety can be compared in our own times only with the often equally well-publicized resignations and ejections from the Communist Party. Even for those sheltered by a private income, like Leslie Stephen when he resigned his fellowship at Trinity Hall, Cambridge, in 1862, and Mrs Humphrey Ward's renegade cleric in her celebrated novel *Robert Elsmere* (1888), the disruption of careers and loss of direction could be severe afflictions. Many resorted to periodical journalism, either for a substitute pulpit or merely for money, and some, like Froude, and his friend Arthur Hugh Clough after he had resigned from Oriel, thought desperately of teaching

3 Margaret Maison, *The Victorian Vision: Studies in the Religious Novel* (New York, 1961), ch.10.
4 Leo J. Henkin, *Darwinism in the English Novel 1860-1910* (New York, 1963), p.80.

in the colonies. Mr Hale, in Mrs Gaskell's *North and South* (1855), made a scarcely less heroic decision than this and had to abide by it, by giving private lessons in a manufacturing town after he had given up his comfortable country living. Froude was fortunate to find a second vocation as a historian, but the same could hardly be said of Clough's later career.

Those who had turned Catholic were often little better off. Newman's own later life was one of considerable neglect and frustration. As he said, at first 'we were necessarily treated like children, being grown men'. A kindly Anglican mourned over a former colleague set to herd with Irish priests in a dingy town presbytery 'with only a print or two and a few books' as reminders of the old comfortable life at Balliol. Those who, like Trollope's Mr Arabin in *Barchester Towers* (1857), had come through their misery of indecision confirmed for the Church of England could well consider themselves fortunate. At least, however, Catholic converts, if unencumbered with wives — as fellows of colleges necessarily were until 1871 — could pursue their vocations as priests. How much worse things could be for the dissenting minister, at the mercy of his congregation and unfitted for his ill-paid post by growing religious doubts, is shown in William Hale White's novel *The Autobiography of Mark Rutherford* (1881) and its sequel *The Deliverance*. Without a vocation, without influence or money, Mark Rutherford is driven to the drudgery of clerking, and leads a life of pathetic endurance far removed from the glamorous secular preaching of Mrs Ward's Robert Elmsmere.

So far, of course, we have considered those who, in life or in fiction, could be considered as martyrs to conscience. But there were also martyrs to other people's consciences. Two of the clerical contributors to *Essays and Reviews*, the manifesto of liberal Anglicanism whose publication caused such excitement in 1860, were prosecuted for heresy and suspended, though their convictions were quashed on appeal; another, Benjamin Jowett, had his salary as Professor of Greek at Oxford withheld. More serious was the ejection of the liberal theologian, F.D. Maurice, from the chair of theology at King's College, London, chiefly because he refused to accept the orthodox theory of damnation. It was this episode to which Tennyson referred in the poem he addressed to his friend Maurice:

> should eighty thousand college-councils
> Thunder 'Anathema', friend, at you.

It is worth dwelling on the secular penalties of conversion or unbelief, because it is often hard in our time to avoid a feeling of irritation with the advertised pathos of Victorian Doubt. Other people's melancholy is apt to look like self-indulgence when sympathy with its idiom has waned; as J.M. Keynes impatiently said of Henry Sidgwick, the Cambridge agnostic saint of the previous generation: 'He never did anything but wonder whether Christianity was true and prove that it wasn't and hope that it was.'[5]

> We are most hopeless who had once most hope
> We are most wretched that had most believed.
> Christ is not risen.   (Clough, *Easter Day 1849*)

Clough's malaise, like that of his friend Matthew Arnold, had, as they well understood, much in common with that Romantic malady of restless, unfocused melancholy and paralysis of will which affected or was affected by so many young Europeans in the years after the end of the Napoleonic wars; it is not without reason that Arnold recalls Byron's Childe Harold in his *Stanzas from the Grande Chartreuse (Poems, 1855)*. The famous reference in the same poem to

> Wandering between two worlds, one dead,
> The other powerless to be born,

though the place and the tenor of the poem lend it a religious reference, might well, if uttered by some contemporary French *enfant du siècle*, for example, have carried a more immediately social or political implication. What is striking in Arnold, Clough, Tennyson and even Carlyle is the persistence of the theological idiom. The Christian sense of sin and belief in judgement, the Christian assumption of personal immortality, with its accompanying appreciation of the world as a moral order, a true cosmos, and hence of the eternal significance of each act and each individual life, were still terribly real in early Victorian England.

Much of this intensity must be traced, directly or indirectly, to the Evangelical movement of the early years of the century. The

5 R.F. Harrod, *The Life of John Maynard Keynes* (London, 1952), p.116.

Evangelicals had set out to, as they saw it, re-Christianize their country. The leadership of the movement lay in the hands of the Clapham Sect, a group of devout Low Church Anglicans living in the substantial houses around Clapham Common, in the first decades of the century. Besides Wilberforce, they included Leslie Stephen's grandfather, Sir James Stephen, and Zachary Macaulay, the father of the historian. Anglican Evangelicalism had much in common with the more emotional and enthusiastic type of Nonconformity, particularly Methodism; the older dissenting sects tended to be drier and more exclusive, like the Independents and Baptists so unsympathetically described in *Mark Rutherford* and in Charles Kingsley's *Alton Locke* (1849) respectively. Intellectually, as a creed, the simplicities of Evangelical piety, based chiefly on Bible reading and the personal experience of conversion, were to prove fragile when confronted by the rigour and subtleties of Tractarian scholarship and theology, or by liberal criticism of the Scriptures. The Evangelicals disapproved of secular literature, and they have been repaid; the portraits of Evangelicals, and their allies among the Dissenters, in Victorian literature are not flattering: Trollope's Mr Slope, Charlotte Brontë's Mr Brocklehurst and Dickens's caricatures, Chadband and Stiggins; for a sympathetic portrait of the Evangelical mentality one has to turn to the agnostic George Eliot. But the enduring effects of Evangelical 'seriousness' were apparent in many aspects of early Victorian social and intellectual life: in the outward pieties of Sabbath keeping and family prayers; in a prudish literature and a sober clergy; above all in an intense, even strained, religious scrupulousness and self-awareness, as marked in the Broad Churchman Thomas Arnold, or, with appropriate nuances, in the High Churchman Hurrell Froude, as in those who, like Newman himself, had been specifically exposed to the influences of Evangelical piety. Here lay the origin of what in the Epilogue to Clough's *Dipsychus* is called 'this over-excitation of the religious sense'.

In particular, the religious temper of the English clergy ensured that if the liberalism of the age seemed to put the church in danger, and to undermine Christian faith, the resistance would be bitter and the casualties would often feel their case acutely. It was the conviction that the church *was* in danger, from a liberalizing secular state, that provided the first impetus to the Tractarian movement at

Oxford in the early 1830s. The church as an institution had suffered, though hardly severely, from the reforming attentions of the Whig government elected after the first Reform Act. Irish bishoprics had been suppressed, English ones pruned; the Bishop of Barchester was not as rich as he used to be. To the Tractarians such tampering with the Church of the Apostles was abhorrent in principle. Not that, like Trollope's Archdeacon Grantly, who was a more old-fashioned kind of High Churchman, they cherished the church's temporal possessions for their own sake. Hurrell Froude even so far defied his contemporaries' sense of fitness as to deny that a priest need be a gentleman; the powers conferred by ordination transcended such distinctions. But their sense of the sacredness of the priestly office, and of the authority of the church hierarchy, left no room for interference by reforming legislators.

Inevitably, in exalting the priest as the successor of the Apostles and the historic church as the indispensible medium of divine grace through the sacraments, the Tractarians were drawn closer to the Roman church, and as inevitably some were drawn into it. After the shocking defections of the 1840s and 1850s, the second phase of the Oxford Movement, now generally christened Puseyism or Anglo-Catholicism, centred more on liturgical innovations than theology; candles, crucifixes, copes and incense were no less offensive to Low Churchmen than Catholic doctrines, and far more noticeable to the laity; in popular Low Church literature the 'ritualist' priest became a villain to rival the Jesuit and the atheist. *Cousin Mabel's Experience of Ritualism* (1867) was the alluring title of one novel. The innovators were more often to be found in the slum parishes of the cities than in country vicarages, and by the end of the century many Anglo-Catholic clergy had won respect by combining ritualism with social work, even sometimes embracing 'advanced' socialistic opinions which would have horrified their Tractarian predecessors, and which in the mid-century had been confined to a few Broad Churchmen, notably Charles Kingsley and F.D. Maurice, the 'Christian Socialists' — though 'socialist' was always rather a misnomer.

The influence of the Oxford Movement, and Newman in particular, on Victorian literature has been extensively studied. It is most evident in Arnold and Walter Pater. A central Tractarian doctrine had been a belief in the importance of 'holiness'. The life of holiness was sanctified by the sacraments and ideally expressed itself, in a character like Newman's, in a graceful, reserved, even elegant fastidiousness and purity of thought and demeanour which deliberately repudiated the contrived exhortations and drawing of banal religious 'lessons' from everyday events which had often characterized the Evangelicals. Newman himself, like Keble and Pusey, was not a ritualist or liturgical aesthete, but the character which Tractarian holiness assumed in him had much in common, when stripped of the sacramental and dogmatic foundation which to Newman was all-important, with the aestheticism to which Arnold was drawn and which Pater preached. Grace, restraint and a kind of religious fastidiousness are stressed notes in Pater's aesthetic dandyism. One of the more bizarre connections in cultural history is that by which, indirectly, the Oxford Movement can be linked with Ruskin, the Pre-Raphaelites and the French symbolists, among the sources of the aesthetic movement of the 1880s and 1890s.

But there is another aspect of the indirect legacy of the Oxford Movement which deserves attention: its power of repulsion. Seen with a hostile eye — and after Newman's defection many eyes were hostile — the elegances of Tractarian holiness looked like affectation, and the sinuosities of Tractarian theological argument like equivocation or downright dishonesty. It was the charge of dishonesty brought by Kingsley against Newman which provoked the latter's memorable reply, the *Apologia Pro Vita Sua* (1864). Patriotism was involved, as well as theology. Catholicism was alien, the religion of reactionary Italian prelates and of the numerous Irish immigrants, squalid and diseased, tragic refugees from the famine of 1846. The defections of English clergymen, and the tactlessly timed re-establishment of the Catholic hierarchy in England in 1850, seemed to the more excitable like attempted subversion by a foreign power. Kingsley's *Westward Ho!* (1855) was one fictional manifestation of this mood, as well as of the patriotic ardours induced by the Crimean War. For Kingsley, a display of robust masculinity and a distrust of speculative intellect became distinctively anti-Tractarian virtues, as well as reassuringly English ones. If aestheticism owed something obliquely to the Oxford Movement, so, still more obliquely, did philistinism, the 'Muscular Christianity' which Kingsley was accused of preaching, and the anti-intellectualism and cult of athletics so marked in the public schools, and even the universities, in the second half of the century. Kingsley belonged to an older tradition of strenuous exercise, a tradition of field sports and nature rambles, but he played, together with his friend and fellow Christian Socialist, Thomas Hughes, author of *Tom Brown's Schooldays* (1857), a notable part in fostering the new educational *mores*: hard training and simple thinking were esteemed as marks of 'manliness' and remedies for 'effeminacy' and 'morbid introspection', long after Kingsley's association of the latter with Tractarianism had become irrelevant.[6]

Before we turn from Oxford High Churchmanship to consider the causes of doubt and unbelief, some important qualifications are in order. For the suggestion that the High Oxford road led only to Rome or to a more ritualistic form of Anglicanism misses an important connection. The influence of Newman and his fellow Tractarians was no insurance against religious doubt; on the contrary, it might indirectly help to promote it. The strained attention to fundamental theological propositions which the Tractarian dilemmas fostered was inimical to an easygoing acceptance of the faith of one's fathers, even, or perhaps most, when the Oxford Tracts claimed to be reaffirming it. The Tractarians would not let sleeping dogmas lie, and more conventional Anglicans were often forced to ask themselves whether *that* was what they believed.

Since the seventeenth century, English Protestants had been proud of the superior rationality of their creed compared with the superstitions of Rome. Tractarian logicians like W.G. Ward turned this argument back on them, delightedly displaying the arguments of David Hume to show that rationalism ended in total scepticism. There was to be no comfortable middle way: the authority of the church or belief in nothing were the proffered alternatives. Clearly, the horn of Ward's dilemma that he did not recommend was as sharp as the one he did, and there is evidence that Ward, who was Clough's tutor at Oriel, blamed himself for his pupil's debility of faith and will. Another double-edged Tractarian weapon was the case of miracles. Catholics traditionally accepted the miracles of the early Christian centuries as genuine, along with those in the New Testament; Protestants endorsed only the latter. One of the inspirations of Newman's edition of *Lives of the English*

Saints (1844-5), to which the young J.A. Froude contributed, was to show the continuity of the miraculous in the church's history. But the continuity could be read either way, and Froude said he had found 'only the continuity of illusion'. Instead of the church's miracles being vindicated, the New Testament ones became incredible. Again, Froude had embraced what, from his mentor's point of view, was the wrong horn of the Protestant's dilemma.

A second qualification is even more important. The losing of faith, for each individual, is a process which is fluid, amorphous, singular and confused almost by definition: difficult often for even the subject to analyse or to recall accurately once it has passed. We necessarily treat unique cases as exemplary, and abridge in a phrase the muddled hesitations and revulsions of months or years. For some the loss of faith was clearly something like a spiritual disaster; others claimed to find the process easy and natural. Leslie Stephen wrote: 'When I ceased to accept the teaching of my youth, it was not so much a process of giving up belief as of discovering that I had never really believed.' How much this was a former self represented to harmonize with a newer one we cannot tell, and nor, no doubt, could he.[7]

Finally, to have done with qualifications, there is a temptation to exaggerate the effects of what was novel: the new, so-called 'Higher Criticism' of the Bible, and the new geology and biology. But there were older qualms which the uncompromising Christianity of Evangelicals and Tractarians was bound to provoke afresh. One of the chief arguments of the eighteenth-century Deists, frequently repeated by working-class radicals in early nineteenth-century England, was the contention that the central Christian doctrines of Adam's Fall and original sin, of Christ's Atonement and of eternal punishment, were morally intolerable and presupposed a God who was a monster of wickedness. These reflections, particularly the idea of eternal damnation, troubled tender Victorian consciences. This is notably the case with two younger brothers of leading Tractarians. J.A. Froude's novel *The Nemesis of Faith* shows his young clerical hero as much troubled by the morality as by the truth of Christian dogmas — the same, incidentally, was true of 'Mark Rutherford' — while similar ethical qualms played the chief part in leading

7 F.W. Maitland, *The Life and Letters of Leslie Stephen* (London, 1906), p.133.

Francis Newman to his own idiosyncratic branch of unorthodoxy. With these reservations firmly in mind we can turn with a modest confidence to the more notorious causes of unbelief: biblical criticism and science. It seems likely that among highly educated Anglicans, and particularly clergymen, it was the former which generally came first and cut deepest. Theology, biblical commentary, historical criticism and the handling of texts were, after all, their culture in a way that science, despite the eager amateur geologists and entomologists, was not, though Tennyson and Kingsley were notable exceptions. The notion that science had 'disproved' the Bible, however, was readily assimilable; questions raised by ancient texts in Greek and Hebrew and their mainly German modern commentators were mercifully forbidding. German scholarship, and particularly that of the Tübingen school of biblical critics in the 1830s, was fundamental to the nineteenth-century historical reappraisal of the Scriptures, which is one reason for the relative slowness of its reception in England; a major landmark in the process was the anonymous translation in 1846 of David Friedrich Strauss's *Life of Jesus* by Marian Evans, not yet calling herself George Eliot. The futility of Mr Casaubon's scholarship because of his deficiency in German is remembered by all readers of *Middlemarch* (1872). 'Mark Rutherford' observed that the President of his Dissenting College found the task of vindicating Christianity 'all the easier because he knew nothing of German literature; and indeed, the word "German" was a term of reproach signifying something very awful, although nobody knew exactly what it was.' Knowledge of German and German biblical criticism became the mark of an up-to-date cleric and educated Christian in the 1850s and 1860s. As Mark Pattison, who was to be one of the contributors to *Essays and Reviews*, put it, writing in 1857 on the current state of theology: 'at present, European speculation is transacted by Germans, as our financial affairs are by Jews.'[8]

The vital issue in the Higher Criticism, and particularly in the work of Strauss, was the biblical miracles, and especially those of the New Testament. Jesus' divinity, and hence the validity of his

8 'The Present State of Theology in Germany', *Westminster Review*, N.S., 11 (1857), p.332.

Atonement and promise of eternal life, were generally held to rest squarely upon the credibility of the Gospel miracles, particularly, of course, the Resurrection. No miracles, no resurrection; no divine Redeemer, no assurance of a hereafter or of the ultimate meaningfulness of existence. Of course, at first sight there is nothing very new about this. Miracles had always been central to the dispute between believer and unbeliever, and Hume had given the case against them its classic logical formulation in the mid-eighteenth century. But the approach of the Tübingen school was more insidious, though in a sense Strauss begged the central question; for him it was an axiom that miracles do not happen. What, then, he asked, is the process by which they come to be believed? Because the question of their possibility was begged, Matthew Arnold was right, in *Literature and Dogma* (1873), to resort to a favourite vagueness to explain the strength of the Higher Critic's case: 'For it is what we call the Time-Spirit which is sapping the proof from miracles — it is the "Zeit-Geist" itself. Whether we attack them, or whether we defend them, does not much matter. The human mind, as its experience widens, is turning away from them.' But Arnold went on to state very precisely the difference that characterized the new and subtler attack on miracles: 'And for this reason: it sees, *as its experience widens, how they arise.*' The argument was not logical or scientific, though in a sense it rested on assumptions similar to those of science, but historical.

The eighteenth-century sceptic, in explaining the origin of miracles, had tended to favour a theory of priestly subterfuge. The newer argument was more subtle. Man was a myth-making animal. Strauss, in formulating his explanation of the divine character ascribed to Jesus in the Gospels, was drawing on more than half a century of German historical and classical scholarship devoted to tracking the folk-soul or collective consciousness. Biblical criticism of this kind was a relatively late outgrowth of this essentially Romantic enthusiasm. It had fostered belief in the collective authorship of the Homeric poems; it had inspired research into comparative mythology; Niebuhr, the historian of Rome, had tried to uncover the folk ballads and traditions which he believed underlay Livy's account of early Roman history. Strauss applied the same technique to the Gospels. It was a natural development. To quote Arnold again: referring to the process by which the miraculous stories recounted by the Greek historians Herodotus and Plutarch grew up, he goes on: 'But we shall find ourselves inevitably led, sooner or later, to extend the same rule to all miraculous stories.'

The high culture of the nineteenth century was historical and textual to a degree now perhaps difficult to appreciate; a highly educated man could find that to preserve his faith he must divide his mind, drawing an apparently arbitrary line between the way he read the Bible and the way the most authoritative modern scholarship taught him he must read the classical and historical texts on which his secular culture was largely founded. Arnold's niece, Mrs Humphrey Ward, set herself in *Robert Elsmere* to give a fictional account of a sensitive mind losing its faith rather than endure such an intellectual dismembering.

> He pored feverishly on one test point after another, on the Pentateuch, the Prophets, the relation of the New Testament to the thoughts and beliefs of its time, the Gospel of St John, the intellectual and moral conditions surrounding the formation of the canon. His mind swayed hither and thither, driven from each resting place in turn by the pressure of some new difficulty. And — let it be said again — all through, the only constant element in the whole dismal process was his trained historical sense ... the keen instrument he had sharpened so laboriously on indifferent material now ploughed its agonizing way, bit by bit, into the most intimate processes of thought and faith.

Elsmere had already read Darwin's *Origin of Species*, and it had made little impression on him. Surprising at first sight, this rings true. Nevertheless, the scientific challenge had come increasingly to accompany the historical as a threat to orthodox faith. Only one of the essays in *Essays and Reviews*, and that one of the least controversial — partly, it is true, because its author was the only non-clerical contributor — had touched on it: the essay examined the implications of the new geology for the chronology of Genesis. Geology as such, however, was already slightly old hat by 1860. From the 1830s onwards, Christians were pressed to accustom themselves to geological estimates of the age of the earth running into many hundreds of millions of years, and a good many had done so. Naturally there were obstinate fundamentalists, but the change required, though in one sense enormous, was textually not great. A few words had to be interpreted metaphorically; no central Christian dogma was involved. Psychologically, of course, the effect could be considerable. The reassuring stability of the world was in an important respect undermined: geological change was perennial, not simply the aftermath of Noah's Flood; and the biblical events began to look a little parochial as a fragment of the world's history. For those who could see it, a world of indifferent process was already beginning to displace one of tidy design and moral drama.

> The hills are shadows, and they flow
> From form to form, and nothing stands
> (Tennyson, *In Memoriam*, LXXIII, 1850)

More disturbing was the fossil evidence of what had happened to the animal world. Increasingly it became necessary to envisage not just one creation but a whole succession, in different geological epochs, and massive extinctions too, not confined to the Flood. Again it was not so much the literal word of Genesis as the moral character of the creation and its author that was impugned. Tennyson, as we know, wrestled with the problem in *In Memoriam*. How could such cosmic ruthlessness and waste be reconciled with the notion of ultimate moral purpose, and with

> one far-off divine event,
> To which the whole creation moves?
> (*In Memoriam*, LXXXI)

So far, however, the new geological time scale and the palaeontological record did not include man, who was still allowed a reassuringly recent entrance in approximately 4000 BC. The archaeological evidence for the antiquity of man was only accepted by the scientific world at the end of the 1850s, and by that time the issue was overshadowed by the publication of *The Origin of Species* (1859). Evolution was already, of course, an old hypothesis, with a number of proponents in the eighteenth century and even in ancient Greece. But it was not generally accepted by the scientific world, and its credit among scientists was diminished rather than advanced by the anonymous publication in 1844 of Robert

Chambers's notorious *Vestiges of Creation*. Those with a taste for such speculations might muse on Chambers's evolutionary ideas, but to a scientist like Huxley, though no Christian, the *Vestiges* was rubbish. What scientists debated or rejected, Christians might surely choose to ignore, or denounce from a safe distance; in scientific terms there was hardly more need for the Christian to be upset by the evolutionary speculations of Erasmus Darwin or Lamarck than to be perturbed that Anaximander of Miletus had said that everything was descended from fishes. This was an important point, because what was new in the Victorian era was the reluctance of unbelief. Sceptics there had always been, because some men found scepticism congenial to their cast of mind, but not generally among naturally Christian souls.

The Origin transformed the situation as far as evolution was concerned, not only because, *pace* Elsmere, it is an immensely impressive book, but because within a decade of its publication it was generally accepted by the scientific world. The Christian establishment had somehow to come to terms with it or condemn itself to perpetual warfare with the new clerisy of science. There were three major points on which Darwinism conflicted with traditional Christian belief. The first, of course, is the literal word of the Scriptures; the author of Genesis was a successive creationist, not an evolutionist. By 1859, however, biblical literalism of this kind was becoming a fairly unsophisticated Christian position. One rather sophisticated version of literalism, however, was that presented by a member of the Plymouth Brethren, Philip Gosse, in his book *Omphalos* (1857), replying to pre-Darwinian versions of evolution. Gosse has been immortalized by his son Edmund, in his novel *Father and Son* (1907), which stands beside Samuel Butler's *The Way of All Flesh* (1903) as a classic semi-fictional, semi-autobiographical study of the father — son relationship in a narrowly Christian Victorian household. In *Omphalos* Gosse took a position which, granted the hypothesis, was logically impregnable: God had created the world *as if* species had evolved, complete with fossils, just as he had created Adam with a navel — hence the title 'Omphalos', the Greek for navel — though he had needed no umbilical cord. The apparent evidence of evolution was a test of man's adherence to the word of God in the Scriptures. Interestingly, this argument was overwhelmingly rejected on moral grounds:

God would not have been guilty of such deceit.

If the literal sense of words had been all that was at stake, the same accommodations could no doubt have been generally extended to biology as to geology. The other two issues were much more intractable. Darwin's explanation of evolution was natural selection: competition for survival among organisms acting on the occurrence of chance mutations. The anxieties raised by the palaeontological proof of the extinction of species, which Tennyson had expressed in *In Memoriam*, seemed awfully confirmed; a soulless and pitiless mechanism, operating through blind chance and at enormous cost in waste and suffering, had been shown to be capable of producing all the beautiful and intricate contrivances of structure and fitness which had hitherto required a benign creative architect or superintending divine Providence for their explanation. It would be harder, in future, to find reflective responses to nature untinged with wryness.

Third, evolution unfortunately included man. Darwin mentions man only once, cryptically, in *The Origin*; his caution was deliberate, but it was useless. Darwinism was everywhere hailed popularly as 'the monkey theory' — monkeys also are mentioned only once in *The Origin*, quite insignificantly — because of the immediate seizure of the implication that man must be cousin to, or, as was vulgarly held, descended from, the apes. Huxley added to the excitement with his essay *Man's Place in Nature*, in 1863, proclaiming that on anatomical grounds alone man was indisputably to be classified in the order of apes. There were loudly proclaimed fears for morality, as there were when Darwin published *The Descent of Man* in 1871. 'Society must fall to pieces if Darwinism be true,' said the *Family Herald*.[9] If man were taught to see himself as a brute, might he not behave like one and 'reel back into the beast'? To believers in the Christian doctrine of the Incarnation the Darwinian idea could be violently repugnant: God had assumed the vesture of a member of the order of apes. Bishop Wilberforce put the orthodox case with uncommon precision in his review of *The Origin*:

> Man's derived supremacy over the earth; man's power of
> articulate speech; man's gift of reason; man's free will and

9 Owen Chadwick, *The Victorian Church*, 2 vols (London, 1966), Vol. II, p.34.

responsibility; man's fall and man's redemption; the incarnation of the Eternal Son; the indwelling of the Eternal Spirit, — all are equally and utterly irreconcilable with the degrading notion of the brute origin of him who was created in the image of God, and redeemed by the Eternal Son assuming to himself his nature.

What was at stake here was nothing less than man's special relationship with God, epitomized in his creation in God's image and the incarnation of Christ as man. And in that relationship was contained every religious hope, and particularly, of course, the hope of a life beyond the grave.

> My own dim life should teach me this,
> That life shall live for evermore
> Else earth is darkness at the core
> And dust and ashes all that is.
>
> (*In Memoriam*, XXXIV)

The religious history of the later Victorian period strikes one as characterized chiefly by the attempts of Christians to accommodate themselves to the changed intellectual circumstances, and the attempts of agnostics to provide themselves with larger hopes. Both attempts, inevitably, were often overstretched, with much tormenting of religious vocabulary to make it mean what none of its earlier users had ever dreamed of its meaning. Arnold's readers may legitimately have wondered what right 'morality touched by emotion' had to the name of religion.

As the Christian establishment became more accommodating, the distinction between doubt and orthodoxy, between the Christian and the devoutly inclined theist or agnostic, often became hard to draw except in terms of a rather arbitrary personal decision. The Anglican accommodations included an acceptance of evolution, and even of natural selection, provided it was seen only as the mechanism chosen by divine providence to achieve its ends. Darwin had offered an olive branch at the end of *The Origin*; Kingsley seems to have been the first cleric to seize it; he was already familiar with evolution, as is striking evinced in the dream passage in *Alton Locke* (1849), in which the hero, while delirious, relives the evolutionary process. Increasingly, evolution was seen as the preparation for man, and biblical history as the record of man's spiritual progress. Without its evolutionary prelude, this was already a favourite Broad Church doctrine, borrowed largely, like so much else, from Germany: Frederick Temple's introductory essay in *Essays and Reviews*, 'The Education of the World', presented a version of it. Comparative religion flourished, under the aegis of Kingsley's nephew-by-marriage, the Sanscrit scholar Max Müller; all religions were aspects of man's search for the divine, though Christianity might be conceded to be the 'highest', while the Bible expressed profound religious truths sometimes 'poetically' rather than literally.

But among agnostics, too, the inclination to restore meaning to the world by moralizing evolution as a progressive and in some sense purposive force, though it found little sanction in Darwin, was frequently irresistible. Samuel Butler's and Bernard Shaw's Lamarckian versions of purposive evolution, accompanied by condemnation of Darwinism as soulless and mechanical in a fashion which recalled the Christian denunciations of the 1860s, were only the most explicit examples. Indeed, once the Christian had accepted evolution as a fact, there could be much in common between his and the agnostic's attitudes to it. Both, after all, tended to be in favour of striving upward and onward. Browning's Paracelsus was a prophet in more senses than one, foreseeing, one might say, the intellectual climate of the later nineteenth century:

> all tended to mankind,
> And, man produced, all has its end thus far:
> But in completed man begins anew
> A tendency to God. Prognostics told
> Man's near approach; so in man's self arise
> August anticipations, symbols, types
> Of a dim splendour ever on before ...
>
> *(Paracelsus*, 1835)

Among believers there was also an increasing emphasis on the ethical sublimity of the person of Christ, and a disposition to regard it, and the believer's response to it, as the authentication of his divinity — variously understood. Agnosticism, too, had its ethical aspect, fervent or arid. One moral variant of agnosticism, for example, was a conscious, dry-eyed stoicism in the face of an indifferent universe. Again, in some newly fledged agnostics, the first emotion seems to have been genuine relief at having done with equivocation; in this mood, the dedication to truth of which Huxley devoutly spoke, a more positive counterpart to Tennyson's 'honest doubt', seemed sufficient exercise for agnostic piety. Leslie Stephen certainly felt something like this, and expressed it in his essay 'An Agnostic's Apology' (1876). Still, self-congratulation on one's intellectual honesty is perhaps slightly meagre as a response to the universe, and it is not surprising that some agnostics sought more emphatic affirmations. Stephen himself, in a letter to a friend, was careful, albeit bluffly, to reaffirm morality: 'I now believe in nothing, to put it shortly; but I do not the less believe in morality, etc., etc. I mean to live and die like a gentleman if possible'.[10] Others experienced more difficulty in putting it shortly, and found more strenuous terms for the ways gentlemen lived. Agnostics and theists closest to Christian sentiment, like Arnold and the fictional Robert Elsmere, found continuing inspiration in the human person of Jesus. Some, again, were drawn to the Comtist Religion of Humanity, which had been making headway in England since the early 1840s, and more found a bleak but bracing anchorage in stern Carlylean notions of duty and work. These solutions were by no means mutually exclusive: George Eliot could be said to have embraced all three. Indeed, the world of the agnostic often seems a bewilderingly eclectic one, with aspiring surrogate deities, science, art, progress, righteousness, humanity, duty, with their attendant prophets, jostling to occupy the empty altars. Perhaps the ablest and most entertaining anatomy of this confusion was the satirical *roman-à-clef, The New Republic* (1877), by Froude's nephew W.H. Mallock. The novel is a dialogue, in the manner of Peacock, in which, thinly disguised, the leading prophets of the seventies — Huxley, Spencer, Jowett, Arnold, Ruskin and Pater — are the protagonists. It has been pointed out that the conflict between faith and scepticism in the mid-century was only possible because the disputants had so much in common: similar notions of fact, of veracity and of morality. But Mallock's book is consciously part of the aftermath; standards are divergent, cross-purposes and misunderstandings frequent, and there is a

10 Maitland, op. cit. p.144.

flippancy of tone which foreshadows the 1890s.

One major prophet is missing: Carlyle. He was an old man, and his direct influence was less frequently noted. But in the mid-Victorian period his persuasiveness for those whose Christian faith was lost had been immense. J.A. Froude, Carlyle's biographer, writing in 1890, is again an important witness:

> The present generation which has grown up in an open spiritual ocean, which has got used to it and has learned to swim for itself, will never know what it was to find the lights all drifting, the compasses all awry, and nothing left to steer by except the stars. In this condition the best and bravest of my own contemporaries determined to have done with insincerity, to find ground under their feet, to let the uncertain remain uncertain, but to learn how much and what we could honestly regard as true, and believe that, and live by it. Tennyson was the voice of this feeling in poetry; Carlyle ... in prose.[11]

What Froude found he could believe and live by was the voice of duty in the accents of Carlyle. The retort belongs to his friend Clough, long since dead, who had also been touched by Carlyle's influence:

> I tremble for something factitious,
> Some malpractice of the heart and illegitimate process,
> We are so prone to these things, with our terrible notions of
>   duty.

> *(Amours de Voyage*, 1849)

Froude did not tremble; there is little doubt that he was the more representative of his contemporaries.

11 J.A. Froude, *Carlyle's Life in London*, 2 vols (1890), Vol. I, p.311.

Select bibliography

General works
Chadwick, O. *The Victorian Church*. 2 vols. London, 1966.
Cockshut, A.O.J. *Anglican Attitudes*. London, 1959.
Cockshut, A.O.J. *The Unbelievers: English Agnostic Thought 1840-1890*. London, 1964.
Cockshut, A.O.J. *Religious Controversies of the Nineteenth Century*. London, 1966.
Houghton, W. *The Victorian Frame of Mind 1830-1870*. New Haven, Conn., 1957.
Symondson, A. (ed.) *The Victorian Crisis of Faith*. London, 1970.
Willey, B. *Nineteenth Century Studies*. London, 1949.
Willey, B. *More Nineteenth Century Studies: A Group of Honest Doubters*. London, 1956.

The Oxford Movement
Chadwick, O. *The Mind of the Oxford Movement*. London, 1960.
Chapman, R. *Faith and Revolt: Studies in the Literary Influence of the Oxford Movement*. London, 1970.
Prickett, S. *Romanticism and Religion: The Tradition of Wordsworth and Coleridge in the Victorian Church*. Cambridge, 1976.

Science and religion
Eiseley, L. *Darwin's Century*. London, 1959.
Gillespie, C.G. *Genesis and Geology: The Impact of Scientific Discoveries upon Religious Beliefs in the Decades before Darwin*. Cambridge, Mass., 1951.
Irvine, W. *Apes, Angels and the Victorians*. London, 1956.

Biography
Annan, N. *Leslie Stephen*. Harvard, 1952.
Faber, G. *Jowett: A Portrait with a Background*. London, 1957.
Newsome, D. *The Parting of Friends: A Study of the Wilberforces and Henry Manning*. London, 1966.

9 The role of women: from self-sacrifice to self-awareness

CAROL DYHOUSE

The many Victorian texts which attempted to define 'womanliness' or 'the feminine sphere of duties' were characterized by an insistence on the virtues of self-sacrifice. According to the formula of Mrs Ellis, one of the most popular writers on the subject, true womanly behaviour was inspired by 'the spirit of devotedness', or 'the power of throwing every consideration of self into the balance as nothing' when ministering unto men. In his well-known essay, *Of Queens' Gardens*, published in *Sesame and Lilies* (1865), Ruskin similarly emphasized his conviction that a woman should be educated 'not for self-development, but for self-renunciation'. Self-abnegation was not only prescribed as womanly, it was considered a religious duty. In *The Daughters of England* (1845) Mrs Ellis observed that she must take it for granted that her young reader, as a Christian woman, had already determined 'not to live for herself so much as others, but above all, not to live for this world, so much as for eternity'.

The total sacrifice of oneself to others and other-worldly goals was unlikely to be a painless process, but 'gentle resignation' or a 'quiet air of patient suffering' were held to enhance the beauty of a woman who strove towards the ideal. It was often assumed, in any case, that a woman was *born* to suffer. The respected physician Dr Gregory, for instance, in *A Father's Legacy to his Daughters* (1774) assured them:

Your whole life is often a life of suffering. You cannot plunge into business, or dissipate yourselves in pleasure and riot, as men too often do, when under the pressure of misfortunes. You must bear your sorrows in silence, unknown and unpitied. You must often put on a face of serenity and cheerfulness, when your hearts are torn with anguish, or sinking in despair.

A modern reader who finds many of the heroines of Victorian fiction curiously undeveloped in character should remember that in the eyes of the nineteenth-century reading public the very distinction of idealized figures such as Agnes in *David Copperfield*, Mrs Gaskell's Ruth or George Eliot's Romola depended upon their fathomless capacity for self-sacrifice, their absolute devotion to others. Both Ruth and Romola are martyrs, *Matres Dolorosae*, ultimately 'purified' by their suffering. Heroines who ventured any protest against the social expectations of the time were, at least until the 1860s, somewhat scarce. Caroline Helstone in Charlotte Brontë's *Shirley* reveals a healthy indignation when she asks herself whether there is not 'a terrible hollowness, mockery, want, craving, in that existence which is given away to others for want of something of your own to bestow on it', but she is protesting against what she perceives to be the socially prescribed role of the 'old maid', not of women in general.

If self-denial was extolled as a virtue of both male and female conduct, it was almost invariably prescribed for women in conjunction with the *passive* virtues of patience, resignation and silent suffering. In a man's education, self-denial was more generally associated with the *activist* ethic of self-help, hard work and self-reliance. These activist, 'Smilesian' values ranked high in the culture of Victorian England. A society that enshrined independence as one of the highest human virtues constantly emphasized the desirability of women being kept in a totally dependent role. It is not difficult to understand the feelings of indignity and resentment expressed by feminists who could only experience passivity as humiliating impotence.

The ideal of the dependent woman, confined to the domestic circle, was succinctly expressed in the writings of Ruskin and Coventry Patmore, who saw the home as a sanctuary, a haven of spirituality presided over by an ethereal angel-wife. Social theorists such as Herbert Spencer suggested that the dependence of women might be used as a measure of social progress. Spencer, like Auguste Comte, believed that in the 'highest type' of civilization women would be completely 'freed' or 'protected' from any kind of productive work outside the home. In view of ideals and theories of this kind, the fact that large numbers of women in nineteenth-century England had no choice other than to seek work outside the home, in order to support themselves or their families, was commonly seen by contemporaries as a definite social problem.

A life of considerable hardship undoubtedly awaited many of the middle-class women in Victorian times who needed to earn a living. Women educated for dependency might suddenly find themselves without support, and opportunities for remunerative employment were simply not there. Exactly how many single women must have sat at home like the Brontë sisters, racking their brains miserably to find alternatives to governessing, we shall never know, but a problem much commented upon by contemporaries was the problem of 'surplus women'. The census figures revealed a significant imbalance between the sexes in England and Wales; there were over half a million more women than men in the population at mid-century. Harriet Martineau, Jessie Boucherett and others protested angrily against society's inclination to regard the 'Old Maid' as an object of contempt rather than real sympathy, while it denied her the opportunity of leading a dignified life earning her own living.

Both William Thompson, in his *Appeal*, as early as 1825, and John Stuart Mill in *The Subjection of Women* (1869), protested against what they saw as the slave-like position of the dependent married woman, confined within the home. Most of the early feminists, however, tended to think of employment outside the home as an *alternative* to marriage; they rarely envisaged the possibility of combining the two. Around the turn of the present century, a growing number of feminists approached a more radical redefinition of the married woman's role. Emily Pfeiffer, in *Woman and Work* (1888), and Olive Schreiner, in *Woman and Labour* (1911), both pointed to the growing tendency, among the middle classes, to have smaller families than in the past. Time could lie heavily on the hands of the middle-aged woman whose children no longer required her ministrations. Like Mrs Transome in George Eliot's *Felix Holt*, these women might become painfully reminded that they had 'selves larger than their maternity'. There can be no doubt, however, that the majority of nineteenth-century feminists focused their attention on the plight of the *single* woman.

During the late 1850s and 1860s a group of middle-class feminists generally known as the Langham Place Circle on account of their headquarters, the Ladies' Institute in Langham Place, began an energetic campaign to widen the scope of employment available to women. Some recent historians have been inclined to emphasize the limitations of this movement. It may be argued that the inroads that women made into the professions in the nineteenth century were slight, and that when a significant expansion of employment opportunities did come about, late in the century, this was related to autonomous changes in the structure of the economy, having little or nothing to do with the demands of the feminists. Certainly the marked expansion of the service sector of the late Victorian economy, which opened up jobs in clerical and secretarial work, eventually made it easier for women to find work of some kind. But expanding opportunities for employment are not in themselves an adequate index of emancipation. The achievements of Victorian feminism have to be measured ultimately in terms of changing attitudes. In this respect, some of the most significant gains of the period 1860-1900 were made in the sphere of education.

The practice of educating middle-class girls in the first half of the century resembled (if it did not represent) a kind of decorative packaging of consumption goods for display in the marriage mart. Some of the earliest attempts to improve upon this notoriously flimsy process were born directly out of the realization that, even for a middle-class lady, employment might be necessary for survival. The feminists of the Langham Place Circle were always acutely aware of the expediency of combining their campaign to widen employment opportunities with pressure for educational reform. Jessie Boucherett, Adelaide Proctor, Barbara Bodichon and others were all involved in a variety of educational ventures. Emily Davies, also connected with the group in the 1860s, devoted the whole of her career to various schemes for improving the structure of secondary and higher education for middle-class girls. She was an inveterate opponent of any scheme of reform inspired by a conception of specifically feminine aptitude, of any suggestion of a curriculum especially tailored for women. At times she may have clung to her principles rather more obdurately than most, but many other feminists sympathized with her viewpoint. Frances Mary Buss, Sophia Jex-Blake and Barbara Bodichon were all driven by the conviction that, given the appropriate training, women might aspire to levels of success in academic and practical life on a par with those achieved by men. They certainly believed that girls needed to measure their ability against established intellectual standards in order to gain self-confidence, and to prove themselves capable of benefiting from whatever was deemed to be the best kind of education available at the time.

The North London Collegiate School for Girls, which was opened by Frances Buss in 1850, aimed to provide:

> such teaching as shall place the pupil *en rapport* with the world she is about to enter, and shall inculcate and inspire industry, frugality, self-dependence, self-control, a definite plan of life, the preference of the claims of the future to present enjoyment, and a steady self-advancement for the sake of others as well as for one's own.[1]

These aims and the ethos of the school amply reflected the 'Smilesian' ideology of the age. Pupils at the North London Collegiate were not encouraged to cherish any vision of leisured dependence as their goal in life. Both Frances Buss and Emily Davies continually emphasized the likelihood of a girl from a middle-class family needing to be able to earn a living of some kind. At the same time, they were certainly not blind to the fact that the majority of adolescent girls looked upon marriage as a preferable alternative. Both were interested in the effect of aspirations upon performance — it seemed to them crucial to encourage girls to define some kind of personal goal in life, vocational or otherwise, in addition to that of marriage, if they were to profit from any education offered to them. Maria Grey, who with her sister Emily Shirreff played a leading role in the formation of the Girls' Public Day School Company (1872), shared these convic-

---

1 M. Gurney, *Are We to Have Education for our Middle-Class Girls? Or, The History of Camden Collegiate Schools* (1872), p.9.

tions. In a paper delivered to the Social Science Congress in 1871, she argued:

> So long as marriage is held out as the only aim of a girl's life, ... So long will all attempts at improvement fail ... marriage should not be the first object of a woman's life, any more then of a man's; girls should be trained from childhood to the idea that they, like their brothers, must take their share in the work of life ... they should not only be allowed, but induced to work for their own maintenance.

In the 1860s the *Saturday Review* confidently predicted that the advocates of higher education for women were doomed to failure. It repeatedly reassured its readers that girls needed to be pleasing to men, and there was 'a strong and ineradicable male instinct that a learned, or even an over-accomplished, young woman' was 'one of the most intolerable monsters in creation'. Yet in the last quarter of a century academic achievement became a source of healthy pride among the growing numbers of women students who distinguished themselves in university examinations. The warnings voiced by medical practitioners and gynaecologists in the 1880s, who had argued that the risks of serious constitutional disturbance in university-educated women were disproportionately high, proved unfounded. Education itself gave women both the confidence and the competence to defend themselves against these pseudo-scientific arguments.

The movement to reform the education of the middle-class girl succeeded precisely in so far as Ruskin's maxim was turned on its head, and women were educated into self-respect rather than for self-abnegation; into a healthy awareness of their potential as human beings, capable of taking an interest in the world outside the home. Even by 1900, educational opportunities were still pitifully narrow; university studies were the preserve of a very small minority indeed. But without the general progress made in the educational sphere from the 1860s, the battles to secure the franchise fought between the 1890s and 1918 would probably have been long delayed.

We need to be cautious in handling evidence relating to working women's lives. Since the idea of the dependent woman lay at the heart of bourgeois notions of respectability, any historian has to some extent to try to discount the bias of middle-class Victorian observers who would automatically look upon women who worked with pity or indignation. Contemporaries were frequently shocked and confounded to discover that young girls, particularly in the cotton mills, sometimes valued their independence highly, and were inclined to delay marriage in order to prolong the enjoyment of a regular wage and the fellowship of the factory. Married women, equally, might welcome their return to the mill as a respite from home. Neither of these groups was likely to merit a sympathetic hearing from middle-class moralists, nor to feature as heroines in a novel by Elizabeth Gaskell, for instance, or Charlotte Elizabeth Tonna.

However, women workers in the cotton industry were in a comparatively favourable position — particularly in the second half of the century, when hours and conditions had been regularized, and during periods of steady employment. There is no doubt at all that most of the work available to women throughout the century was unskilled, very badly paid, and carried out in totally unenviable conditions. Certain 'sweated' trades like dressmaking attracted what was probably a disproportionate notoriety; in most industries women represented a pool of 'cheap and docile' labour, and they were commonly employed at a half or even a third of the wage which a man would have received for the same job. Even as late as 1900, by far the biggest single category of work available for women was indoor domestic service, which employed 1,330,783 women. While it is obviously hazardous to generalize about the conditions that prevailed in an infinite variety of private households, 'going into service' commonly offered the working-class girl an even less attractive prospect than did 'governessing slavery' her middle-class counterpart. Indeed, some measure of the unpopularity of domestic service can be derived from the alacrity with which, particularly towards the end of the century when openings were widening, girls seem to have seized upon opportunities for almost any other kind of employment.

Self-sacrifice was something built into the very structure of many working women's lives. If mill-girls sometimes realized all too clearly that marriage might herald the beginning of a lifetime of hardship, of repeated pregnancies and of a constant struggle to feed a growing family on an inadequate income, perhaps the majority of single girls still found the circumstances of earning their own living so uncongenial that they dreamed of marriage as an escape. Many must have found their illusions rudely shattered in later life. In any case, a large number of working-class wives had no choice other than to seek work outside the home in order to supplement the family income, or even to maintain the family entirely when their husbands were unemployed. Widows with young children usually led lives of incalculable hardship, as the Minority Report on the Poor Law emphasized in 1909.

Working-class women rarely kept diaries; we know very little about their attitudes to their own lives. In 1915 the Women's Co-operative Guild published a volume entitled *Maternity: Letters from Working Women*, representing a series of letters from working-class women describing their experience of childbearing in late Victorian and early twentieth-century Britain. The women who wrote these letters were almost all from families where the husband was comparatively well paid by the average standards of the working class at the time, yet they refer to continual shortages of money for food. It was common for a woman to stint herself in order to feed her husband and family. Pregnancy, as Herbert Samuel recognized in his preface to the volume, meant the onset of a period of especial hardship for the working woman, who had to scrape and save precisely at the time when she ought to have been well nourished, in order to put by money for the inevitable expenses of her confinement. Many of the letters reflect an acceptance of hardship as inevitable; some are tempered, here and there, by a lively undercurrent of resentment at what could indeed be perceived as the selfishness of men; others are imbued with a near-fatalistic attitude to the overwork, ill health and suffering which constituted such a large part of these women's lives.

The complaint that working women tended to be apathetic, indifferent, even passively resigned to their own exploitation, was often voiced by those who applied themselves to the task of encouraging trade-union organizations among women in the late nineteenth century. A witness before the Royal Commission on Labour in 1893-4 argued that one of the reasons why the long hours and miserable conditions suffered by many of the shop-girls in London had gone so long unchecked was that the girls had 'the patience and endurance of martyrs' and rarely complained. The matter was put in a nutshell by the Honorary Secretary of the Leeds Society of Workwomen: 'Trade Unionism means rebellion,' she pointed out, 'and the orthodox teaching for women is submission.'[2] The problems that confronted organizers were daunting in the extreme. Low earnings, in part a reflection of the absence of union protection, also made it difficult for women to afford regular subscriptions. Married women workers found it almost impossible to find the time to participate in union affairs. 'When a man has done his day's work he becomes free,' argued Will Thorne, of the Gasworkers' and General Labourers' Union, 'and that is not so with women.'[3]

Nineteenth-century feminism has often been portrayed as a middle-class movement which remained almost wholly out of touch with the problems of working-class women, but although true in some respects the picture has probably been exaggerated. A good deal has been written about the careers of figures like Eleanor Marx and Annie Besant, both of whom combined their feminist perspective with socialism and were involved in trade-union activity among women in the 1880s. From the 1860s onwards a growing number of middle-class women of all shades of political opinion and outlook worked energetically to promote the various kinds of organization which they believed would enable working women to learn strategies of self-defence, to secure some measure of control over their lives and conditions of employment. Pioneers of women's trade-union organization like Emma Paterson, Emily Faithfull, Emilia Dilke and Clementina Black have as yet received little recognition from historians.

The Women's Trade Union League (originally 'The Women's Protective and Provident League') had been founded by Emma Paterson in 1874. In its early years the League's effectiveness as an instrument for improving wages and conditions was constrained by an official determination to work mainly for harmony between employers and employed. Strikes were deprecated, and energies channelled into the 'Provident' rather than the 'Protective' side of the movement. Against a background of social unrest and 'New

2 Quoted in B. Drake, *Women in Trade Unions* (London, n.d.), p.41.
3 Ibid. p.42.

Union' activity in the 1880s, and stimulated by the challenge of the more radical elements among its own membership, the League embarked upon a more active phase of its history.

One aspect of this departure was an energetic campaign to encourage male trade unions to open their ranks to women. The earlier policy had favoured the promotion of separate women's organizations, a policy that had stemmed in part from the stubborn hostility of many male trade-unionists to the idea of female membership. In 1889 a scheme was devised whereby any union admitting women was invited to affiliate with the League at the cost of a halfpenny per annum per female member; in return, the League offered the services of a woman organizer. This proved highly successful, and between fifty and sixty societies took advantage of the offer in the 1890s.

One factor that impeded cooperation among those who sought variously to further the interests of working women in the late nineteenth century was a major controversy over the question of factory legislation for women. According to the Marquess of Salisbury, the principle of factory legislation in Britain had always been to protect 'those who, for some reason or other, are subject to other people, and are not able to take care of themselves',[4] in other words, women and children. This attitude infuriated some feminists: Emma Paterson, Jessie Boucherett and the Fawcetts, for instance, remained obdurately opposed to legal restrictions on specifically female employment on the grounds that these would handicap women with no choice other than to compete with men in the labour market. Equally important was the conviction shared by many feminists and trade-unionists that women needed to learn self-defence through the principles of combination rather than rely upon the protective legislation imposed by a male Parliament. The issues were debated with a good deal of acrimony on all sides. Beatrice Webb, for instance, wrote savagely accusing feminists and 'capitalists' wives and daughters' of having confused working women in regard to their real interests, by exaggerating the importance of personal freedom and obscuring the benefits of factory regulation.[5] During the 1890s the policy of the Women's

4 Debate in House of Lords on Factory and Workshops Bill, 23 July 1891. Reprinted from Hansard in pamphlet form (1891), p.4.
5 B. Webb, *Women and the Factory Acts*, Fabian Tract No. 67 (1896), p.9.

Trade Union League swung in favour of the idea of protective legislation for women, abandoning its original stance, defined by Emma Paterson, of opposition. Members who looked askance on this departure tended to join separate societies, such as the Women's Employment Defence League, which had the object of opposing any further restrictions on female labour.

Even at the end of the century, many organizations of working-class women, particularly outside the textile industry, continued to rely fairly heavily upon middle-class leadership and support. It was partly Emma Paterson's desire to free the women's trade-union movement from the middle-class tutelage of the League that had prompted her to found a Women's Trades Council in 1882, but this venture had only survived her own death (in 1886) by two years. The outlook among those who sought to encourage the development of independent unionism among working women cannot, even by 1900, have been unduly sanguine: the 1901 census revealed that, out of a total of 4,171,751 women and girls returned as being occupied, only 122,047 belonged to a trade union of any kind. Even so, it should be emphasized that membership figures had more than trebled between 1884 and 1900. Further, the problems of the female wage-earner had attracted a good deal of publicity during these years. The Royal Commission on Labour reported on women's employment in 1894, and the same year saw the foundation of the Women's Industrial Council, an organization that operated as a central bureau for research into many aspects of women's work until the outbreak of the First World War.

During the second half of the nineteenth century, middle-class patterns of domestic life, embodying the ideal of the husband as breadwinner who kept his wife at home, began to filter down the social scale. Rising real wages, particularly in skilled occupations after 1870, helped to raise the social aspirations of working men, who felt increasingly that a wife who went out to work constituted some kind of slur on their capability as male providers for the family. State elementary schools probably played an important role in conditioning this social outlook in the last decades of the century. School readers with titles like *Girls at Home* (1895) both reflected and transmitted the values and attitudes of the respectable middle class. Ironically, the period in which the ideals of the feminist minority began to make their impact on the education of the middle-class girl was also the period in which the curriculum of her Board School counterpart was shaped by a mounting emphasis upon skills of domestic economy and housecraft. This tendency can be seen partly as a response to the pressures of those who believed that either social stability, on the one hand, or the solution to a variety of social problems (ranging from temperance reform to the servant shortage), on the other, depended upon upgrading the status of housework among schoolgirls and strengthening the nation's homes.

Given the conspicuously unattractive prospects of women in the labour market, many wives of working men would have welcomed the opportunity of staying at home. It is equally certain, however, that many of these women came to feel oppressed by the drudgery of the domestic routine and the social isolation which so often followed. In 1901 Seebohm Rowntree felt constrained to comment on the lives of the better-paid workmens' wives whom he visited while investigating social conditions in York:

> No-one can fail to be struck by the monotony which charac-
> terises the life of most married women of the working-class.
> Probably this monotony is least marked in the slum districts
> where life is lived more in common, and where the women
> are constantly in and out of each other's houses, or meet and
> gossip in the courts and streets. But with advance in the social
> scale, family life becomes more private, and the women, left
> in the house all day while their husbands are at work, are
> largely thrown upon their own resources. These, as a rule, are
> sadly limited, and in the deadening monotony of their lives
> these women too often become mere hopeless drudges.[6]

The position of the housebound woman of the working class was far less enviable than that of her middle-class counterpart. She had no spare money for domestic help. In the evenings and at weekends, as Rowntree pointed out, her husband was likely to seek relaxation with his mates in the pub, leaving his wife alone yet again with their children. Lacking education and deprived of adult companionship, her life was often cripplingly narrow.

The growth of the Womens' Co-operative Guild, founded in

6 B.S. Rowntree, *Poverty: A Study in Town Life* (London, 1901), pp.77-8.

1883, pointed to a new self-awareness and self-assertion among women of this kind. The twin objects of the Guild were first, as the name implies, to foster the growth of cooperative ideals; and, second, to combat the isolation and impotence of married working-class women in the home. The range of activity was wide: in the late nineteenth century Guildswomen worked in harness with other feminist organizations seeking to promote trade-unionism among women, and voicing the demand for suffrage; after 1900 they were to play an important role in campaigning for public provision for maternal health and infant welfare. Between 1883 and the 1920s, however, some of the most important activities took place at the local level. By the 1890s, the Guild had managed to build up a network of more than 100 branches, and under the energetic leadership of Margaret Llewellyn Davies, who served as General Secretary between 1889 and 1921, many branches developed an enduring interest in educational projects. Discussion groups received advice on possible courses of study, with recommended reading lists, from Guild headquarters. Branch secretaries were continually urged to try to wean the attention of their members away from 'housewifely' or domestic subjects, and to stimulate an active interest in social and political affairs.

Readers of D.H. Lawrence's novel, *Sons and Lovers* (1913), will remember how Mrs Morel finds self-respect and a new purpose in life from her work for the Bestwood branch of the Womens' Co-operative Guild:

> when the children were old enough to be left, Mrs Morel joined the Womens' Guild. It was a little club of women attached to the Co-operative Wholesale Society, which met on Monday night in the long room over the grocery shop of the Bestwood 'Co-op'. The women were supposed to discuss the benefits to be derived from co-operation and other social questions. Sometimes Mrs Morel read a paper. It seemed queer to the children to see their mother who was always fussy about the house, sitting writing in her rapid fashion, thinking, referring to books, and writing again. They felt for her on such occasions the deepest respect.

Lawrence describes how these activities were resented by hostile husbands, who found their wives getting too independent, and referred to the Guild deprecatingly as the 'clat-fart shop — that is, the gossip-shop'. He explained this by showing that the discussions provided a new frame of reference, a new standard of comparison whereby 'the women could look at their homes, at the conditions of their own lives, and find fault'.

The opportunities for study and discussion groups pioneered by the Guild undoubtedly helped a small but significant section of working women to gain confidence through expressing their views in public, simultaneously helping them to move towards an objective awareness of their problems and social position. This new self-awareness could certainly have the effect of disturbing many men, and Lawrence's insights are corroborated by the testimony of Alice Acland, the founder of the Guild, who later recorded the kinds of suspicion her efforts had encountered in the 1880s. In the first instance, the feminists of that period, she remembered, 'were sometimes strange in their personal appearance. Co-operative menfolk were fearful that I intended to lead their wives and daughters to adopt similar styles of dress and speech. So I had to walk with the utmost caution.'[7]

More importantly, she recollected how she had been charged with 'stirring up unrest and discontent among the women'. Looking back with the benefit of hindsight from the year 1921, she believed that she had merely given voice to the unrest, to that 'desire for a wider outlook that was rising in the minds of all women' towards the end of the Victorian era.

The Victorian discussion over the nature of woman's role in society reached its height in the 1890s, a decade in which most newspapers, magazines and respectable monthly journals featured articles on 'The Woman Question' — some of them sociological and serious, many polemical and satirical in vein. A number of catchphrases were coined to describe the 'emancipated' women of the time. The 'Unwomanly Woman', for instance, was introduced by G.B. Shaw in *The Quintessence of Ibsenism* (1891). More enduringly, 'The New Woman' emerged as a commonplace of journalistic observation, taking her place, as Holbrook Jackson pointed out, alongside 'The New Hedonism', 'New Realism', 'New Unionism', and

7 Quoted in C. Webb, *The Woman with the Basket* (Manchester, 1927), pp.21-2.

numerous other *fin-de-siècle* social phenomena celebrated for their fashionable modernity.

The production in London of Ibsen's play *A Doll's House* in 1889 aroused a storm of public controversy. In a series of famous articles published in the *Daily Telegraph*, Clement Scott waged war against what he considered to be Ibsen's poisonous and subversive doctrines, his defamation of the sacred temple of the home and family life. Walter Besant, who had already revealed a deep-rooted antipathy towards feminism in his satirical novel *The Revolt of Man* (1882), wrote a short story entitled *The Doll's House — And After*, which appeared in *The English Illustrated Magazine* (January 1890). This cautionary tale catalogued an exaggerated series of disasters which Besant imagined Nora's wickedness might have perpetrated upon her family — her husband driven to drink, her son to forgery, her daughter to suicide. Other alternative sequels to *A Doll's House*, penned by defenders of Ibsen, like Shaw, Israel Zangwill and Eleanor Marx, soon followed.[8] In *The Quintessence of Ibsenism* Shaw addressed himself to the defence of the 'Unwomanly Woman', by which he meant women who, like Nora, challenged the cherished conventional belief that women found their supreme fulfilment in sacrificing themselves wholly to the interests of husband or child. 'No man', argued Shaw, 'would ever pretend that his soul found supreme satisfaction in self-sacrifice.'

The 'New', 'Unwomanly' woman quickly became a popular subject in both drama and fiction, often playing a leading role in novels that explored problems of conventional marriage and married life. Among the best-known works by English writers interested in both 'The Woman Question' and 'The Marriage Question' in this decade were Thomas Hardy's *Jude the Obscure* (1895), George Gissing's *The Odd Women* (1893) and Grant Allen's notorious bestseller, *The Woman Who Did* (1895). There was also a host of minor works by woman novelists of the 1890s which I shall return to shortly.

Some idea of the popular image of the 'New Woman' in the 1890s can be gleaned from the pages of *Punch*, particularly between 1893 and 1895. She was generally middle class and

8 G.B. Shaw, 'Still After The Doll's House', *Time* (February 1890); E. Marx and I. Zangwill, 'A Doll's House Repaired', *Time* (March 1891).

educated — almost invariably at Girton or Newnham; she smoked, rode a bicycle, and eschewed the frills and furbelows of conventional femininity in favour of tweedy knickerbockers or 'rational dress'. The 'New Woman' was often depicted perusing the pages of 'advanced' or 'decadent' literature — Ibsen or Zola, George Egerton or *The Yellow Book*. The stereotype frequently figures in the minor literature of the 1890s, such as Grant Allen's novel, *The Typewriter Girl* (1897), for instance, or Lynn Linton's *The One Too Many* (1894). There were slight variations on the general motif. Sometimes the 'New Woman' was shown as a neurotic prey to hysteria and morbid self-analysis, with a constitution allegedly enfeebled by over-education and too much strain on the intellect — Laura, in *The One Too Many*, is a good example of this type, while Sue Bridehead in *Jude The Obscure* shares some of the same characteristics. Alternatively, the 'advanced woman' was likely to be credited with a hale and hearty constitution; with a bluff good humour likely to manifest itself in backslapping or the tendency to refer to intimates (whether male or female) as 'jolly good chaps'. She was nothing if not self-possessed, given to advertising her 'advanced views' without blushing and usually, of course, in a loud voice. Effie Chegwin in *The One Too Many*, and Sylvia Craven in Shaw's *The Philanderer* (1907) illustrate this second variant. In both cases the 'New Woman' is caricatured as a social deviant — and both imply pathology — in the first case, neuroticism, or mental instability, in the second, a sexual ambivalence or tendency toward androgyny.

To some extent these stereotypes of 'The New Woman' reveal more about the psychological anxieties of a society confronted by the demands of the feminists than about the character of the feminist movement itself. The feminist and suffragist organizations of the 1890s tended to be dominated by women who were preoccupied with establishing the 'respectability' of their movement. They were anxious to avoid any association with radical, unconventional behaviour or 'advanced views' on explosive issues like sexual morality and personal freedom. In their keen desire to forestall any reputation for impropriety or eccentricity, many feminists angrily dismissed the literary image of the 'New Woman' as a figment of the journalistic imagination or, more commonly, of degenerate male fantasy.

A novel that particularly enraged feminists was Grant Allen's *The Woman Who Did*, published in 1895. Grant Allen, a prolific journalist and writer on popular scientific subjects, had developed a somewhat ambiguous perspective on 'The Woman Question', which preoccupied his attention increasingly in the 1880s and 1890s. A freethinker who rebelled against what he saw as the constraints and hypocrisies of conventional marriage, he saw himself as a leading advocate of both women's emancipation and the 'Higher Social Morality'. At the same time he confessed himself acutely afraid that women bent on securing freedom would overlook what he considered to be a cardinal principle of natural law; namely that women could only ever find their true fulfilment in maternity.[9] *The Woman Who Did* was a supremely bathetic tale of a heroine possessed by a sense of mission to regenerate society, which she believed she would best achieve by refusing to marry and raising her illegitimate child alone. Not inappropriately, the novel was described by W.T. Stead as a 'fin-de-siècle apocalypse' — it went through at least twenty editions, earning its author about £1000 p.a. in royalties, in addition to a dreadful reputation. The public was scandalized, the feminists appalled. Millicent Garrett Fawcett felt obliged to publish a savagely satirical article on *The Woman Who Did* in the *Contemporary Review* (1895). The novel itself she found 'feeble and silly to the last degree': Grant Allen's claim to be writing in support of the Woman's Movement was spurious in the extreme. Women were claiming rights of citizenship, Mrs Fawcett emphasized: they wanted social and economic independence; they were certainly not clamouring for anything like 'free love' or the destruction of family life. Altogether, the novel seemed calculated to do a grave misservice to the cause.

The Woman Who Did quickly became a byword for the whole genre of minor popular fiction which focused on the 'New Woman' in the 1890s. In Shaw's play *Getting Married*, for instance, published in 1908, Edith was to be found reading a pamphlet with the title *Do you know what you are going to do?* by 'A Woman Who Has Done It'. The topical literature of the late nineteenth century included a large number of works by women writers like George

9 Grant Allen, 'Plain Words on the Woman Question', *Fortnightly Review*, 46 (1889).

Egerton (Mrs Clairmonte), Emma Frances Brooke, Mona Caird and
Menie Muriel Dowie, all of whom were primarily interested in
exploring the problems of feminine psychology and sexual identity.
These works are well worth unearthing from obscurity, not on
account of any intrinsic literary merit, but rather for their significance for social history.

Along with more important novels like Hardy's *Jude the
Obscure*, the whole of this literature was castigated as 'degenerate'
by what Havelock Ellis dubbed 'the wholesome school' of writers
and literary critics. The average writer of this school, he pointed
out, tended to believe that 'the life of a pure-natured English-
woman after marriage' was 'mainly that of a very broody hen, a
series of merely physiological processes with which he, as a novelist,
had no further concern'.[10] The tone of this 'wholesome school' of
criticism is well conveyed in two articles which were written by
Hugh E.M. Stutfield for *Blackwoods Magazine* in the 1890s, the
first entitled *Tommyrotics* (June 1895), the second, *The Psychology
of Feminism* (January 1897). Stutfield's argument was buttressed
with numerous references to the German critic Max Nordau's
work, *Degeneration*, a grandiose condemnation of the late nineteenth-century *Zeitgeist* which had been translated into English in
1895. Stutfield believed that the interest in 'psychological realism',
which he considered the main feature of the 'new fiction' in
England, was a product of social and artistic decadence. The recent
explosion of writing by those whom he would refer to as 'the yellow
lady novelists' represented one of the most disturbing symptoms of
this decadence. Stimulated on the one hand by the writings of
Ibsen or the 'Scandinavian doctrine of the ego', on the other by
'the unbridled licentiousness' of Continental realism, women
writers in England were developing a tendency towards morbid
introspection, or a constant obsession with self, that he believed
could only be described as pathological.

A cursory glance through some of the stories by George Egerton,
or the work of writers like Sarah Grand or Mona Caird, may well
convince the reader that some of Stutfield's allegations were not
altogether unfounded. For this literature presents us with a

10 Havelock Ellis, *Concerning Jude the Obscure*, first published in *Savoy Magazine*
(October 1896), reprinted (London, 1931), pp.12-13.

complex and often confused picture of women who were struggling towards selfconsciousness. Both egocentricity and a certain obsession with questions of identity were probably inevitable if women were to compensate for that abasement of self-concern relentlessly prescribed for them throughout the Victorian era. In order to be themselves, as Virginia Woolf was to perceive later in the twentieth century, women had to murder the phantom of the 'Angel in the House', who 'sacrificed herself daily, to others'. [11] In attempting to diagnose those tendencies in contemporary literature which he was most anxious to condemn, Stutfield observed that as an ideal of feminine behaviour, 'self-sacrifice is out of fashion altogether in our modern school novelists, and self-development has taken its place'. This tendency, he added ruefully, was 'of recent growth, it was unknown to our mothers and grandmothers'.

We may reject his censoriousness, while still admitting that he was very largely right.

Select bibliography

Basch, F. *Relative Creatures: Victorian Women in Society and the Novel 1837-67*. London, 1974.
Hewitt, M. *Wives and Mothers in Victorian Industry*. London, 1958.
Holbrook Jackson. *The 1890s*. Harmondsworth, 1913.
Holcombe, L. *Victorian Ladies at Work*. Newton Abbot, 1973.
Kamm, J. *Hope Deferred*. London, 1965.
Millett, K. *Sexual Politics*. London, 1971.
Neff, W.F. *Victorian Working Women*. London, 1929.
Pinchbeck, 1. *Women Workers and the Industrial Revolution*. London, 1930.
Rowbotham, S. *Hidden from History*. London, 1973.
Showalter, E. *A Literature of Their Own: English Woman Novelists from Brontë to Lessing*. Princeton, 1977.
Strachey, R. *The Cause*. London, 1928.
Turner, S. *Equality for Some: The Story of Girls' Education*. London, 1974.
Vicinus, M. (ed.) *Suffer and be Still: Women in the Victorian Age*. Bloomington, Ind., and London, 1973.

11 V. Woolf, *Professions for Women*, in *Collected Essays*, ed. Leonard Woolf (London, 1966), Vol. II (1967 ed., p.285).

Part III

Literature and society

10 An essay on *Dombey and Son*

LAURENCE LERNER

As this book has tried to show, an early Victorian observer of landscape and people must have been aware of change, whether brought by factory chimneys to the green meadows, or by new work conditions to human intercourse. If any one thing represented that change to contemporaries, it was probably the railway. The first line (Stockton to Darlington) had been opened in 1825; building began in earnest ten years later, and in the mid-forties there was a railway boom — 2000 miles of line in 1843, 5000 by 1846 The railways were important in many ways. Their cuttings and tunnels transformed the landscape; their belching fires were violent and vivid evidence of the new energy of steam. And they had created new experiences. It was now possible to get from London to Paris in twelve hours: no one had ever travelled at that speed before. Both work and leisure were transformed: three years after *Dombey and Son* was published, special excursion trains were bringing thou-sands of working men and their families to London to see the Great Exhibition. England had become smaller. And the railways meant money: there were fortunes to be made by investors — and savings to be lost, if they were so unfortunate as to invest with George Hudson, the railway king, the blunt entrepreneur who was three times Lord Mayor of York, became a millionaire, and then went bankrupt.

This was only one (thought perhaps the most obvious) of the new achievements of industrial capitalism. Economic enterprise was changing human relationships, and birth and breeding were no longer the only keys to social importance: now there was a new class who had risen from poverty to wealth, sometimes very rapidly. The most famous analysis of this change is that of Marx, who asserted that the bourgeoisie had 'torn asunder the motley feudal ties that bound man to his "natural superiors", and left no other nexus between man and man than naked selfishness, than callous "cash payment".' As units of production grew larger, so the small manufacturer found himself squeezed out: factories replaced cottage industries, and machines replaced craftsmen. The most famous example of this was the handloom weavers (see Chapter 3) who had proliferated to fill a technological niche in the 1790s, and by the 1840s were unable to compete with the power looms. The whole process of industrialism makes work more impersonal, and the readily available symbol of this impersonality is money. The possibility of reducing any goods or activities to their monetary value reveals an abstract way of thinking about men and what they do, an implication that the whole variety of man's achievement can be measured by a standard that ignores the complexity of actual being. Such an abstract scale is necessary for economic organization, but it has always been felt to have dangerous implications. Marx called money 'the alienated activity of mankind'; and modern neo-Marxist terminology regards it as the reification of capitalist activity — the attribution of real existence to a convenient but misleading fiction.

Another great consequence of the Industrial Revolution was the increase in social mobility. In such economic upheaval there were bound to be rearrangements of power and status. Belief in the possibility of rising from humble origins to riches by means of diligence and prudence was central to early Victorian ideology. Its most famous exponent was Samuel Smiles, and the doctrine of self-help clearly assumes a world in which social advancement is both possible and desirable. Beatrice Webb's mother believed that 'it was the bounden duty of every citizen to better his social status; to ignore those beneath him, and to aim steadily at the top of the ladder.'[1] Palmerston saw his society as one 'in which every class in society accepts with cheerfulness the lot which Providence has

1 Beatrice Webb, *My Apprenticeship* (London, 1926), ch. 1.

assigned to it; while at the same time every individual of each class is constantly striving to raise himself in the social scale.'[2] Self-help is the ideology of social mobility.

There, then, in brief is a view of Victorian England, a view which previous chapters of this book have tried to set forth at greater length. All aspects of this view can be found in *Dombey and Son*. The railway is very prominent, from the moment when we see Staggs Gardens, home of the Toodle family, looking as if rent by 'the first shock of a great earthquake'.

> Here, a chaos of carts, overthrown and jumbled together, lay topsy-turvy at the bottom of a steep unnatural hill; there, confused treasures of iron soaked and rusted in something that had accidentally become a pond. Everywhere were bridges that led nowhere; thoroughfares that were wholly impassable; Babel towers of chimneys, wanting half their height.
>
> (chapter 6)

The main feeling here is of enormous energy — destructive, but at the same time exhilarating and creative. The vitality of the prose ('everywhere were bridges that led nowhere') seems to refute any negative feelings that the details might arouse. That steep unnatural hill is as much of an achievement as a monstrosity. For a parallel in Dickens's work, we can turn to *Bleak House*. George the Trooper, on his way to visit Mr Rouncewell the Ironmaster (chapter 63), enters the iron country with its 'coalpits and ashes, high chimneys and red bricks, blighted verdure, scorching fires and a heavy never-lightening cloud of smoke.' This looks at first like dirt and destruction; but once again, as we read on, the description turns out to be warm and favourable. George enters the town 'swart with the dust of the coal roads', and the poetic adjective takes some of the dirt out of being black. He meets one of Rouncewell's hands, and discovers that this new town has a kind of feudal loyalty and pride in its master. Chesney Wold, over which the Dedlocks have ruled for centuries, is a place where you quarrel with your neighbours; it is here, in the manufacturing world that Sir Leicester Dedlock despises, that true community is to be found. Rouncewell's

2 Lord Palmerston in the Don Pacifico debate in the Commons, 1850. Quoted in Asa Briggs, 'The Language of ''Class'' in Early Nineteenth Century England', in Briggs and Saville (eds), *Essays in Labour History* (1960).

hands are at home in their world of muck and brass: 'they are very sinewy and strong, are Rouncewell's hands — a little sooty too.' And none the worse for that, we are clearly meant to feel.

Left alone in Rouncewell's office, George looks round on the unfamiliar scene:

> Tumbled together on the table are some pieces of iron, purposely broken to be tested at various periods of their service, in various capacities. There is iron-dust on everything and the smoke is seen, through the windows, rolling heavily out of the tall chimneys, to mingle with the smoke from a vaporous Babylon of other Chimneys.

The iron is broken as Staggs Gardens was torn open; and once again the energy is seen as a sign of human ingenuity and enterprise. The image of the Babel of chimneys, found in both passages, is not meant to carry any real religious overtones: Dickens is not hinting at the blasphemy of human achievement, as a seventeenth-century writer might have done. The effect is that of an untidy but liberating power, and the prose contains the energy it is celebrating. It is as if Dickens writes with the energy of the Industrial Revolution itself.

When Dickens died, Ruskin wrote to Charles Eliot Norton that though the literary loss was infinite,

> the political one I care less for than you do. Dickens was a pure modernist — a leader of the steam-whistle party *par excellence*.... His hero is essentially the ironmaster: in spite of *Hard Times*, he has advanced by his influence every principle that makes them harder.[3]

Hard Times is Dickens's most famous vision of industrialism, and its unrelenting hostile picture of Coketown has given him the reputation of an enemy of what industrialism was doing to England. But Ruskin was right in placing him on the other side. Bounderby, the industrialist of *Hard Times*, a savage parody of self-help, brutal to his workmen, constantly boasting that he was born in a ditch, must be set against Rouncewell, the true believer in the

3 Ruskin to Charles Eliot Norton, 19 June 1870. Quoted in Stephen Wall (ed.), *Dickens*, Penguin Critical Anthologies (Harmondsworth, 1970).

new, open society; indeed, Bounderby himself is not really an attack on self-help, but on fraudulent claims to it, and the follower of Samuel Smiles could feel his doctrine confirmed as he reflects that the unacceptable face of capitalism turns out to belong to a liar. The horrors of machinery in Coketown must be set against the delight shown by Dickens in the activity of Chatham dockyard: 'twelve hundred hammerers, measurers, caulkers, armourers, forgers, smiths, shipwrights; twelve hundred dingers, clashers, dongers, rattlers, clinkers, bangers bangers bangers.' (*The Uncommercial Traveller*, 26.)

Let us return to the railway, whose role in *Dombey and Son* is steadily beneficient. In chapter 20 we are taken on a railway journey to Leamington with Mr Dombey and Major Bagstock, a bravura passage in which Dickens attempts to reproduce the rhythm of the journey and the bewildering interest of the landscape. Mr Toodle, husband of Paul's nurse, is stoker on that train (later he is promoted to engine-driver, virtue being rewarded in the best Smilesian manner). At home, he is a picture of working-class contentment: 'Mr Toodle, sinewy and swart, was refreshing himself with tea, in the bosom of his family' (chapter 38). Swart again: the word is clearly a label for honest dirt, the badge of industry and satisfaction in work. In relation to Toodle, the railway is realistically presented, and its economic benefits are shown; in relation to Carker it is given a very different, almost allegorical treatment — the train which kills him as a kind of destroying angel: 'He uttered a shriek — looked round — saw the red eyes, bleared and dim, in the daylight, close upon him — was beaten down ... ' (chapter 55). The broken syntax and the dashes convey not only Carker's terror but the very different way in which the train is now seen. Its function is here no longer economic but moral, the instrument of divine punishment.

As well as the railway, *Dombey and Son* shows us the world of finance and the depersonalizing effect of money. Money is perhaps the main theme of the novel: on the title page (probably drawn to Dickens's instructions) is an elaborate framework of ledgers, cash boxes and receipts, held up on one side by a structure of cards. The full title, 'Dealings with the Firm of Dombey and Son', announces the financial theme, and the opening chapter announces immediately the irony of the 'and Son'. To Dombey the child is a necessary completion of the firm's name, not a human being in his own right. That is why Dombey does not love his daughter: her existence has no commercial importance. Dombey's view of the world is depersonalized in just the way that money depersonalizes. The most famous illustration of this is the hiring of Mrs Toodle. Paul's mother having died giving birth to him, it is necessary to engage a wet-nurse, and Dombey insists on regarding this as a purely commercial transaction. 'I desire to make it a question of wages altogether,' he says; and in order to depersonalize Polly Toodle he insists that she be known 'as — say as Richards — an ordinary name, and convenient'. In order to keep it a 'question of wages' Dombey insists:

> It is not at all in this bargain that you need become attached to my child, or that my child need become attached to you.... When you go away from here, you will have concluded what is a mere matter of bargain and sale, hiring and letting: and will stay away. The child will cease to remember you; and you will cease to remember the child. (chapter 2)

Of course this does not happen; and the refusal of human feeling to submit to this alienated activity of hiring and letting is seen when Paul asks for his old nurse on his deathbed, and Dombey is forced into the humiliation of sending for Polly, whom he had earlier dismissed in disgrace. All this has been often pointed out — though no critic, I think, has remarked that the name Richards does in fact stick, and is used by some of the good characters. Do we take this as a sign that the touch of commerce has left its mark on Polly after all; or that even the name given her as a sign of the impersonality of the bargain can be turned to something human and meaningful?

If we are looking for examples of the alienating effect of urban life on human beings, we can find it in one of the most striking features of Dickens's writing, his habit of seeing people as things. No example of this is more striking than Mr Wemmick, the lawyer's clerk in *Great Expectations*, who leads two lives, a warm domestic life in his toy castle at Walworth, and a grim money-making life among criminals and legal machinery at his office. When they walk to work in the morning Wemmick 'got dryer and harder as we went along, and his mouth tightened into a post-office again'. Critics have understandably seen this as the registering of a frightening process: 'He is a schematic and limited, but poetic, embodiment of the utterly alienated man of modern capitalist civilisation.'

Social mobility too can be found in *Dombey and Son*. Like most of Dickens's novels, it offers a panoramic view of English society, and sees some classes rising and some falling. There are two main examples of decline, very different from each other. One is Sol Gills the instrument maker, the kind of old-fashioned craftsman who is overtaken by change. He lives at his shop in the Strand, by the sign of the Wooden Midshipman (the quaint old figure symbolizing the old-fashioned nature of the enterprise). Old gentlemen pause and stare in the window — one of them looks at a ship's telescope 'with all his might and main' — but they never come in to buy. He arouses curiosity, but no longer attracts customers.

The other case of decline is found among the aristocracy. The English commercial classes have always married into the aristocracy, offering money in exchange for birth, and rescuing the fortunes of those who can no longer afford to keep up their traditional position. This is exactly what happens in Mr Dombey's second marriage, and the aristocratic family he marries into is particularly helpless and seedy. It has no young men; but it has Cousin Feenix, who comes from Baden-Baden to give away the bride. '"Confound it," Cousin Feenix says — good natured creature, Cousin Feenix — "when we *do* get a rich City fellow into the family, let us show him some attention; let us do something for him."' The aristocracy, we notice, speak with more directness than the bourgeoisie: Mr Dombey would not have described the situation quite so bluntly. Of course Dickens is mocking Cousin Feenix when he calls him 'good natured', but it is not merely mockery: the broken-down old gentleman's vagueness is seen as somehow preferable to the self-interested ingratiations of Carker, or the chilly correctness of Mr Dombey; and at the end of the novel Feenix (like Sir Leicester Dedlock in *Bleak House*) is shown to have passed a moral test. Dickens is at his best in the dialogue of Cousin Feenix, and there is sharp social observation in the humour. His anecdotes are rambling and pointless, and interspersed with constant assertions that whoever he is speaking to must know whoever he is speaking of:

> I dare say my friend Dombey ... may remember Jack Adams,
> Jack Adams, not Joe; that was his brother. Jack — little Jack —
> man with a cast in his eye, and slight impediment in his
> speech — man who sat for somebody's borough ...
>
> (chapter 36)

This is the speech of someone who assumes a restricted circle, in which everyone knows everyone — an inner élite of privilege. Because such a circle guards its privileges carefully, it assumes that anyone admitted to it is admitted completely, and must know all other members; and because access is difficult, it allows itself the polite fiction of assuming that anyone addressed is a member. The joke here is twofold. In the first place, Feenix's anecdotes are all about worthless hangers-on of a decayed aristocracy: it would be no privilege to know little Jack Adams. And second, Feenix extends this polite fiction so indiscriminately that if he really had a circle to protect he would long since have broken down its walls. What we are seeing is a parody of social privilege, delivered by someone who has lost the substance but retained the forms.

That, then, is a way of reading *Dombey and Son* that will connect it to the material contained in this book, and treat it as a novel about social structure and economic change in industrial England. These are themes that we know interested Dickens, and he saw himself, both in his journalism and in his fiction, as a social reformer. If this essay stopped here, it would have illustrated the theme of our volume, and shown how society and literature can illuminate each other. But it would leave us with a lopsided view of *Dombey and Son*, indeed of literature itself. The book has other aspects, some of them existing in tension with the social novel so far described.

Let us first look at some of its limitations as a social novel. Does it, for instance, really see the railway as a social reality? The answer seems to be, yes, as far as its effects are concerned, but not at all in respect of its causes. One might say that it is not the province of such a story to take us into boardrooms or to the desks of engineers: social institutions are often simply given in fiction, as they so often seem to be in our own experience. But this is a book about a merchant house: if it is really interested in how society works, should it not tell us what the Dombey money does? Should it not (this would have provided a nice irony) tell us whether Dombey and Son have financed the railway? Or at least, whether they belong in the new world of industrial capitalism, or the old world of the Wooden Midshipman?

The lack of social realism in the handling of economic affairs in the book can be seen in the bankruptcy. Why does Dombey and Son go bankrupt? One kind of answer would concern itself with financial policy and shrewd investment, would ask what kind of manager risks the firm's capital to the point of danger? Another kind of answer, far commoner in the history of the novel, uses bankruptcy as a form of poetic justice, a way of bringing the proud man low, and preparing him for redemption. The bankruptcy of Arthur Clennam in *Little Dorrit* is of this kind: it is a way of making Clennam an inmate of the Marshalsea which he had once visited, so that Amy, once an inmate, can visit him. But though this moral patterning is certainly Dickens's main concern, *Little Dorrit* does show some concern with economic forces: Clennam is one of the many victims of Merdle's swindling. In *Dombey and Son* the concern is more purely moral: Dombey has neglected his business and Carker has been reckless, and bankruptcy is their fitting punishment.

If Dickens shows little interest in what makes a banking firm tick, he also shows an unwillingness to consign Sol Gills to the lumber room of economic history. The world of Sol, Walter and Captain Cuttle is the world of human warmth and inefficiency (Captain Cuttle is gloriously unable even to give notice to his landlady and collect his luggage); but Dickens is reluctant to admit that the efficient can do anything which the good cannot. So after bringing Dombey low economically, he must balance it by bringing Sol up; and at the end of the book we discover that 'some of Mr Gills' old investments are coming out wonderfully well.' Fortunately this does little harm to the novel. It is so obviously cursory that we can dismiss it as a moralizing afterthought, and by bringing in some virtually unmentioned 'investments' he does refrain from the far more implausible claim that the shop was not behind the times after all. Yet there is something more deeply wrong here: Dickens seems reluctant not only to admit that a certain kind of goodness is ineffectual, but also that certain kinds of hardness are economically valuable. Of the two Carker brothers, it is not the virtuous James but the ruthless John who represents the men who really ran industrial England, but the virtuous plot insists on granting success, in the end, to James, not John. Dickens would like us to think that the meek inherit the world of railways and finance.

So far, we have seen the avoidance of social realism as an artistic flaw, as a failure to come to grips with the issues raised by the book. But this is too simple a view: for the other kind of novel that sits within the same covers is in some ways even nearer to the heart of Dickens's genius. This other novel can perhaps be most clearly seen in the famous conversation between Mr Dombey and Paul about money:

> 'Papa! What's money?'
> The abrupt question had such immediate reference to the subject of Mr Dombey's thoughts, that Mr Dombey was quite disconcerted.
> 'What is money, Paul?' he answered. 'Money?'
> 'Yes', said the child, laying his hands upon the elbows of his little chair, and turning the old face up towards Mr Dombey's; 'What is money?'
> Mr Dombey was in a difficulty. He would have liked to give him some explanation involving the terms circulating-medium, currency, depreciation of currency, paper, bullion, rates of exchange, value of precious metals in the market, and so forth; but looking down at the little chair, and seeing what a long way down it was, he answered: 'Gold, and silver, and copper. Guineas, shillings, halfpence. You know what they are?'
> 'Oh yes, I know what they are,' said Paul. 'I don't mean that, Papa. I mean, what's money after all?'
> Heaven and Earth, how old his face was as he turned it up again towards his father's.

> (chapter 8)

The literary tradition of the *puer senex*, the boy with the wisdom of an old man, goes back a long way: there are versions of it in late antiquity, and in the Bible. Originally it was a hagiographic device, a way of giving more than human qualities to the saint. Dickens's version enriches that tradition by joining it on to the idea of *sancta simplicitas*: Paul is not wise through precociousness, but precisely because he is so childish. There is a kind of folk-wisdom in this attempt to show that the naïveté of the child goes deeper than the sophistication of the businessman: Paul is like the child who saw that the emperor had no clothes on. The distance Mr Dombey has to look down to the little chair is a moral distance: looking down is also a kind of looking up. Little children do look old, in a way, and we find their earnestness lovable. Dickens wants us to share this warm sentiment, then to consider taking it more seriously.

The realistic novel has not, however, completely given place to the folk-tale; it is still there in the person of Mr Dombey. For Mr Dombey, unable to handle Paul's demand for an ontological definition, offers a functional one instead, explaining what money is by explaining what it does. Ironically, this is the most realistic awareness of economic realities we are ever given: in the course of putting Mr Dombey's view in its place, the novel for once allows him really to develop that view. It is as if the realism, in the act of being rejected, takes on its own life at last.

Shortly after this comes an episode that is clearly designed to show us money in action. In chapter 10 Walter and Captain Cuttle come to see Mr Dombey in Brighton in order to ask for his help to save Sol Gills's business. Shown into the hotel where Mr Dombey is dining with Paul, they tell their story; and it is no doubt the presence of Paul — their good angel — that gains them their request. It is a marvellously comic scene, because of the Captain's obtuse conviction that he has somehow won the confidence of Mr Dombey; and once again it is a scene from a moral fable, but with a realistic undercurrent. It is meant to show the almost magical influence of Paul in saving Walter's uncle; but when Mr Dombey concludes by telling Paul that he can now see 'how powerful money is, and how anxious people are to get it', we may conclude not only that he is hidebound and superficial, but also that he is right, and has been proved right.

It is not easy, and in our space not possible, to trace the full complexity of the interaction of the two narrative modes of *Dombey and Son*. The relation between Mr Dombey and Carker, for instance, can be seen either as something age-old (master and clever servant) or as topical (chairman of the company and managing director). Indeed, we must point out that age-old themes can make social points too. If we see the novel in terms of social history,

Dombey is the 'rich City fellow'; but in his dealings with Carker he seems more like an archetypal aristocrat. He it is who does not need accomplishments because he can employ accomplished dependants — as the feudal lord did not need to write if he had clerks. This is a social insight, of a highly generalized kind — sociological rather than historical, we might say — and it is proffered in scenes in which the two men almost seem to become allegorical figures of Master and Man — yet without ever quite losing their surface particularity.

In conclusion, let us look more carefully at Dickens's famous and inimitable style, and in particular at its most striking feature — the inversion of things and people. We have already described this as an expression of the alienation of industrial man. Since the effects we need to look at are local, it does not greatly matter if we wrench a paragraph out of context, and we can therefore take the opportunity to quote an urban description from another novel.

> Several fruit-brokers had their marts near Todger's; and one of the first impressions wrought upon the stranger's senses was of oranges — of damaged oranges, with blue and green bruises on them, festering in boxes, or mouldering away in cellars.... Strange solitary pumps were found near Todger's hiding themselves for the most part in blind alleys, and keeping company with fire-ladders.... There were ... tall trees, still putting forth their leaves in each succeeding year, with such a languishing remembrance of their kind ... as birds in cages have of theirs. Here, paralysed old watchmen guarded the bodies of the dead at night, year after year, until at last they joined that solemn brotherhood; and saving that they slept below the ground a sounder sleep than even they had ever known above it, and were shut up in another kind of box, their condition can hardly be said to have undergone any material change when they in turn were watched themselves.   (*Martin Chuzzlewit*, chapter 9)

What we see immediately is that it is a half-truth to say that Dickens reduces people to things; at the same time, he animates things, and sees them as people. The oranges rot, and this brings them to life; the pumps are playing hide-and-seek with the eager eyes of the writer; and the feebleness of the trees' growth is important because of the opportunity it gives to explore a human analogy. The passage describes the blighting effect of urban life on the processes of nature, but style and content are locked in splendid opposition: so far from being depressed by what he sees, Dickens is exhilarated by the metaphoric opportunities it gives. To describe this as urban alienation is on one level correct, but it is a description that completely ignores the medium.

Similarly with the old men. They are so old and decrepit they seem to be ceasing to be human; and their feebleness is just what brings them to life in the writing. The parallels and repetitions that tell us how like the dead they are are what impose the author's sensibility on the material. Dickens's interest in the old men is kindled once he can see them as things.

The animation of things is central to his imagination, and even fog (at the beginning of *Bleak House*) or sunlight (at the beginning of *Little Dorrit*) are the occasion of dazzling stylistic performances that give them a more independent life than many of the human characters. If we relate the novels to their social setting, we can see this as alienation. But novels are the product not only of social circumstances but also of a literary tradition and an individual sensibility: relating the prose to these we can see it as expressing something more like delight.

Dickens often saw himself as a realist and as a reformer. He claimed to have shown contemporary London as it really was, not as the flattering eye of literary prejudice liked to glamourize it; and he saw himself as contributing to the removal of social evils, not only in his speeches and journalism, but also in his novels. The aim of this essay has been to show that although this view has much truth it is also very misleading. Dickens's art draws deeply on non-realistic traditions — fable and folk-tale, allegory, comedy and satire; and its attitude to social abuses is profoundly ambivalent. What Dickens the reformer attacked, Dickens the imaginative novelist often saw as inevitable. And even those modern critics who have seen that Dickens feeds on his fantasy as much as his observation have sometimes been reluctant to admit that this leads him away from the theme of industrial capitalist society. The blending in his work of realistic observation and personal fantasy, of moral indignation and pessimistic acceptance, of the immediately topical, the more generally social and the purely timeless, is of a complexity that no one critical method can describe.

208   *The Victorians*

Select bibliography

Dyson, A.E. *The Inimitable Dickens*. London, 1970.
Forster, J. *Life of Charles Dickens*. London, 1872-4.
House, H. *The Dickens World*. Oxford, 1941.
Johnson, E. *Charles Dickens, his Tragedy and Triumph*. London, 1952.
Lucas, J. *The Melancholy Man*. London, 1970. Chapter 4.
Moynahan, J. 'Dealings with the Firm of Dombey & Son: Wetness versus Dryness'. In Gross and Pearson (eds), *Dickens and the Twentieth Century*. London, 1962.
Orwell, G. 'Charles Dickens' (1940). In *Collected Essays*.
Welsh, A. *The City of Dickens*. Oxford, 1971. Part I.
Williams, R. *Culture and Society*. London, 1958. Part I, chapter 5.
Wilson, E. 'Dickens: The Two Scrooges'. In *The Wound and the Bow*. London, 1941.

11 An essay on *The Princess*

LAURENCE LERNER

Why is Tennyson still read today? He was interested in the social and religious issues of his time but so, after all, were scores of other intelligent Victorians. His special gift was the power to enrapture us with words, to create

> Jewels five words long
> That on the stretched forefinger of all time
> Sparkle for ever.

Tennyson's jewels are richly varied. They are the famous examples of pure technique, as in the onomatopoeic

> The moan of doves in immemorial elms,
> And murmuring of innumerable bees;

there is the sharply terrifying simile for the Princess's bitter smile

> that looked
> A stroke of cruel sunshine on the cliff,
> When all the glens are drowned in azure gloom;

or, most mysterious and most haunting, there is the plangent evocation of how the Prince, 'half in doze', seemed

> To float about a glimmering night, and watch
> A full sea glazed with muffled moonlight, swell
> On some dark shore just seen that it was rich.

Perhaps no image captures more movingly the central concern of the Romantic sensibility than the half-glimpsed shore associated with sleep and a more than human sleep. The Tennyson of these effects, is the successor (and equal) of Wordsworth, Shelley and Keats.

It is best, perhaps, to begin with this reminder of an approach to poetry utterly different from the one which this book invites, in order to remind ourselves that in relating a poem to its society we ought never to ignore what makes it poetry. What keeps the masterpieces floating on the sea of immortality, remarked André Gide in a memorable image, is their skin. So it should be with an awareness of its wonderful surface texture that we now proceed to peer beneath the skin of *The Princess*.

That a poem published on Christmas Day, 1847, should deal with higher education for women suggests that Tennyson was not only interested in the social issues but a pioneer: Girton College was not founded till 1869, women gained the right to sit Cambridge local examinations in 1863, and both Cheltenham Ladies College and the North London Collegiate School for Girls date from the 1850s. The classic statement of Victorian feminism, Mill's *Subjection of Women*, was written in 1861, and not published till 1869, and even his wife's pioneering essay in the *Westminster Review* on 'The Enfranchisement of Women' only appeared in 1851. To write a poem about a university for women in the 1840s is surely to be ahead of one's time, and one of Tennyson's early editors claimed that the 'surface thought of England' did not for many years become conscious of anything wrong in the position of women. This is partly true: Tennyson was not an original thinker but he had a good nose for the topical. Of course the education of women, like theories of evolution, has a long history, and it is not difficult to find discussions of it that Tennyson could have read. Mary Wollstonecraft's famous *Vindication of the Rights of Women* (1791) emerged from the ferment of radical thought associated with the French Revolution; and most of the progressive thought on the subject in the early nineteenth century came from France, especially from the early socialists associated with Saint-Simon and Fourier. In England Robert Owen and his followers frequently canvassed the question in the 1820s and 1830s; William Thompson published his *Appeal of one half the Human Race, Women, against the*

*pretensions of the other half, Men, to keep them in political and
thence in Civil and domestic slavery* in 1825, but there is no reason
to think Tennyson knew this work; and in the early 1840s both the
Edinburgh Review and the *Westminster Review* published articles
on the woman question — by which time Tennyson was already
thinking about the poem, if we are to believe his son's statement
that the idea had come to him by 1839, 'when the project of a
Women's College was in the air'. It is not clear what project this is:
John Killham has suggested that the remark may refer to an
anonymous article in *The Metropolitan Magazine* for May 1838,
wrongly ascribed to Caroline Norton and subsequently attacked,
which asserted emphatically:

> Have they [women] not been systematically kept in ignorance
> — and has not every imaginable means been resorted to in
> order to perpetuate that ignorance? I say it, and I say it
> boldly, that there is no post of trust, no important office, for
> which women are not naturally as well qualified as men.

Yet despite these ringing periods, and despite the Owenites, there
is some truth in the claim that the education of women had not
troubled the surface thought of England before 1847. Most of these
earlier discussions were in theoretical and speculative works by
radicals: there was not yet an organized movement, involving the
actual teaching of women. The crucial date for this is perhaps the
founding of Queens College in 1848. Certainly there can hardly
have been such a detailed account of what might actually happen in
a women's college before Tennyson.

The Princess itself was part of the movement: its reception was
hesitant at first, but it was soon popular, and something of the
complexity of the poem can be seen from the very varied reception
it got. Not only did some critics praise and others blame, but they
differed widely about where Tennyson stood. Charles Kingsley
(conservative on the woman question) approved of the way Tennyson showed 'woman, when she takes her stand on the false
masculine ground of intellect, working out her own moral punishment, by desroying in herself the tender heart of flesh', and the
reviewer in *Tait's Edinburgh Magazine*, who thought women's
education an invincible force for good, objected to the way
Tennyson opposed it. The *Eclectic Review* on the other hand saw

Tennyson, as he warmed to his subject, pleading the rights of women 'with a force and an eloquence which the world has scarcely witnessed before'. This should not surprise us; for *The Princess* has both the intricate tensions of a true work of literature, and some of the confusions that result from uncertainty of purpose, and it was natural that some committed readers should take it in the way they liked, and others as a whipping horse for what they disliked.

We turn now to the poem; and the first question to ask, from which all others flow, is why the college fails. There are external troubles — the arrival and discovery of three young men in female disguise, when the college had been forbidden to men on pain of death, provides their first problem; then comes the invasion by the Prince's father, threatening to pluck their palace down if his son is harmed; and finally the battle between fifty warriors of Arac's and fifty of the Prince's countrymen turns the campus into a battlefield and the college halls into a hospital. One view of the fall of the Roman Empire maintains that it was not caused by the invasion of barbarians whom it could easily have assimilated if its institutions had been healthy; and Tennyson similarly makes it clear that the real causes of the downfall are internal. In the first place, the men are able to stay concealed, even after they have been recognized, by appealing to the weaknesses of their discoverers — the feminine softness and sisterly affection of Psyche, the jealousy and ambition of Blanche; by doing this they sow confusion and loss of trust, which leads to the Princess's repudiation of both her deputies. As for the tourney and the consequent nursing, these are quite explicitly the consequences of the Princess's own choice. Her decision to nurse the wounded is one of the climaxes of the poem, and the consequence of this is seen in the bustling lines that open part VII:

> So was their sanctuary violated,
> So their fair college turned to hospital;
> At first with all confusion: by and by
> Sweet order lived again with other laws:
> A kindlier influence reigned; and everywhere
> Low voices with the ministering hand
> Hung round the sick: the maidens came, they talked,
> They sang, they read: till she not fair began

To gather light, and she that was, became
Her former beauty treble; and to and fro
With books, with flowers, with Angel offices,
Like creatures native unto gracious act,
And in their own clear element, they moved.

After the opening confusion, all settles down to the new order — a more appropriate one than the old. For the women now are carrying out their womanly function, caring for their menfolk like the sisters, wives and mothers of traditional idealized femininity. This role makes you beautiful if you aren't, trebles your beauty if you are; for the truly feminine woman ought to be physically attractive, but, after all, it doesn't matter if she isn't. The comparison with angels is almost inevitable: the Victorians believed ('believed'?) in angels as no earlier age ever had, for they used them as similes for the domesticity they really did believe in. The whole passage turns more and more into a sigh of relief: at last these women are doing what they ought to do.

For at last they are conforming to the Victorian ideal: they are turning into those women whom one loves on earth and looks forward to loving 'with a love unknown on earth', as David Copperfield comes to feel about his flawless Agnes; women whom one looks up to and is guided by, for they always help and never answer back. The central statement of this ideal of womanhood is Ruskin's essay 'Of Queens Gardens' (*Sesame and Lilies*, 1865), which insists that the 'mission' and the 'rights' of woman can never 'be separate from the mission and the rights of Man', and then proceeds to define an ideal of 'womanly mind and virtue' that sees her as fitted 'for rule not for battle' (rule, however, to be compatible with true wifely subjection). The educational implication is emphatically that women should have a special syllabus — 'a woman ought to know whatever her husband is likely to know, but to know it in a different way.' Her aim in learning is 'to sympathise in her husband's pleasures, and in those of his best friends.'

This is what all good women really want to be like; and even the strenuous activity of Ida's college cannot fully banish true femininity. All along, she had had grumblers who

Murmured that their May
Was passing: what was learning unto them?

> They wished to marry; they could rule a house;
> Men hated learned women.

And so it is inevitable that once Ida has nursed the Prince they declare their love, each of them purged of earlier follies. This is so obviously the central theme of the final section that modern critics have been led to say that *The Princess* is not really a poem about women's education but about love; that the education of the Prince is quite as important as that of the Princess; and that everything moves towards the eloquent statement of the ideal of marriage, 'nor equal nor unequal':

> Each fulfils
> Defect in each, and always thought in thought,
> Purpose in purpose, will in will, they grow,
> The single pure and perfect animal ...

We know that these lines were favourites with Tennyson himself, and this interpretation of the poem is in one sense obviously right. Yet in another sense it is obviously inadequate. The literary historian dutifully reading the work in the light of the author's intention, is in danger of impoverishing it. Literary conventions, robbed of their social resonance, grow too well behaved to move us to passion, and the convention of perfect womanhood on which the poem ends was in nineteenth-century England locked in tension with the problems of women's education. Any ending that pretends this tension will melt with a kiss is a poor weak thing for all its eloquence.

For the Princess began her college with the conviction that the cause could not afford certain kinds of femininity; and she was right. Her breaking off the betrothal is the most obvious example of this rejection, but it was after all a betrothal to a man she had never seen, and the only reason it offends us is that the Prince is the hero, with whom we already sympathize. A more interesting case is her rejection of the songs. 'Tears, idle tears' is sung by one of her attendants after the geological expedition, and Ida reacts to it as follows:

> She ended with such passion that the tear,
> She sang of, shook and fell, an erring pearl
> Lost in her bosom: but with some disdain

Answered the Princess, 'If indeed there haunt
About the mouldered lodges of the Past
So sweet a voice and vague, fatal to men,
Well needs it we should cram our ears with wool
And so pace by: but thine are fancies hatched
In silken-folded idleness; nor is it
Wiser to weep a true occasion lost,
But trim our sails, and let old bygones be.

The sensibility of the singer is melancholy and feminine: in language appropriate to the conventional graces of womanhood, her tear is a pearl with vaguely sexual associations; it is erring because the grief into which her sexuality overflows draws attention to what is womanly about her. This is exactly the conception of woman that will lead her to find her true vocation nursing rather than studying. Ida's speech is a very perceptive piece of literary criticism: she sees the song as expressing nostalgia, looking back to the past, and so inimical to any reform programme, that must look forward; and she describes it in the language of Tennyson's own lyricism — the sweet voice and vague 'haunts' the 'mouldered lodges' rather as 'a spirit haunts the year's last hours' in an equally nostalgic and dreamy lyric of 1830. Perhaps the most interesting of Ida's remarks is 'fatal to men': the song itself includes a lament for lost love, and Ida seems to see that as itself seductive. The erring tears, wild with all regret, are the signs of 'das ewig Weibliche', and show woman as fulfilling the stereotypes that surely will get in the way of serious study.

That the Princess is right to reject feminine sensibility in this way is made clear by the two occasions on which she yields to it: her acceptance of the tournament, and her agreement to nurse the wounded. The former is perhaps the more interesting. Arac, Ida's brother, admits to not understanding — or not greatly sympathizing with — her scheme, but being a manly and affectionate brother he is willing to fight for her against these foreigners who have annoyed him. And so the future of the college awaits trial by combat, for Ida replies

and whereas I know
Your prowess, Arac, and what mother's blood
You draw from, fight; you failing, I abide
What end soever: fail you will not.

Now why does she agree to this combat? It belongs to the mouldered lodges of the past: settling a woman's future by armed combat is exactly the kind of oppression, of the yoke of custom, which it had been her aim to throw off. We are given no reason for the change of mind, and it is a fair guess that Tennyson himself was uneasy about it, for he causes Arac, when he issues the challenge, to refer vaguely to sending to his sister 'worthy reasons why she should Bide by this issue'. It is an even more revealing example than the next concession, to nurse the wounded (which is more important for the plot), for that at least is a decision consciously and explicitly taken, partly in pique, and partly through the resurgence of her feminine warmth.

There is perhaps one explanation, though not really a justification, for the tourney, which will lead us into a pervasive theme of the poem. The discussion of the Vivian family in the Prologue tells of an ancestress who 'beat her foes with slaughter from her walls', announcing the theme of the martial woman that is resumed in (for instance) the description of the 'eight daughters of the plough' who caught the messenger by the hair

> And so belaboured him on rib and cheek
> They made him wild.

There are naturally comic possibilities to women who fight, and they come out here; but for the most part it is presented in all seriousness. The ancestress is a 'miracle of noble womanhood', a phrase that clashes slightly with the preceding account of how she 'trampled some beneath her horse's heels': we are being told from the beginning that womanhood can be noble for having the military instead of the melting virtues. And so after the Princess has denounced the fancies hatched in silken-folded idleness of 'Tears, idle tears' and 'O swallow, swallow', she reveals that she has herself written poetry of a more appropriate genre:

> ourselves have often tried
> Valkyrian hymns, or into rhythm have dashed
> The passion of the prophetess.

Clearly the exultant hymn of triumph she sings after the tourney — 'Our enemies have fallen, have fallen' — is of her own composition, and it fulfils her programme of looking to the future rather

than the past: its favourite image is of seeds growing, and it ends
with the determination to 'move the stony bases of the world'. It
would not be fair reasoning to claim that the martial strain
associated with the collegiate women justifies the decision to let
Arac fight for them, since settling the fate of women by a fight
between men is precisely associated with the image of woman as
unmartial and helpless; but the confusion is understandable, and
the comparison of Ida, singing her song of triumph, with Deborah
'that great dame of Lapidoth', one of the Old Testament's bloodthirsty women, helps to justify it.

It is just this point which would annoy a feminist. If the
alternative to woman as melting is woman as the warrior, then an
intelligent feminist might feel she had not gained much. Nineteenth-century feminism was a claim to responsible civilian qualities, education, suffrage, the exercise of rational power; if Tennyson
saw emancipated women as either ridiculous or bloodthirsty, he did
not understand anything about emancipation. We must therefore
appeal from the Valkyrian hymns to the serious curriculum of the
college. Psyche's lecture begins with the origin of the solar system
(according to Laplace) and the ascent of man, before coming to its
outline of history — 'the ungracious past' in which women were
kept subordinate. The lecture (which must have lasted for days —
but poetic licence presumably allows some compression) would
have done credit to any of the great Victorian women. It deals
judiciously with chivalry, an issue on which the feminist is naturally
ambivalent:

> When some respect, however slight, was paid
> To woman, superstition all awry.

It makes all the right answers to the stock arguments, for instance
that women's 'heads were less':

> Some men's were small; not they the least of men;
> For often fineness compensated size:
> Besides the brain was like the hand, and grew
> With using; thence the man's, if more was more.

The anatomical argument is sound; and the environmentalism of
the last two lines is crucial to feminism. Because the conservative
view has so often stressed the 'natural' qualities of women, it

becomes important for the radicals to minimize the role of nature and emphasize nurture. This view is prominent in Mary Wollstonecraft's *Vindication*, which insisted that women were systematically degraded by the trivial attentions men paid them, and that the heart as well as the understanding could be cultivated; it was developed by Mill, and indeed it tends to be an element in any radical programme. And so the impulsive Lilia, whose outburst in the Prologue sets off the whole story, showed a true grasp of essentials when she said, naïvely but perceptively:

It is but bringing up; no more than that.

It is important to emphasize the seriousness of Psyche's lecture, because there are such clear elements of burlesque in the situation. There is clearly a parallel intended between the women's college and the academy of the four young men in *Love's Labour's Lost*, in which they impose strict statutes on themselves for three years' study — limited sleep and food, no women admitted — and break them, when the ladies appear, on the very first day. Shakespeare was clearly writing a burlesque, but he gave no such description of what was actually being studied; and if it was Tennyson's intention to make fun of the women's college, then we must appeal from intention to achievement: no poet can be sure that he will direct the reader's sympathies as he wishes to, and the academic study that we are subsequently intended to find mistaken, even comic, can kindle in the description with a true thirst for knowledge. And Tennyson's intention was in any case not so simple, as he knew when he called the poem a medley: the mingling of burlesque and serious, of

A Gothic ruin and a Grecian house,
A talk of colleges and ladies' rights,
A feudal knight in silken masquerade,

produced a result for which the narrator feels obliged to apologize in the Conclusion, and critics have taken this apology as an uneasy admission of failure, an awareness that the changes of tone are more than the poem can compass. Many of them have felt that Tennyson should have had the courage to write a genuine burlesque, that he damaged his poem by constantly reverting to the serious. The extreme version of this view is no doubt that implied by W.S.

Gilbert, whose libretto for the burlesque opera *Princess Ida* (1884)
reduced the syllabus of the college to absurdity:

> They've a firmly rooted notion
> They can cross the Polar Ocean,
> And they'll find perpetual motion,
> If they can — if they can.

To judge the poem against a unity of tone that it does not attain to
is to offer a criticism based on an awareness of aesthetic and stylistic
problems. A criticism based on social awareness, on the other hand,
is more likely to wish away the burlesque, and to feel that only
when the poem enters into the women's studies with genuine
sympathy does it rise to the treatment that its subject deserves.

What is the price of social change? Most of the intelligent
resistance to the emancipation of women in the nineteenth century
was afraid that the traditional feminine functions in society would
be damaged, perhaps destroyed. A good example of such moderate
opinion is the hesitant progressivism of George Eliot. Of all the
aims of women's emancipation George Eliot was least sympathetic
to suffrage, and most to education: education for women, after all,
is a reform that could always be supported on conservative grounds,
that women will better carry out their traditional functions if
educated. In a letter to Emily Davies (8 August 1868) she supports
this position, and shows an understanding for the 'vulgar alarm'
that women might be 'unsexed' by education.

> We can no more afford to part with that exquisite type of
> gentleness, tenderness, possible maternity suffusing a
> woman's being with affectionateness, which makes what we
> mean by the female character than we can afford to part with
> the human love, the mutual subjection of soul between a
> man and a woman.

As we watch the arguments over this question in Victorian times we
can see taking shape, behind the battle between reformers and
conservatives, that other alignment by which moderate reformers
claim that you can have your cake and eat it, while radical reformers
accept that the price which the conservatives fear will probably have
to be paid. By this standard, Emily Davies was a radical: she did not
see how the prospect of college life could be described without

revealing 'how infinitely pleasanter it will be than home'. It is not surprising, then, to find a radical feminist of our own day claiming, as Germaine Greer does, that the nineteenth-century conservatives were right in their belief that women's emancipation would destroy the family.

This issue is active in *The Princess* in a way that deeply involves the structure of the poem. The point can be briefly put: are two views of the role of woman being displayed or three? Ida's initial challenge was to the convention that beats women down, and we were given a simple contrast between the status quo and the emancipation of women. That would mean that for Ida to abandon her college and marry the Prince was simple defeat, and this is not the note on which Tennyson wishes to end: he wants the end to sound like a compromise, a way of making both sides abandon what is untenable in their position. There must therefore be an expression of male chauvinism as extreme as the feminist rebellion of the women, and this is provided by the Prince's father:

> Man to command and woman to obey;
> All else confusion.

There is the simplest form of authoritarianism with a strong dash of sexual gloating

> — We hunt them for the beauty of their skins;
> They love us for it, and we ride them down —

in contrast to which the final union of the lovers will emerge as the golden mean:

> Each fulfils
> Defect in each, and always thought in thought,
> Purpose in purpose, will in will, they grow —

Turning from the poem to its age, we can ask a similar question about the ideal of the angel in the house. To the radical feminist, this is an ingenious psychological con-trick, a way of exalting woman with homage — which costs nothing — while doing her out of her rights. To most of the Victorians it was a new and enlightened view of woman, contrasted with the older, cruder doctrine of authority and subordination. The former sees only a twofold contrast; the latter sees the doctrine as the golden mean between oppression and emancipation.

It is hardly possible to say which of these two views is right, for the choice between them depends on our way of looking at past ideology. It is a choice between a diachronic approach within the history of ideas, and a more sociological approach that stresses the function of an ideal in contemporary society. Neither approach is 'right'; each tells us different things. The first will lead us to the 'right' reading of the poem if we confine ourselves to the strictest intentionalism: Tennyson certainly intended us to see a threefold contrast and, in the end, a golden mean. But to the modern reader this reading goes against the grain. It is hard for us to see so old-fashioned an ideal as the angel in the house as something new and challenging; historical imagination can help us to overcome this limitation, but sociological imagination (so much better developed in this century) prevents us from ignoring the ways in which it can be seen as a form of oppression. The marriage of Ida and the Prince is surely a reversion to the status quo. The college is not going to be reopened, Psyche will give no more lectures, and when Cyril's ardour has cooled she will not be able to stop him singing Moll and Meg with the boys. And Ida will no doubt be happy and angelic, but in a way highly acceptable to conventional readers, for whom as for us the Prince's final line — 'Lay thy sweet hands in mine and trust to me' — sounds indistinguishable from the climax of a hundred contemporary romances. One can understand Emily Davies's complaint that *The Princess* set feminism back by twenty years.

Yet what else could Tennyson have done? A poet must rest his poem on the poetry he can write; and Tennyson's poetry is, in terms of the concepts he used, deeply feminine. The best of the songs which the women sang 'between the rougher voices of the men' contain the most marvellous writing of all: they are the skin which keeps *The Princess* afloat. And they express nostalgia, passion, melancholy and sexual love: they 'moan about the retrospect'. Ida was right, as a practical politician, to reject them, but it meant rejecting Tennyson: what could he do in return except betray her?

222   *The Victorians*

Select bibliography

The Poems of Tennyson. Ed. Christopher Ricks. London, 1969.

Bergonzi, B. 'Feminism and Femininity in *The Princess*'. In Armstrong (ed.), *The Major Victorian Poets: Reconsiderations.* London, 1969.

Danzig, A. 'Tennyson's *The Princess*: A Definition of Love'. *Victorian Poetry*, 4 (1966), pp. 83 ff.

Davies, E. *The Higher Education of Women.* London and New York, 1866.

Houghton, W. *The Victorian Frame of Mind.* New Haven, Conn., 1957. Chapter 13.

Jump, J.D. (ed.) *Tenyson: The Critical Heritage.* London, 1967. Contains J.W. Marston on *The Princess* (*Athanaeum*, 1 January 1848) and Charles Kingsley on *In Memoriam* and earlier works (*Fraser's Magazine*, September 1850).

Killham, J. *Tennyson and The Princess.* London, 1958.

Palmer, D.J. (ed.) *Writers and their Background: Tennyson.* London, 1973.

Ricks, C. *Tennyson.* London, 1972. Chapter 7.

Shannon, E.F., Jr. *Tennyson and the Reviewers.* Cambridge, Mass., 1952.

Strachey, R. *The Cause.* London, 1928.

Tennyson, Hallam, Lord. *Tennyson: A Memoir.* London, 1897. Chapter 12.

Index

b) *Subjects*

Labour movement, 87
Labour Party, 84-5
landscapes, 22-3, 28, 31
Langham Place Circle, 177
law reform, 7, 105-6
living standards (1830-60), 57-69,
(1860-1900), 73-5
London, 80-4

magazines, 23, 146
miracles, 161-5
money, 4, 11, 196, 199-200, 204-5
mortality, 64
'Muscular Christianity', 160-1

natural selection, 168-9
New English Art Club, 152
Nonconformists, 106
North London Collegiate School
for Girls, 178, 210
nostalgia, 12, 44, 123, 125-37

Oxford Tractarian Movement, 123,
127, 153, 158-60

paganism, 30
painting, 120-1, 140-4, 150-2;
see also illustration
Parliamentary Reform, 97-100
paternalism, 15
pathos, 7, 22
photography, 140
poetry, 25-45, 143
Poor Law, 5, 112-14, 181
poor relief, 112-14, 130-1
poverty, 62-4, 65, 66, 67-8, 73,
77-9, 112, 114
Pre-Raphaelites, 120, 131, 141-3,
151, 160
professions, 93
prostitution, 7, 8
Public Health Acts (1848), (1875),
116
public schools, 109

railways, 53, 55-6, 195, 197, 199
realism, 9, 10-11, 14, 19, 21, 152,
203, 207
Reform Act, First, (1832), 90, 97,
98
religious belief, 155-7, 161-72
restoration, 134-5
revolution, 76-7, 86, 124
Romanticism, 12, 13, 26, 122
Royal Commission on Labour
(1893-4), 181, 184

Sale of Food and Drugs Act (1875),
116
sanitation, 115-17
satire, 10, 14, 146
savings banks, 92, 114
science, 42, 151, 163, 165-71
scriptures, 167
secret ballot, 99
self-sacrifice, 174-5, 180-1, 188
sentiment, 7, 9, 152
sexuality, 8, 20, 151, 191
social change, 16-19, 219
Social Democratic Foundation, 85,
86
social justice, 71-2, 75-6
social mobility, 8-9, 196-7, 201
social reform, 7, 76-8
socialism, 84-8
Society for the Protection of
Ancient Buildings, 135
specialization of workers, 53
steam engines, 52
symbolism, 4-6

textile industries, 53-4, 55, 57,
61-2, 180, 196
Tractarians *see* Oxford Tractarian
Movement
trade unions, 92, 114, 182-3
traditionalism, 123, 125-37